Kok Cheow Yeoh

The Influences of Computer on Idea Formation in Design

Kok Cheow Yeoh

The Influences of Computer on Idea Formation in Design

A Human-computer Combination in Discovering
the Creative Process of Design

VDM Verlag Dr. Müller

Imprint

Bibliographic information by the German National Library: The German National Library lists this publication at the German National Bibliography; detailed bibliographic information is available on the Internet at http://dnb.d-nb.de.

Cover image: www.purestockx.com

Publisher:
VDM Verlag Dr. Müller Aktiengesellschaft & Co. KG , Dudweiler Landstr. 125 a, 66123 Saarbrücken, Germany,
Phone +49 681 9100-698, Fax +49 681 9100-988,
Email: info@vdm-verlag.de

Zugl.: Lubbock, Texas Tech University, Diss., 2002

Produced in USA and UK by:
Lightning Source Inc., La Vergne, Tennessee, USA
Lightning Source UK Ltd., Milton Keynes, UK
BookSurge LLC, 5341 Dorchester Road, Suite 16, North Charleston, SC 29418, USA

ISBN: 978-3-8364-5303-5

ACKNOWLEDGEMENTS

In pursuing a doctorate, I voluntarily left the practice of graphic design to confront the abstract area of design. The route was not easy to take and I wish to express my gratitude to the following academic mentors for their advice, support, and encouragement: Dr. Dennis Fehr, Dr. Ed Check, Prof. Carla Tedeschi from the School of Art, Dr. Yung-mei Tsai from the Department of Sociology, Anthropology and Social Work, and Dr. Frank Durso from the Department of Psychology.

My heartfelt thanks go to Dr. Fehr, who provided an enormous amount of internal security to proactively make the Interdisciplinary Program of Fine Art at Texas Tech University work for me. You detected my personal and moral uniqueness and provided the academic and ethical guidelines for realizing the potentiality within me. Throughout my studies, you treated me as a friend and colleague rather than as a graduate student.

Dr. Tsai, your constructive suggestions, efforts, patience, and temperance deserve to be applauded. Your dedication to students inspires me to become a better educator. Prof. Tedeschi, thank you for facilitating my data collection and letting me teach some great Design Communication classes in the School of Art.

I am indebted to my mother, Madam Beh, Bi Yeang, whose hardship and endurance throughout my academic pursuit provided me with the impetus to attain my goals. You have raised, loved, inspired, and supported me. Education was always a high priority in your upbringing of me. This degree is my gift to you, Ma.

I would like to thank my brother, Yeoh, Kok Jin who has always supported and encouraged my idealistic goals. My ability to pursue a doctorate while being far from my family and home is due to the fact that they have been a constant stream of unfailing emotional and financial support that I could never repay. I am eternally grateful.

I extend sincere appreciation to Mr. and Mrs. Mah, Peng Cheah. I am most appreciative of the Mah family for their inspiration as well as their efforts in instilling the positive effects of education in my early childhood.

I would also like to extend a heartfelt thank you to James Magro and his mother, Sarah, for being a positive force in my life. James has agonized with me every step of this arduous goal. Your contribution has been central to the completion of this dissertation. To James Carter, thank you for always being there for me.

Amy Broadbent, to you, I express my gratitude for initiating my first freelance design project after my graduation from the Academy of Art College in San Francisco in 1992. Many thanks to Tariq Khan and Rashid Nasim for opening doors of opportunity for me to explore and experience life in the United States of America. I also wish to acknowledge Lonnie Wheeler, Jr., who has proofread the numerous drafts of this dissertation. Thank you for your help.

There are many names that are unmentioned, but everyone has been inspirational in my wild spirits for discovery, adventure, and creativity in life. Last, but not least, thank you Siddhartha Gautama for your spiritual guidance. Amitha Buddha.

TABLE OF CONTENTS

APPENDIX

LIST OF TABLES

LIST OF FIGURES

CHAPTER I

INTRODUCTION

Computer technology has profoundly changed the way we function in society. Graphic designers are translating ideas from screen to print and in some cases, depending on the nature of the project, online and motion media. As a tool, computers are utilized as a means to an end. While there could be many feasible solutions to a particular problem, the design process ends when the designer produces a single, realizable artifact or result. Regardless of the objectives or tools used for the project, ideation is an initial stage that is necessary in the design process. However, many factors such as deadlines, budgets, production and logistical concerns, as well as client-imposed restrictions can influence the design process.

Because rapid technological advancement is capable of impacting the ideation process, I see my research as a form of ongoing explanation in an environment that engages in an iterative process where the design is subject to assessment, refinement, elimination, selection, and production. This research explores accumulated knowledge about the creative process as it relates to computer usage. Through a lens that narrowly defines the graphic design profession within a market-driven framework, it involves the troika of designer, client, and audience.

The process is narrowly defined here as the search for a solution to a design problem and in reality, the field is expansive, diverse, and multi-faceted. Depending on the nature of the project, the project is a complex blend of functions and objectives. However, the human-computer combination becomes an interesting platform for this research because technological expertise is essential within the creative process of graphic design.

Background of the study

In 1984 when Apple Inc. introduced a user-friendly desktop named Macintosh, the field of graphic design changed tremendously. What was once thought of as the traditional manual design processes and tools in graphic design are now laid out on a computer screen, replacing and integrating drafting instruments, coloring materials, measurement tools, and more.

Presently, technology permeates our lives at every level—from workplace to home, from high culture to popular entertainment. In the field of graphic design, computer

1

technology has become an ideation and production tool. Graphic design students use computer technology to conceive ideas and to bring their ideas to fruition with combinations of software knowledge and hardware availability. When a printer is used with a computer, the finished product is visually pleasing and professional looking, thus extending the computer's simulated visual form into tangible product.

Presently, it is nearly impossible to practice graphic design by using traditional manual processes. Photographs can now be digitally manipulated. Text can be word-processed and laid out on a computer screen for electronic pre-press output. The benefits are irresistible—three-dimensional display capability and connectivity of multiple peripherals allows sophisticated new possibilities.

Once it became apparent that the computer could efficiently execute work faster than before, educators across the nation equipped our educational institutions with digital technology in response to industry standards and demands (Leonard & LeCroy, 1985; McCoy, 1998; Papert, 1987; Rossman, 1998). Introducing technology into pedagogy also introduces a unique problem. These technological opportunities and challenges influenced by personal computers have drastically transformed the field of graphic design and it has a profound effect on how we teach, learn, and work (Blauvelt, 1998; Davis, 1998; Keedy, 1994; Rubinstein, 1994; Wild, 1998).

With increasing influence of technology, design is democratized and the design process no longer is in the bailiwick of the graphic designer. The technological change has exerted considerable influence and as a result, some jobs are disappearing while new ones are created. Because the field of graphic design does not require certification, unlike their architectural counterparts, everyone with accessibility to computer software and hardware can essentially become desktop publishers. However, it takes specialty and concentration in design to become a good communicator of visual ideas. Graphic design students are well-prepared for the task. In the definition section for "desktop publishing," some clarifications between a desktop publisher and a graphic designer are provided to avoid confusions between the two terms.

Technology is an expensive endeavor that requires constant upgrading and re-learning. Other administrative considerations such as infrastructure, networking capabilities, qualified technical support staff, software management, course scheduling and so forth are factors in determining a strong academic curriculum which directly relates to computer technology. It has also created a knowledge-based class of how much one knows technologically. Those who are equipped with computer skills are able to compete far better with those who are without (Volti, 2001).

American Institute of Graphic Arts (AIGA) and the National Association of Schools of Art and Design (NASAD) advise academic institutions to be financially committed and instructionally-prepared to arm graduates with technological expertise, which is critical to the practice of graphic design (n.d.). They also reported that nationally many schools with graphic design courses or programs either underestimate this obligation or they simply fail to respond in a timely manner. As a result, graduates become unprepared and unqualified for the jobs that they are trained to work in. Because many aspects of graphic design education are visually-based and when the computer becomes an important tool in the design processes, the very nature of creativity itself may be affected.

This is because traditional hand processes such as paste up of mechanicals, photo-typesetting and retouching are now being replaced by electronic output and digital mechanisms. Graphic design students have to draw images on the computer, manipulate images digitally, produce digital page layouts, write in word-processing programs, and use appropriate technological resources for applicable design tasks. Finally, they also have to understand the electronic pre-press preparations and web-based applications. Not only does the medium offer a broad variety of artistic practices and disciplines, it also has a wide-ranging impact on design representation and the design process (Hanna & Barber, 2001; Lawson & Ming Loke, 1997).

This has a profound effect on how we acquire knowledge, develop interpersonal relations, foster self-development, and experience our sense of individuality. These phenomena serve as the basis for my interest in studying the impacts of computer technology. Specifically, the study investigates the impact of software and hardware in undergraduate students on ideation within the problem-solving aspect of the design process.

Context of the study

In order to understand the practice of graphic design and the processes involved, it is relevant to discuss the factors that shape the field. On the very basic level, even the terms used to describe the field varies. We may have heard of descriptors as graphic communications, communication design, and graphic arts, visual design, communication arts, commercial art, just to name a few. Graphic arts may refer to the technical components such as printing and pre-press. According to the American Institute of Graphic Arts, "graphic

3

design is the profession that plans and executes the design of visual communication according to the needs of audiences and in the context for which communication is intended" (n.d.).

In graphic design, communication takes place because someone wants to communicate a message, advertise a product, set up a company, sell a magazine, or whatever scenarios that demand consumers and audiences to respond to it. Graphic designers are engaged at different phases in the creation processes. The objective of visual communication is to convey information that will in turn cause an effect in the public's knowledge, attitudes, and behavior. In order to do so, the communication has to be based on human cognition, behavior, perception, preferences, and other perceivable value systems including age, educational level, environment, and occupation.

Certainly, visual skillfulness and proficiency are important dimensions in communications because effective communicational strategies call for responsiveness in achieving the intended objectives. The ability to sell an idea or to communicate a message requires skill in understanding, analyzing, and interpreting information.

Finding an effective solution to a problem is not easy. The challenge is having to work through the restrictions imposed by the nature of the design process and the complex situation in which it serves. This includes not just the audience which the message is intended; it also involves budgetary concerns as well as timing. Since meeting deadlines is paramount to the designer-client relationship, student designers must learn to be decisive, efficient, and goal-oriented.

Within the arts, graphic design is one of the first few to include computer technology in its repertoire and it is accepted with mixed blessings. Because of technological advancements, graphic designers have lost ground as technology enables clients to figure out how to exercise control over digital documents, eliminating the needs for graphic designers (Glaser, 1995). Technology also, according to Glaser (1995), contributes to "overpopulation" of graphic designers (p. 256). This view is further supported by Blauvelt (1998) who added that every personal computer owner can become a desktop publisher. Some begged to differ by suggesting that compared with the conventional methods of drawings done by hand, computers are far better. (Mercedes, 1996; Mills, 1994; Truckenbrod, 1990).

The technological hardware and software used by graphic designers change rapidly. As we face a world of accelerating change, due in large part to the advent of computer science and technology, change in job skills, interpersonal relations, social standards and norms, learning in close interaction and adjustment with day to day life is now more important than ever before because of the rapid changes that occur in contemporary society.

In order to provide a holistic solution, graphic design educators are mirroring "real world" situations to narrow the gap between what is being preached and what is being practiced. This is because the tendency toward promoting a professional approach rather than general education at colleges and universities has been steadily increasing for the past two decades (Swanson, 1998). Educational learning is based on the learner's total experience and learning institutions need to fit their students' and the industry's needs to function effectively in the real world.

Historically, the designer, the client, and the audience are the three players that are involved in the paradigm of visual communications. The designer creates a message or a solution for the client who intends to target it for a specific audience. The designer is like a mediator for ideas. A graphic designer does not manufacture a product that can be sampled, tried or tasted. Although he or she can show examples of work produced for other companies, design ability, business acumen, ethics, ability to communicate effectively and deliverance of what is promised are tested. Adding to the mix is the reality that many projects have fixed deadlines and services must be geared to that reality. In the real world, delays are likely to occur and adjustments have to be made. Working with the constraints of time and money in mind, compromises are sometimes necessary. Preparing oneself to take an active, participatory role and learning how to plan marketplace strategies and management realities will reward one to function more effectively.

Simulating reality-based projects, the task of teaching is to make connections to the outside world where real problems exist. Outside the context of use, problem solving cannot be effective if the situation is unreal. The suggestions are outlined in chapter V in recommendations for educators. From the client's perspective, the end result is the goal. From the standpoint of market-oriented business disciplines, computer technology is a machinery of expediency and productivity. From the learning institution's standpoint, technique and technological skills will be a large part of a design curriculum. The extrapolation of the meaning of technology takes on more importance because the essence of using a technological tool is learning the underlying values and rationales of communicating ideas or solving a problem.

In actualizing one's design potentials, a designer may do experimentations. For graphic designers, making any form of decision answers a great number of questions. By presenting many design solutions, some of which may be totally new concepts, they establish a balance of presenting visual and technical information by using technology as tool to develop their vision. For a designer, technology is not just a means of productivity, it is also a means for addressing and responding to change in the creative process and communication environments.

As we enter the 21st century with technology continuing to shape our lives, market-driven employers are demanding and expecting every graduate to have the ability to conceive ideas in digital formats. Consequently, students are forced to be creative, innovative, analytical, organized, and disciplined in making their ideas visible by using new technology. Selling an intangible service like design involves special considerations. The design business is changing and with increased competition for work, designers have to be more aggressive and inventive than ever before. Designers are in a business and they must respond to the demands of customers with their own needs and ideas.

Technology and society are constantly interacting. In an advanced and expanding society, we are apt to apply technocracy into solving problems or performing tasks. One thing is valued over another, one sense or skill is amplified over the other especially in a competitive, capitalistic, and fast-paced economy. Every tool has its potentiality but embedded within it are ideological and technical biases. Technology has its advantages and disadvantages depending upon whose hands it happens to fall into. Technology is not the problem but rather how it is being used.

In our tool-using culture, the computer can be seen as physical and psychological extensions according to Marshall McLuhan (1967). Since the 1960s, he popularized his famous observation, *the medium is the message*, which suggests that electronic medium itself impacts us as much as the information it conveys. Throughout the ages, humans have *extended* themselves through a variety of inventions that seem to provide for their shortcomings. The microscope is an extension of the eye and the telephone is an extension of the ear. He sees technology as an extension of mankind, both physically and psychologically. According to him, electricity and television are both extensions and externalizations of our consciousness. People spend more time watching television while print media is competing for people's time and attention, and depending on the context, money. In order to perceive and understand these media, we are not required to go through

6

any training. All is needed is our ordinary perceptual skills. The same can be said about radio and telephone. If one understands spoken language, the message can be sent.

Extending this line of thought, all media can be seen as extensions of some human faculty-psychic or physical. If the computer is seen as a medium rather than as a tool, then this has a direct impact on how design is conceived. Computers as the media can alter the environment, raising unique implications. This is because apart from being the medium of message, computers are also the medium that facilitate the transmission of numerous messages to other forms of media, especially when boundaries have blurred, particularly when it is virtually impossible nowadays to practice graphic design without using the computer.

Graphic design is more than a discipline; it is an interdisciplinary field of different disciplines (Poggenpohl, 1984; Swanson, 1995) which converge to create communicational objects to address a certain message or to solve a particular problem to an audience. When students use the computer to layout type, they are required to become typesetters. Graphic design is a form of communication which means that graphic designers need to be better cross-disciplinarians and broadly educated. They communicate and draw ideas from marketing, history, science, sociology, contemporary issues, and so forth. It is an intellectual, cultural, and social activity albeit the technological aspect is a dependent component.

<u>Purpose of the study</u>

The purpose of my research is to investigate whether the usage of computer software and hardware for graphic design projects in one major U.S. university's graphic design program could encourage or diminish design students' creativity within the ideation phase. Because graphic design projects usually result in a final product of some sort, it is pertinent for this study to address additional components within the design process as well as other factors that may impact the outcome of a design.

In a limited sense, it is about how undergraduate students' creativity is affected when the aid of computer technology comes into place. In essence, I am interested in understanding the process of idea creation. In order to do so, design process, thought process, technical issues, and individual notions are reflectively collected through a set of questionnaires distributed in classroom settings. The method affords a theory that explains the process and consequences which involve the interactions and actins of people using tools, processes, and materials.

7

In this research, I analyze reflective data where meanings are ascribed based on experiences of 68 participants from 14 undergraduate classes in a major university in Southwest United States. Because computer software and hardware are now part of the design process in graphic design pedagogy, this inductive analysis will allow for categories and patterns to emerge from the data rather than being imposed on data prior to data collection. The methodology allows me to investigate the views, values, beliefs, feelings, assumptions, and ideologies of the participants.

The intent of this research is to explain a process. I am interested in understanding the process of creation which involves four different areas: thoughts surrounding the issue of creative process, the graphic design processes, proficiency on technical issues and individual notions of self-concept. Every project assigned is different in the research subjects' courses and while they ideate with different media, the respondents are participating in an environment that consists of internal and external factors that can influence the outlook of their design solutions. I am concerned with understanding social phenomena interpreted from the students' perspectives in an authentic context by capturing their experiences.

My interest in this area is motivated by professional experience as a graphic designer, creative director, freelancer, and educator. The aim of data collecting is to yield to a possible outcome in assisting in theory development. I intend to construct a theory about the process of graphic design. By expressing systematically certain terms and concepts, analyzing the field from three relevant literatures—marketing, graphic design, and creativity—I can delineate meaning, significance, and legitimacy. Information gathered from this research may suggest implications regarding the strengths and limitations of computers in education, whether or not computer technology can stimulate nor hinder creativity, and how computer technology influences the graphic design process.

Blauvelt (1995) wrote that as we become more and more technologically advanced, the need to link graphic design to theories becomes important. Contrary to popular belief that theory is an immaterial abstraction, it is something that is "fashioned, refashioned, and self-fashioned—not merely fashionable, preordained, or predestined" (Blauvelt, 1998, p. 72). As something that already exists, theory can allow graphic designers to actively redefine their practice from within, unlike social scientists who often observe from the outside.

By critically examining their world and role from within, much like Paulo Freire's *Pedagogy of the Oppressed*, educators and students have an advantageous position to tackle some ramifications that resulted from internal and external factors. Graphic designers should

8

proactively reconstruct their roles to cope with the change rather than submitting passively to it. By bridging a theoretical framework that integrally engages in the process of making graphic design and a practical framework that understands the definitions and limitations of graphic design as a form of social practice, educators, students, and practitioners can cope with changes.

Embracing their views, I undertook this endeavor to generate discussions about the field and I wish to produce a theory for graphic design in the area of ideation to provide insights, new perspectives and new understandings in the area of creativity in graphic design students using computer technology. It is impossible to provide a complete description of the field, but rather to develop a theory that accounts for much of the relevant behavior in which there is a sequence of cognitive activities, actions and thoughts by people and interactivity between them and computer technology.

<u>Hypotheses</u>

What I am investigating, in a limited sense, is how undergraduate students solve graphic design problems with the aid of computer technology. Because they are in an environment that is constantly simulating a real world where emphasis is placed on providing effective solutions within a market-driven framework, four hypotheses tested by my study are described in the following:

1. The field of graphic design in the marketplace at large has no meaning or value except in relation to a client. Within this context of art and commerce, graphic designers are aware that it takes looking at problems from the client's perspective, not just their own. Graphic design is willy-nilly chained to communicative interests whether they function within economic, apolitical, propagandistic, or selfless agendas. Responding to expediency, computer technology is utilized as a tool within the design process. Graphic design education is responding to these changes and as they respond they also initiate changes forming interdependent and synergistic relationships between education and practice. Educators are simulating an environment where their students are trained to meet the demands and standards of a market-driven field. This in itself is an example of a market-driven principle.

2. Creativity in achieving the most effective solution is strongly motivated by the demands of the market. Because of this, the specific kind of creativity that

9

corresponds to a market-driven framework is valued. The creative process becomes a form of commodity in the marketplace because it is artistically and entrepreneurially intertwined.

3. In my view, computer technology has the potential of creating a synergy between the mind and the potentiality of technology. As a catalyst for creativity within the design process, technology becomes the facilitator in supporting creativity. Students can recognize the problem, analyze and synthesize it to create many ideas or solutions but the design process is complicated by the fact that an effective solution has to be accepted or validated in the construct in which it exists, which in this case is confined within a market-driven context.

4. Because of these contexts, it may seem that creativity may be compromised or overshadowed by these factors. Yet when computers are used, new ideas can be created because they are being facilitated by interactions between human minds and machines. Therefore, human creativity is still an important factor. The trick is to find a balance between idealism and functionalism.

Information I gather may provide a framework for understanding larger implications such as:

1. How does computer technology influence the students' ideation?
2. Can computer technology neither stimulate nor hinder creativity?
3. What are the strengths and limitations of computers in education?

The commonalities of these perspectives serve as a lens to examine the creativity in undergraduates' ideation.

Significance of the study

It is not my interest to view graphic design as a form of vocational training, but rather as a field that is constantly involved in discovery and renewal. The idea is to interweave educational training with a "real world" sense of practicality as a platform to contribute to the field. Through such approach, graphic design educators and practitioners can actively observe and redefine the practice from within. This study is important for three reasons:

1. To understand if computer technology can impact the students' creativity especially in the design process. And by doing so, the study may also define the strengths and limitations of computers in design education.

2. To investigate how graphic design students construct and visualize (problem-solve) their concepts and solutions in visual discourse.

3. To construct a theory about the practice of graphic design by expressing in systematic terms or concepts the analysis of the design process in order to give it meaning, significance, and legitimacy in service-oriented and market driven contexts.

As technology and society continue to evolve, my research will continue to track the benefits or drawbacks of computer software and hardware.

<u>Limitations</u>

With the proliferation of reading and research materials related to my research question, it is impossible to completely cover the subject. Polling an entire student population in the Southwestern United States would not only be too time-consuming but also it would be impossible given the constraints under which I must work. As market researchers usually study only a small sample or a large group to determine its characteristics, my study is limited to one major university.

This study does not involve analyzing or predicting specific tasks of computing technology nor does it seek to analyze or predict human mentality on creativity. This study seeks to understand the influence of computer software and hardware on undergraduate students' creativity in completing their design projects using computer technology and in doing so, whether their creativity was enhanced or compromised in the area of ideation.

The research subjects are already solving problems in digital environments and computer usage at the final stage of their assignments is a must. This is not an exception but the rule and this qualifies them as subjects to this research. I seek to implement objectivity through distance and limited involvement. Research subjects who have experienced the process I am studying are perfect for this study because I am interested in reporting their reflective opinions. They react more naturally in the classroom compared to artificially restricted, manipulated conditions if the research were conducted under artificial conditions.

In order to maximize the opportunities for data collection to allow for time constraints, self-administered questionnaires are used. This research depends on an uninterrupted design development process where students have accessibility to both computer software and hardware within or outside of university campus. Because students may enroll in different classes, they may be repeating the similar research methodology but in

11

different class settings with different assignments. Because I may not be in all the classes to proctor the questionnaire, instructors are left with the questionnaire and a detailed instructional sheet for them to carry out the survey. Appendix B shows a copy of the reduced instructional sheet for the instructor. The actual sheet measures 8.5" x 11" and is printed on a beige card stock for identification purposes.

The question of what constitutes creativity needs to be addressed here. Creativity consists of at least a few observable components: (a) the person, (b) the process, (c) the product, and (d) the environment. For this particular study, although the interactions between the four components are observed and eventually documented in the questionnaire, data gathered is a reflective account of the respondents. By their own nature, reflective narrations generated by respondents for this case study tend to reflect what they think is relevant to them and can only report what they remember.

Although they serve as valuable sources for hypotheses for future empirical data, these "introspective" data are at the same time, "retrospective" as respondents look back into their previous experiences. Such data are open to interpretations which mean that any possibility of testing is possible due to the empirically verifiable nature afforded by the "retrospective" documentations.

It is important to report that I cannot document what exactly goes on in the respondents' minds as they think of ideas during the ideation stage, but their ideas are documented in the process notebook as required by some instructors. A process notebook is a collection of ideas from initial sketches to final visuals. The purpose of the notebook is to document the students' thought and design processes. Depending on the course and the instructor, a process notebook can be elaborate or a hodgepodge of research materials, visuals, idea explorations, and computer printouts bound in a volume. Moreover, as they respond to the questionnaires, their reports about the design process are documented, which then become observable and verifiable since anyone can read them.

When I seek knowledge about design, it is also a category which I belong especially when I function professionally as a graphic designer. The result is therefore intertwined and creates an intimate relationship between the seeker and the knowledge. My academic and professional backgrounds have always been shaped by how well I can provide solutions to my clients. Therefore, my backgrounds may inhibit my impartial judgment in my research but they also provide the impetus that fuels my interest in this area of research.

Throughout years of practice in the field of graphic design, I acquired an understanding of how things work, why, and what will happen under certain conditions. This reality of a phenomenon is faithfully taken into my research situation to help in understanding events and actions as they are observed, seen, and heard. Strauss and Corbin (1990) claim that one can draw from his or her professional experience. This can result in a richer knowledge base and insight to draw upon. However, they warn that the same experience can also block one from things that have become habitual.

Anyhow, the idea of documenting one's mental processes as a metacognitive ability presents an interesting approach and support for this research. The integrity of data and the plausibility of its explanation depend on how the students respond to the written questionnaire. The assumption is that by keeping the questionnaire short and simple, it would be easy for students to report their own mental processes since all descriptions and interpretations are conveyed verbally rather than numerically.

The research subjects' ability to express themselves in a written format would have varied from person to person. Taking into consideration that the ideation process is a non-verbal task, the fluency and articulation in writing as required in answering the questionnaire does not necessarily reflect their creative abilities. Individuals who are comfortable expressing their thought may have higher number of memories or simply because they are being helpful in the research. It is entirely possible that some subjects who are creative may have a lower ability in written articulation and some of them may have a lower ability in articulating their thoughts. Some who are not as creative may be more expressive in their responses.

It is also possible that the respondents are reticent in expressing their thoughts. Therefore, it is only the expressed aspects that are being discussed and analyzed for the research. Subjects that report their mental process in a written format may have subconsciously allowed writing ability and other technical and environmental factors to become confounding variables in this research.

By understanding the impact of computer technology on the students' creativity especially in the design process, my theories about creativity and the ideation process presented in this study are by no means conclusive or grandiose in approach. It is made out of frameworks from which the design process, marketplace, and creativity are combined to give the theory meaning, significance, and legitimacy in service-oriented and market-driven contexts.

I must admit that there is a possibility that the theory generated from this research and the empirical world will mismatch because my research is linked to the data collected. The information itself is characteristically derived from participants and their interpretations are reflective in nature. Furthermore, the field of graphic design is constantly changing. Therefore, theory itself is subjected to modification and reformulation. However, in order to generate possible explanations, theories are being made answerable to the facts. It is prudent to consider how the theory from this research is helpful in the areas to which I make recommendations. It is my hope that my theory will stimulate a variety of research and study and excite educators and students to apply the theory to their educational goals.

Definition of terms

In the following paragraphs, I would like to define a few key terms that are used throughout the chapters. To avoid confusion, I must clarify at the outset about the terms used in this study, not just for the methodology but also some ideas that may otherwise have larger implications in different contexts. The first section of definitions is devoted to terms used in the methodology. Because of the systematic stages observed in the methodology, the terms described in the following section are not alphabetized.

Properties and dimensional locations

The first step in data analysis is to conceptualize it. *Conceptualization* or the basic building blocks of theory or labels placed on events or other instances of phenomena are identified by their *properties* and *dimensions*. Properties are attributes or characteristics pertaining to a category in open coding that serve to provide more detail about each category. Dimensions mean that I view properties along a continuum to locate examples that represent extremes on the continuum in the data.

For example, the computer, as a facilitator (category), engages the students in exploring more ideas (a property), which leads to the possibilities on a continuum of figuring out problems that eventually lead to an effective solution (dimensional location). Both properties and dimensional locations form the basis for making relationships between categories and subcategories.

Open coding

Open coding is about generating initial categories. This means that every observation, sentence, and paragraph in the questionnaire is closely scrutinized, and selected data are given a discrete label. Data are broken down into distinct parts, closely examined, compared for similarities and differences, and questions are raised about the phenomena as reflected in the data. Because new data can be "raw" and generic, it is important at this stage to conceptualize them or to name them. The analytic procedures require making comparisons and asking questions (Strauss & Corbin, 1990).

Questions such as: what is this data about?, what does it represent?, and how does it relate to my hypotheses? are asked. I also compare categories with sub-categories as I go along so that similar phenomena can be given the same name. Once I have identified a particular phenomenon in data, I begin to group concepts around them that seem to pertain to the same phenomena. This process is called *categorizing* (Strauss & Corbin, 1990, p. 65). Concepts or themes with similar properties are grouped together and arranged and rearranged until they are "saturated."

Axial coding

If *open coding* breaks down the data to allow identification of categories, properties, and dimensional locations, *axial coding* puts those data back together for connections to be made between a category and subcategories. In the second phase known as *axial coding*, one *open coding* category is selected and positioned at the center of the process being explored (as the core phenomenon), and then relates other categories to it.

Phenomenon

A *phenomenon* is "the central idea, event, happening, about which a set of actions/interactions is directed as managing or handling, or to which the set is related" (Strauss & Corbin, 1990, p. 100). Simply put, think of it as a variable. There are four other variables in the process of data analyzing:

Causal conditions

1. *Causal conditions* refer to the events or incidents that lead to the occurrence or development of a phenomenon. In the context of this study, if I am interested in the phenomenon of creativity, I might discover that using a computer can lead to

15

discovering new ideas. Using the paradigm model, a discovery event may be diagramed like this:

Causal condition ▶ **Phenomenon**
Using computer technology   Discovery

Properties of computer technology	**Dimensional profiles of discovery**	
The kinds of programs used	effects	personalization
Features within the program	creativity	continuity
Peripherals (auxiliary devices) attached	stimulation	sensation
Performance	limitations	productivity
Solution	performance	application

Context and intervening conditions

2. *Context and intervening conditions* are specific and general situational factors that influence the strategies. A contextual condition refers to "a specific set of properties that pertain to a phenomenon [but they also refer to] the particular set of conditions within which the action/interaction strategies are taken to manage, handle, carry out, and respond to a specific phenomenon" (Strauss & Corbin, 1990, p. 101). To clarify this, let us return to my example of using computer technology. Assuming that it leads to discovery, I need to know the specifics about the cause, as well as the properties to use the technology effectively. Intervening conditions are broader and more general structural context pertaining to a phenomenon. Exemplary conditions include time, space, culture, technological status, economic status, career, history, biography, and so forth.

Action/Interaction strategies

3. *Action/Interaction Strategies* are actions taken in response to the core phenomenon. This is defined as the action/interaction. It is purposeful and goal-oriented because in responding to a phenomenon as it exists in context or under a specific type of conditions, one has to manage, handle, carry out, or respond to a set of actions. However, not all action/interaction is purposeful because there are always intervening conditions. In this case, it is the lack of training in computer technology, one has limited accessibility to technology, peripheral problems, and so on.

4. *Consequences* (outcomes from using the strategies). It may be actual or potential and it may happen in the present or in the future. This stage involves drawing a diagram, called a *coding paradigm* to analyze the data collected. Coding paradigm is a form of visual picture of theory generated which portrays the interrelationship of causal conditions, strategies, contextual and intervening conditions, and consequences.

Selective coding

From here, a central phenomenon is identified and categorized to identify a *core category*. This is the stage of *selective coding* where other categories are being methodically related to other categories, relationships validated, and to fill in categories that need further refinement and development. The entire procedure leads to generating a theory based on data collected. The theory generated is an abstract explanation or understanding of a process about a substantive topic grounded in the data. The final theory generated is limited to those categories, their properties, dimensions, and statements of relationship that are in the actual data collected.

Quite a simplification, the model looks something like this: A (causal conditions) ▶B (phenomenon) ▶ C (context) ▶ D (intervening conditions) and ▶ E (action/interaction strategies) ▶ F (consequences). The model addresses how different kinds of broad (intervening conditions) and specific awareness (context) become conditions for action/interaction, how they are maintained (strategies), how they change (process), and what it means for those involved (consequences). Once the data are related on a conceptual level and also the property and dimensional levels for each major category, a rudimentary skeleton for theory can be either diagrammatically or narratively presented.

This denotes the end of the first section of definitions devoted to methodology and the following sections are for technical or generic terms that pertain to the study.

Client

A client is the decision-maker and the invoice payer who commissions a designer. He or she could be a business owner, a marketing and sales professional, or a publisher. A freelancing graphic designer may serve an art director or the creative director for the client. Creative directors may sometimes be principles of their own design firms and although they are mainly responsible for originating ideas and concepts, they are also responsible for managing the project, supervising the entire design processes, coordinating resources, and supervising the whole processes and production process (Sebastian, 2001). Roles between them blend and become less definable as responsibilities become expanded and specialized due to automation of the design processes.

Creativity

The objective of this research is to determine if creativity is affected when students use computer technology. For this study, creativity is narrowly viewed in terms of how undergraduates solve graphic design problems in a design communications program at a major university. I do not intend to give a holistic definition of creativity but rather a definition that pertains to my study.

Creativity, for the context of this study is defined as using problem solving ideas in leading to tangible products or message. When "creativity" or "creative" is used in connection with graphic design, it is to be assumed that productivity of ideas and novelty are involved. Hanna; et al. (2001) and Sawahata (1999) defined creativity as problem-solving using effective methods, informed by an understanding of social, cultural, historical, and technical aspects of communication to achieve a desired goal. We exercise creative thinking not only to communicate, but to solve problems. More importantly, part of this process is to realize that a problem exists.

Design

Using the term "design," which has hitherto been loosely used, I would like to clarify and define its reference in this research. The term itself covers a large variety of human activities and products. However, when singly used in the chapters, design is referred solely to the field of graphic design, unless specified. The field has since diversified and evolved into many areas of specialty. In a recent poster, the American Institute of Graphic Arts (2002) listed the following design occupations:

1. Advertising designers
2. Animators
3. Brand designers
4. Environmental graphic designers
5. Exhibition designers
6. Experience designers

7. Gaming designers

8. Graphic designers

9. Illustrators

10. Information architects

11. Information designers

12. Interaction designers

13. Interface designers

14. Motion graphics designers

15. Package designers

16. Publication designers

17. Typeface designers

18. Web designers.

Nobody will deny that the professions listed above deal with information and the communication of this information. Emerging from this list is a broadened definition for the functions which goes beyond the standards of aesthetical enhancements and problem-solving. Students preparing to assume these roles in graphic design make the public aware of the informational forces that require them to be highly specialized and competitive in a field subjected to unrelenting commercial pressure to produce new visual forms that are visually enticing and lucidly communicative. It is clear that graphic design is no longer a submissive advertising subset or marketing derivative.

Desktop publishing

Desktop publishing is the use of personal computers or computer workstations and various kinds of software to produce different types of printed materials with a high-resolution printer (usually a laser printer). Desktop publishers have a choice of selecting from a variety of fonts and sizes, column justifications, page layouts, and image libraries for document creation and editing. Small businesses or an individual can produce professional-quality materials inexpensively and quickly without the need for outside and often expensive typesetting or printing facilities.

As the professional boundaries become blurred, it is important for me to attempt to accurately define the difference between a desktop publisher and a graphic designer. Like graphic designers, desktop publishers use computers but the professional and responsibilities of graphic designers are beyond the scope of a desktop publisher. This is because graphic designers are trained in design sensibilities as well as technical knowledge and they are able to offer options beyond any standard desktop publishing. Trainings in conceptual, formal, and technological skills prepare student designers and as a result, they have great fluency in the visual language.

While there are components of graphic design that may be shared with desktop publishing such as page layout, graphics and image-editing aspects, graphic designers typically graduate from a four-year undergraduate professional degree program. This prepares them in areas of corporate identity, packaging design, collateral design, web design, computer graphics, and other art and design areas. A listing of professions for graphic designers is listed in "design" in this definition section.

Graphic design

Graphic design is defined here as the range of practices, information and objects that define the field. Within the discipline of the graphic design, practice deals with boundaries that fall within its own breadth and also what the field excludes. In other words, the field has its innuendoes and biases. Graphic design is different from other forms of applied art because the field combines artistic creativity and commercial viability. Graphic design has a purpose primarily because of the audience to which it is trying to target. A graphic designer is concerned with reaching out and influencing a mass audience. Every creation is meant to "sell" something, either a message or a product.

Even the label of graphic design is non-standard by all means. Graphic communications, communication design, design communication, commercial art, and graphic arts, just to name a few are the commonly heard descriptions for the field. Compounding this, the professional status of graphic design remains questionable by the Department of Labor and there is no governing body to supervise the profession of graphic design compared to those of the American Institute of Architects (McCoy, 1998). Having access to technological tools does not create a professional, nor does having licensure of the field. What should happen is an appreciation and understanding of the graphic design process in raising the quality of graphics and publishing.

Graphic designers may not save the world and though design is not everything, both somehow manage to permeate many aspects of our lives. Because everything around us is "designed" by someone and we may not commission for them, we get the outcome regardless. Directional signage at airport terminals aids in getting passengers onto the right plane at the right place in the right time. Slick advertisements inform us about new products. Clever packaging not only protects the merchandise but also acts as a "billboard" attracting store customers. Annual reports attract new investors while retaining old ones. Instructional manuals provide trouble-shooting directions, and the list goes on. Although graphic designers do not design a product per se, they work with marketing or personnel and we need to realize that our role is to help "sell" something.

In a market-driven context, the "design" in graphic design has evolved into a commercial enterprise which means it is a matter of efficiency as time is being equated with money (Schreuders, 1977). Businesses hire design studios or freelance graphic designers to fulfill their graphic needs. Much of the impact of design depends on the way it is constructed: the material used and the underlying message it sends. Therefore, it is not surprising that graphic designers are very much aware of how people react to ideas and the elements and principles of designs.

Some historians track the historical development of graphic design back to the Industrial Revolution when it gained its momentum in a capitalistic society that constantly responds to shifting needs in a socio-economic environment (Meggs, 1998). Because of the nature of graphic design and the protocol used therein, a distinctive way of looking at and thinking about the field is that it is psychologically and philosophically conditioned by the discipline, people that are part of the field, the process employed and the environment which all of these factors interdependent on to produce a desired end result. The end result is achieved through a combination of metaphors, signs, symbols, colors, type, and images serving, design, advertising, sales, and service entities.

Whether freelancing or employed by a firm, graphic designers use a variety of print, electronic, and film media to create art that meets a client's needs. Most graphic designers use computer software to help in the creation and production of their design projects. Depending on the commission, they may create promotional displays and marketing brochures for new products, visual designs of annual reports and other corporate literature, or distinctive logos for products or businesses.

Graphic design can be found in such diverse opportunities in the following careers: design direction, art direction, multimedia and web page design, layout, package design, exhibition design, retail identity, sign system design, and environmental graphics. As for career options, graphic designers can choose to work in publishing houses, advertising agencies, corporate in-house agencies, printers, newspaper and magazine publishers, production houses, service bureaus, catalog publishers, financial institutions, television stations, movie studios and so forth.

Market-driven

The word "market" is derived from the Latin word, *mercari*, which means to buy or trade and it can be goods or services sold or traded (Curry, 1999). Market-driven is described as "a company that produces goods, services or modifications based upon what consumers demand [or] an economic system in which supply, demand and price are the determinants of which products will enter the marketplace" (Curry, 1999, p. 178). The relationship between a marketer and the consumer is built upon sales transactions. There is some sort of gain taking place in the marketplace, regardless of one buying or selling. Even in the briefest transaction between the buyer and seller creates a relationship. The concerted effort is the initial utilization of ideas that results in a saleable product or services.

Problem-solving

In this study, students problem-solve their designs by using computer technology. Academically, it constitutes an educational method in which learning takes place through discoveries that result from investigations made by the student. *Problem-solving* is defined as the ability to analyze, identify, interpret, connect, and apply a set of visually pleasing, technologically adept, socially responsive, and intellectually effective solutions through concepts and skills to solve project-based assignments.

Problem-solving is also definable as a heuristic which is a speculative formulation serving as a guide in the investigation or solution of a problem where one considers a wide range of alternatives with methodical processes to reach the desired and effective end result. Within the context of graphic design, I interpret problem solving as finding an effective solution to a task or project.

The credit goes to Graham Wallas and John Dewey for the conception of thinking as a problem-solving activity. The connection between artistic creation and problem solving can be traced back to 1926 when Graham Wallas identified four steps in the process of problem-solving: (a) preparation, (b) incubation, (c) inspiration, and (d) verification (Couger, 1995). Incubation is the term used for unconscious generation of potential solutions (Glover et al., 1989).

John Dewey added that problem solving "comprised of defining the problem, identifying the alternatives, and selecting the best alternatives" (Couger, 1995, p. 110). Often times, the solution is found only through the process of solving a problem because we have not been exposed to it yet. This reinforces the concept of discovery. Perhaps the most remarkable feature of problem solving was that problem solvers had to formulate the problem as well as propose a solution to it.

Sketching

Sketching is defined as a rough or tentative drawing representing the ideas often made as a preliminary study in a design. In this study, hasty or incomplete drawings, doodles, sketches, or any sort of outlines that lead to compositional formation of ideas are documented on either paper with writing utensils or directly on the computer throughout the process. Although the study does not use students' initial sketches for analysis, several questions in the questionnaires are designed to solicit ideas about the students' reflections about sketching.

Technology

Within the arts, graphic design is one of the first few to include computer technology in its repertoire and it is accepted with mixed blessings. For the purpose of this research, computer technology refers to computer software and hardware which operate in the Apple Macintosh operating system and IBM-compatible personal computers running on Microsoft Windows. Both these systems are capable of displaying images with the graphic user interface (GUI). Whenever a single word of technology is mentioned in the writing, it is to imply that both computer software and hardware are mentioned in the discussion unless specified otherwise.

CHAPTER II
REVIEW OF RELATED LITERATURE

<u>Overview of the Literature</u>

Graphic design is a young field and research is limited and theoretical research is not abundant. In the past, the derivative contents of most texts are extended general principles of communication, advertising, and marketing concepts. In its humble beginning, texts about graphic design relied primarily on information in fields other than graphic design itself but graphic designers and scholars' strong interests have produced enough materials and discussions to provide incentives in advancing the field as a competitive profession.

Textbooks for graphic design courses no longer rely on research or theories developed by scholars outside the design field. Although writing about graphic design continues to draw from other disciplines, mainly because of its adaptive and interdisciplinary backgrounds, it is now a substantive field in its own right, with enough bases of knowledge, theories, and research to support from within. It is liberating to learn that some literatures derived for this study are written by practicing professionals who are also educators.

Computer technology, made possible by hardware and software contributes to print and electronic media as it is now one of the major devices used in conceptualizing, developing, and producing materials for graphic designers. Existing research attempts to understand the problematic computer's impact on its users especially in the field of graphic design pedagogy and practice but no empirically supported literature specifically addresses the impact of technology in the ideation process in graphic design. Current literature offers little guidance as to how to identify and capture the essence of creativity amongst graphic designer and to translate those cognitive explanations during the ideation process. Most studies speculate on emerging issues in the areas of design practice and process especially the integration of computer into our educational system in graphic design courses.

Because of these integrations, technology affects the way we learn, study, and work. After perusal and study of related literature and appraisal of the scope and ambition of other recent dissertations in the field, I find that most educators or researchers are more interested in the influence, impact, benefit, and drawback of computer technology. Several researchers are also interested in using the technology's capability to benefit our cognition but there is very little research focusing specifically in graphic design process of ideation.

Research that attempts to understand the cognitive processes of writers while working at the word processor exists but none exists for studying the computer's impact on the creative thought process on graphic designers and studio artists until Alvey's (1991) research came along, particularly in exploring the relationship between the artist and the electronic design station. Enormous reliance upon technology in the arts prompted Heinz-Glaeser (1999) to conduct an Internet survey of the public and to interview thirty practicing artists to determine the positive and negative effects of computer technology. She discovers the following: decrease of communication skills, integration of diverse artistic modes, technology being used as a tool to enhance the arts and the desire to retain knowledge of traditional art practice.

Freedman and Relan (1992) conducted a case study on eleven undergraduate art education majors enrolled in a university computer graphics course to determine how computer graphics influence their educational experiences and what kinds of experiences the computers are capable of enhancing. They concluded that these students shifted from a focus on manipulative and technical aspects of generating graphics to formal and conceptual aspects as they gained computer experience.

Becker (1982) and Rosenblum (1978) identified that the equipments or tools used embody not only the aesthetics but they also create a "convention" that is determined by the characteristics and idiosyncrasies of the tool or equipment. Conventions will dictate the materials and styles that designers or artists use. In this case, an example of a convention applied to graphic design is thinking of the scale of design. The scale of a monitor is consistently designed to match a magazine layout. Another example is the output from a printer that is determined by the design's dimensions. Another way of thinking about tradition is when they create, student graphic designers are creating within the traditions of a convention in which an intended target audience can identify with and respond to, as long as the designer stays within an acceptable convention (Schreuders, 1977).

However, after mastering the techniques of a computer program and understanding the conventions, designers may strive to transcend the program. The predictability of the software may force the designer to break the rules of the convention (Johnson, 1995). Different software program offer different capabilities for performing functions in art and design. As the artist learns the technical aspects of the program, he or she identifies the features and possibilities of the medium. Based on this observation, the intricacies of the

25

machine can stand in the way of expression, particularly when the users are not familiar with the program.

Academic institutions are not immune to technological change. Rossman (1998) reported that as colleges and universities invest heavily in computer technology, not many are interested in developing students' awareness about how thinking is reshaped by technological innovations. This disturbing trend lies in the tool-using advocates' inability to foresee the consequences of technological usage and the nearsightedness of furthering human progress through technological innovation without considering its implications. He is concerned that as we embrace technology, we intentionally and unknowingly push our agendas onto the society. He is concerned with what Postman (1993) describes as "technopoly" (p. 71). Postman expressed that

> Technopoly eliminates alternatives to itself in precisely the way Aldous Huxley outlined in Brave New World. It does not make them illegal. It does not make them immoral. It does not even make them unpopular. It makes them invisible and, therefore, irrelevant. And it does so by redefining what we mean by religion, by art, by family, by politics, by truth, by privacy, by intelligence, so that our definitions fit its new requirements. Technopoly, in other words, is totalitarian technocracy. (p. 48)

Everything must surrender to the supremacy of technocracy. Historically, Western technocracies stem from medieval Europe and perhaps the most monumental invention ever to happen to mankind is that of printing, which helped to facilitate the spread of knowledge (Postman, 1993). German printing pioneer, Johann Gutenberg's invention in the 15th century changed the way information is disseminated. Printing spread rapidly and began to replace hand-printed texts for a wider audience and it has permanently influenced all aspects of human life.

The invention of a system of printing of movable type meant that information becomes much more accessible to general populace rather than elite groups in high places. It is worth stressing that the printing method itself does not revolutionize how we learn, but rather a complex system of socio and economic factors that led to the success. In technocracy, tools take on a leading role in the society that accepts them. Without much of our modern inventions, we would not have progressed this far.

Volti (2001) warned us about the impact of technology in his book, Society and Technological Change. Trusting that technocracy is the solution, we are lulled into thinking that they could solve society's problem. According to Volti (2001), technocracy is defined as the governance of society by engineers, other people with technical expertise, and those who attempt to develop policies based on technical and scientific principles. In our quest to improve human conditions, we invent and implement technology before we can fully foresee the totality of its impact on society. This is because most of the time, we are forced to deal with the problem at hand.

Ogburn (as cited in Volti, 2001, p. 267) who coined the term "cultural lag," describes that as technology progresses, many things such as habits, thoughts, values, and social arrangements often fail to change at the same speed as technological innovation. Cultural changes come more slowly than the technological changes that instigate it.

The versatile usage of the computer is irresistible to many. It is now possible to display and interactively manipulate models of nonexistent objects with computers. Computer technology enables self-directed work that allows for a high degree of initiative, spontaneity and experimentation which often yields multiple solutions and original ideas in an environment free from anxiety and time pressure without abandoning sense of responsibility.

The multifaceted abilities of computer technology allow designers and artists to include sound, images, text, and movement. Other elements such as voice, music, sequence, and time are now part of the features in creating and delivering multidimensional experiences for both the creators and the viewers. Because no other medium can facilitate this kind of diverse integration, computers can become a vehicle for educators to be experimental in their teaching methods.

Truckenbrod (1990) believed that the integrative elements of technology can be used to stimulate creative thinking and creations for new forms of artistic expressions surpassing the traditional limitations of art and design. Coupled with her own book, she developed a course entitled Experimental Computer Imaging at the School of the Art Institute of Chicago. Students are encouraged to experiment and explore their creative thought processes through digital photography with video digitizers that provide opportunities for students to draw, sketch, paint and create imagery. They interpret and create various abstract ideas visually and from there audio is added. This forms an interesting visual-aural synthesis. Her students are also introduced to animation that explore movement and time as well as compositional explorations. The class culminates into a final compact disc project where their work will be exhibited via telecommunication, broadcasted to a worldwide audience.

Justice (1998) is not so sure. She argues that technology is hastening the teaching and learning process. Although she agrees that technology has given designers the opportunity to do more, everything related to the field from academic institutions, educators, students to businesses and employers are being incited into the demands of an ongoing acquisitions of the latest hardware and software. Not only must universities provide expensive technological facilities, but educators and students must constantly retrain themselves to learn new software and hardware, interact with technology personnel, and maximize the limited time available for design courses without compromising the quality of their work. When educators relearn technology, they have to learn it on their own and to find a slot in their busy schedule to sneak in creativity in their teaching methods.

Postman agrees. He stated that computers are "not integrated into the culture," but instead "they attack the culture" (Postman, 1992, p. 28). Not only must universities provide expensive technological facilities, educators and students must constantly retrain themselves to learn new software and hardware, interact with technology personnel, and maximize the limited time available for design courses without compromising the quality of their work. The computer has also forced us to speed things up in terms of learning and having to enforce and institute the teachings. As a result, we now have to face the constant challenge of having to relearn new knowledge to keep up.

Technological tools radically change the way we work and live because every medium has the potential to re-characterize the world we live in. New technologies do not alter us but it changes the environment in which we live. There is not much of a choice in terms of realizing ideas because modern design is "technologically infected," (Bonsiepe, 1965, p.163) whereby the exchange of ideas becomes dependent on a device to actualize it. We become helpless to resist its spread and find ourselves adapting to it. Technology generates what Mok (1996) calls the "multiplicity phenomenon" (p. xiii) where he sees a growth in digital communication technology from printed to online media.

Pulitzer Prize-winning journalist and New York Times foreign affairs columnist Thomas L. Friedman (2001), in describing digital Darwinism, warns us that the key to winning is "adapt or die, get wired or get killed" (¶ 3). If we do not subscribe to this theory of digital evolution, do we lose out? In many ways, Friedman is right. At the current rate which software is updated or rendered obsolete, universities are facing the challenge of keeping up with changes in technology. Lacking well-trained educators and a lack of general knowledge about software and its capabilities are just some of the salient problems faced by academic institutions.

Due to the speed of information age, what we know today may be rendered obsolete tomorrow. At the rate which software is being updated by their manufacturers, universities have to face the challenge of keeping up to date with changes in newer versions that promise to deliver more and better features. Justice (1998) stressed that the days of an instructor knowing everything is over because they suffer under the weighty demands of technology and time. Faculty tasks greatly expand when they teach or rely on technologies in their classrooms. Not only must they learn the new software and hardware, they must provide a different studio setup, interact with technology personnel, and maintain computer setups at school as well as at home.

Computer technology has introduced a unique factor into design pedagogy. In order to solve the problem, LeCroy and Leonard (1985) contend that not only must educators acquire some technical skills in dealing with computer technologies, they must also integrate these applications into actual lessons. They also add that features such as creativity, instructional objectives, content relevancy, user friendliness, feedback capabilities, motivational devices are some of the features that are necessary to use computers as a tool of instruction. Instructional objectives must match teaching strategies, and assessments to meet student needs and achieve learning outcomes.

According to Blauvelt (1998), the interrelatedness of "cognitive interaction, cultural reflexivity, and technological innovation shape the field of graphic design" (p. 76). As an educator, he proposes that graduate education should focus on research because it is important to acknowledge the fact that graphic design does not begin nor end in the objects it makes or the solution it presents. In different stages of designed artifacts from their production to distribution to consumption, a realistic model of learning recognizes that in every step of the way, change does take place and it may influence preceding and subsequent stages, resulting in a dynamic and cyclical stage.

Mills (1994) published a paper about using computers to enhance human creativity. He disagrees with the notion that computers are tools of efficiency but rather that it should be used to help us work smarter. For one, computers can give us more accurate understanding of complex information. Given the limitations of our human body and the conditions in which we have to work in, errors are common. Our cognitive weaknesses, amongst others include the tendency to give greater weight to recent events when computer neither get emotional or forgetful.

We also overemphasize, allow for and filter out biases, and dramatize our experiences (Mills, 1994). This is not to say that computers are error-free but Mills' idea is that computers are better equipped to make experimentation with various analytical skills more efficiently than human beings. He agreed that in the end, human expertise is still needed to interpret "computer-generated intellectual semiprocessed goods" (Mills, 1994, p. 219). Computers do not solve complex problems, they serve by preparing our work and that frees us to focus on the solutions.

A relatively low cost computer system setup with text and graphics layout programs, attached to a printer and scanner can serve as a powerful partner for teachers to enhance more creative projects especially when visual aspect and textual meaning are concerned. Computers can be a stimulant for creative activity. Sullivan (1988) claimed that in her advanced writing class held in her classroom, she was able to assign various projects such as newsletter, business cards, résumés, learn basic software and graphics concepts, and write miscellaneous papers.

These activities emphasize the "visual dimensions of writing" which helps to improve the quality of her students' work as well as their ability in discussing the "visual dimensions of meaning" (Sullivan, 1988, p. 346). The benefits are clear. Her students learn some useful skills and teachers are given a means for teaching visual and verbal elements. She further adds that one of her students was offered a job on the spot during a job interview after the interviewer became impressed with her class newsletter.

Like Sullivan, Rubinstein (1994) is also appreciative that software technology has given her, a former typesetter and color separator, the instantaneous ability to produce work that is comparable to well-trained graphic designer. The software package she uses is equipped with multiple templates that could be altered, making it easy for anyone with accessibility to the software to produce anything from stationery items to book cover design. According to her, design professionals are ignorant about the fact that anyone who has a computer and a book of design history would be able to imitate great designers.

Keedy (1994) communicated similar ideas but he insists that computers are allowing more people who never had prior knowledge about design to experiment with design. He warns that change is inevitable due to technological, ideological, and cultural complexity. One positive change is in the attitude and perception of designers not relegating themselves as service providers to their clients but rather a facilitator between their clients in a cultural context that defines the field as a whole.

As argued, most educators, researchers, and graphic designers are able to use the computer technology effectively only if they invest time and money into learning the software, to master the skills necessary to use the "tool" effectively and finally to constantly upgrade their knowledge and system to keep up with current technologies. Taking a more proactive approach in their papers, Leonard and LeCroy (1985) advocated that instead of arguing about the pros and cons of computers in our society, we need to train educators in dealing with technology that seems to be here to stay. This is because teachers are the most important resources in a classroom. Apart from that, software is the next most important investment, not hardware because software needs to be constantly updated and the availability of different kinds of software becomes important to accompany course materials.

The possibilities are boundless with digital applications but it has also brought with it some ethical ramifications. Ethical ramifications are exactly what Milton Glaser's (1995) fiery rhetoric when he proclaims, "The war is over," which shows his loathsome hostility towards computer technology. As an educator at the School of Visual Arts in New York for more than thirty years and the designer of the "I Love NY" logo, he confidently asserts that because of technological advancements, graphic designers have lost ground as technology enables clients to figure out how to exercise control over digital documents, eliminating the needs for graphic designers. He further adds that the argument within the field is whether computers can aid or hinder creativity.

The computer in fact, is no longer a tool, it is also the medium. Every designer plays the interchangeable roles of author, designer, and producer (Cullen, 1998; Glaser, 1995). Although the computers are empowering and democratic, clients are now able to control the design processes by micromanaging every step from start to production. Technology also, according to Glaser (1995), contributes to excessive population of graphic designers. They are now industrial workers in a field that does not necessarily require them to be either creative or competent. He contends that a person with six weeks of computer training can become a designer in a corporation without the knowledge of form, color, art history or aesthetics in general that was once thought of as essential. If his arguments hold ground, the unprecedented power of technology is changing the way the very nature of graphic design profession itself.

31

When designers collaborate directly with computer technology, they are indirectly being either constrained or liberated by programmers, software and hardware engineers, and interface designers whose "authorship" is being embedded in the program and hardware designs (Johnson, 1995). The computer is a highly technical device and manufacturers have to make sure that they are "user-friendly," including software designed to run on them. Graphical user interface (GUI) that is represented in windows, menus, and icons are technical programming that is turned into actuality to facilitate the so-called "friendly" interface design and their operating systems.

Elements that we are familiar with such as metaphorical icons and pull-down menus are being replicated onto a computer screen. As friendly as they may look, users are forced to learn and conform to the conventions created by software with embedded cues that all users must consciously interpret. One example is the trash icon in the Apple Macintosh computer. The trash is designed with the idea that we remove files by dragging them into the trash but in order to eject a floppy disk or a CD-ROM, they too must also be "trashed" by dragging them into the trash icon.

Without GUI, accessing intangible virtual data may seem even harder because it requires different organizational models and they are: linear, hierarchical, web, parallel, matrix, overlay, and spatial zoom. From these models, five data types of text, audio, music, pictures, and moving pictures are supported (Mok, 1996). Students can unlimitedly combine them for possible creations in design.

Communication is an important part of design and when the means of communication change, it is inevitable that we will either change or be affected by it. As technology continues to broaden its boundaries, we need new names and descriptors to conceptualize their discursive, symbolic, and influential effects. In coping with the advancement of technology, we develop new language to cope with change brought about by technology. Several researchers (Dix, 1998; Gozzi, Jr., 1999; Simons, 2001) recommend that we use metaphors, analogies, and similes because they are usually perceived as imaginative and engaging in communicating complex ideas. This is because metaphor becomes important as a cognitive mechanism for us to understand deep concepts about technology and electronic media.

Along this line of thought, visual metaphors should also be exercised in ideation. This is not a new phenomenon. Computer software companies are already utilizing them in the interface design with icons that we already understand. In accessing the application, a user's interaction with the software is through a graphic user interface with tools and navigational devices that let users manipulate their ideas on the screen. Ideating with metaphors need to be concise and economical in their delivery of an otherwise abstract idea.

As the medium is internalized as a metaphor, it becomes "naturalized" (Gozzi, 1999, p. 17) as we are familiarized with its symbolic forms, genres, and conventions that are dispersed through our educational and social cultures. Understanding the language of technology may be complex but with the usage of both visual and lingual metaphors, we are making the unfamiliar a familiar element, which can be a helpful tool in teaching as well as communicating otherwise abstract ideas.

Unlike the restrictive "conventions" created by software, our "naturalization" of computing discourse can liberate us in understanding a language that is otherwise ambiguous. Understanding computing discourse is important because digital media have no tactile depth. The ability to understand information can be improved through the summarizing effect of graphics. The likelihood to accurately convey messages from sender to receiver is increased if the appearances of the graphics create or expand interests. Information presented in icons reduces the likelihood of information overload.

Within the many choices of design directions, designers need to understand that in order for the message to go through, successful interpretation requires the audience to be able to decode or interpret the message, regardless of how obvious or inconspicuous it is. The computer plays a formative role in a graphic designer's repertoire and since it can affect the outcome of a final design, designers need to be responsive to change and cognizant about the eccentricity of technology.

Concerned with the utilization of computers at an early conceptual design process, especially in the three-dimensional fields, Lawson and Ming Loke (1997) published a paper arguing that existing CAD (Computer-aided design) lack three-dimensional input tools, inadequate interface metaphors, and the system's inability to sustain parallel thoughts. Because of these, they believe that although there is a widespread of computer graphics, it falls short of enhancing creativity in especially dimensional design of architecture, industrial design, and the like. By studying sketches by American architect, Robert Venturi, they notice that early elevational sketches are explored in order to produce many solutions but existing CAD systems tend to focus only on the resolution itself instead of aiding in the "creative uncertainty" during an early stage of the design process (p. 174).

The popularity of illustration and image editing software programs create an interesting dilemma for its users. On one hand, it is a powerful tool but on the other, it has raised legal, moral, and ethical questions about manipulation, alteration, appropriation, exploitation and piracy of images (Mercedes, 1996). Though copyright laws in the United States are fairly clear and direct, they prove deficient and ambiguous in addressing ramifications raised by an electronic age. It states that "any taking from copyrighted material, no matter how small a portion is taken, is still unlawful unless it falls under the doctrine of 'fair use'" (Walker & Herman, 1994, p. 32).

"Fair use" refers to images used for non-commercial purposes which include education, research, criticism, or news-collecting. Parody is added to the fair use principle and the courts decide what constitutes fair use, usually on a case-by-case basis (Mercedes, 1996). Issues such as what constitutes a copied, a derived, or a new work is unclear. Designers and educators constantly struggle with these issues because the law is behind current technology in its laggard pursuit in interpreting what copyright is really about.

Modern scanning technologies make digitization of images excessively easy especially for someone who is trained and experienced. If an image is distorted to a degree where it is no longer recognizable, especially in collage, it becomes perfectly acceptable because it now constitutes a new piece of art (Ashford, 1994). Pop artist, Andy Warhol appropriates images of canned soups and celebrities to create his famous collage, transforming commercial influence into art. This compounds the issue of ownership because the new digital methods of making, sharing, and distributing information, change and redefine the way we construct our socio-cultural values.

There is no doubt that computer technologies provide design and production access to the public. In <u>How high do we set the bar for design education?</u>, Davis (1998) presented alarming evidence that the ratio of students to professionals in graphic design far exceeds that of other design disciplines such as architecture and industrial design. Her experience has been that clients cannot differentiate the difference between a professional and an amateur job or they do not seem to care and are sure they are not willing to pay for it. Because the supply outstrips the demand for graphic designers and there is no licensing or certification for the field, anyone can consider themselves as graphic designers, regardless of any academic and professional background. Needless to say, it is a known fact that one does not need certification or a college degree to become a graphic designer.

On the contrary, the National Association of Schools of Art and Design (NASAD) is the government-authorized body for accrediting graphic design programs. Because of their general and fine arts-based criteria for colleges and universities, they are not helpful in improving the overall quality of design programs in the United States. Educators need to realize that the survival of the field is more dependent on strategic changes in business, social, and communication environments, and not so much on traditional education in art-based concepts.

In the past, few of us had the means to technologies owned or operated by the rich or the powerful. Computer technology is now easily available, thanks to pricing competitiveness of the computer technology industry. Not just in our own homes or workplace but also in formal and informal education, we can participate in activities such as image manipulation, design, and desktop or web-site publishing. With the falling prices of computer systems, it is inevitable that this invention is here to stay.

To proclaim that graphic design is something that only a graphic designer can do is surpassingly vulgar especially in this day and age of computerdom. Computer technology has made it possible for anyone to be an author or designer. The profusion of technology has enabled many designs to be produced ubiquitously. With the abundance of computer technology in terms of software and their availability, the design process has been democratized, making it available to everyone. Technology changes the traditional role of graphic designers from paste-up to desktop publisher, and in fact, this view is further strengthened by Salchow (1993) who coyly thanked Apple Macintosh computers because "any novice can do graphic design and may legally advertise this expertise" (p. 83).

As McCoy (1998) mapped the trajectory of graphic design from its humble beginning into the future, she heedfully cautioned her readers about the impact of technology. Because of computer technology, design, reproduction processes, media, and distribution channels are forever changed. The professional boundaries are blurring with designers doing more than ever and clients relying on nonprofessional desktop publishing. Even educators are severely challenged to respond and to incorporate the new interactive information and communication technologies into the graphic design curricula.

Because of these possibilities, graphic designers are needed especially in the field of time-based interactive media, computer interfaces and designs that require incorporation of sound, motion, time, and virtual space. Wild (1998) concurred by stating that such an increase in media options beyond print makes all communication problems more complex

35

and these changes also split audiences into many "micromarkets" (p. 39) that will result in "micromarketing" (p. 40). In a media saturated society, major campaigns are needed to grab people's attention. This is where the designers and marketers come in.

As we face challenges and opportunities, divergent thinkers who display creative potentiality seek to quantifiably identify as many options as possible based on given information while convergent thinkers who are linear-oriented, narrow their options to a few choices, generally based on a conventionally accepted single best answer to a solution (Cropley, 2001). The concept of creativity as divergent thought is made popular by J.P. Guilford in his 1950 APA presidential address which set the tone for laying the foundations of contemporary research on creativity.

In 1967, he proposed the well-known tridimensional model of intelligence, the "structure of intellect." Briefly, there are five *operations* (cognition, memory, divergent production, convergent production, and evolution), described as the different ways in which we can handle four different kinds of informational *contents* (figural, symbolic, semantic, behavioral) which lead to six different types of *products* (units, classes, relations, systems, transformations, and, implications) or the outcomes of information processing. (Glover, et al., 1989, p. 15). The overall evaluation of Guilford's system is beyond the scope for this case study. His general ideas about divergent thinking are presented because of the implications of his views on creativity.

Theoretical framework

The theoretical framework for this study is framed by a few areas. Three relevant fields of thought are examined: (a) market-driven framework; (b) graphic design processes, and (c) theories and models of creativity. The study is concentrated on graphic design methods, technology associated with the field, and design pedagogical perspectives more than any other, but all the perspectives add important dimensions to the concept. These three models are lengthy partly due to the fact that I intend to illustrate the complexity and diverse body of knowledge available. This knowledge combines to influence the outcome of a design. It is also important to familiarize the reader about the position I take and to situate the research through a selectively defined lens of the three relevant fields.

My own personal interest and professional experience as a graphic designer, creative director, freelancer, and educator are strong motivational factors for the pursuit of the study. As a graphic designer schooled and trained in the field since 1986, it is difficult for me not to think of the field bound in servitude to corporate and economic values. Even in the absence of a market-drive economy, graphic design is a form of visual communication that thrives on solving a problem because if that is not the case, "then it is simply self-indulgence" (Landa, 1998, p. 10). Fine arts may allow its constituents to create in isolation but applied arts such as graphic design differ in this area. While a design can be created in isolation during its initial stages, it soon has to stand the grueling processes of assessment, refinement, elimination, selection, and finally, production.

It is impossible to engage the services of creative visual thinking without considering the practicalities and to approach graphic design as a problem-solving discipline. The first step in selling a product, promoting a service, or simply communicating a message is to define the problem. To achieve this, one must develop a concise idea of what one wish to accomplish. By answering who is the intended audience, what is the objective, what elements are required to produce the project, cost involved, the most appropriate production methods, format, pieces to be produced, due date, parties involved, approval, distribution, etc, one can determine and propose an end result to be projected.

Graphic designers establish a balance of presenting visual and technical information by using technology as tool and medium to develop their visual ideas. They collaboratively conceive, execute, and materialize ideas from sketch to finish using both non-technological devices to execute a solution for a client. The end result can be achieved through a combination of metaphors, signs, symbols, colors, type and images.

An idea or product is appropriate if it meets some goal or criterion. Graphic design is a "communicative activity," a field that is idea- and market-driven, with budgetary concerns as well as client-imposed restrictions (Ilyin, 1994, p. 116). The practice and process of design is oriented to reality within social acceptance which explains why the field corresponds to market demand. In this collaborative effort, a graphic designer is not just a producer of a body of works and ideas, but also one that expresses their place in contemporary culture. The client that commissioned the work is a component of our cultural context that the designer happened to be participating in and responsible for.

In the first framework, market-driven, I will discuss some literatures and models about marketing in the context of graphic design. It will be helpful to take into account how the roles of marketing changes the way companies function and their relations to graphic design. It is also important to examine the role of marketing as a facilitator in a market-driven framework and how the nature of marketing influences the relationship between businesses and graphic design. It provides the framework for my research on the cross-section of design and business.

The second framework, the graphic design processes, discusses the procedures. This is also the section where I highlight the relevancy of graphic design in a marketplace. By providing information about the graphic design processes, I hope to elucidate readers with an understanding how the design process is developed, factors that influence the process, as well as some benchmarks that pertain to the design processes. The market-driven framework situates the graphic design process within a relationship based on client-designer relationships. It can be seen as an external factor that drives one aspect of the field. Ironically, a project needs both internal and external factors and they must not contradict each other to work.

In the third section, creativity framework, it is best to describe how creativity is intertwined in the design process that it becomes important to describe the concepts, approaches, phases, and methods rather than creativity all by itself. However, by exploring these differing views, I am attempting to make sense of some of the research evidence that has been accumulated on creativity. This section is not intended to provide a comprehensive understanding of the vast ideas of creativity. Rather, it seeks to provide readers with contextual and relevant information to aid in the understanding of this research. Because they are interconnected, there will be some overlapping of framework in the discussion.

Market-driven framework

For the purpose of our discussion, the word "company" may indicate commissioner, an individual, a company, an institution that hires, utilize, promote, patronize, sponsor, or use graphic design. Market-driven means that it is not "marketing" driven. In order to be market-driven, businesses have to be more than simply customer or service oriented because the main goal is to develop a total marketing and advertising program that includes products or services, prices, distribution, and communications that respond to changing customer needs and preferences.

In describing the origin of graphic design, McCoy (1998) writes that it is "a spontaneous response to the communication needs of the industrial revolution in capitalist market-based economies, invented to sell the fruits of mass production in growing consumer societies" (p. 3). The graphic design profession was born out of the needs of the industrial revolution capitalist to sow their fruits of mass production to the market-based economies

38

(McCoy, 1998). She further adds that as a society becomes more and more civilized, especially free-market countries, the need for graphic design to exist as they become tied to cultural and political agendas. From a client's perspective whom the graphic designer typically works for, end results are the final goal.

In a general sense, every product contains information that has the potential to communicate a message or to solve a problem. The utilization of marketing programs or graphic design itself is intended to tackle the aforementioned goals. The principal communication methods for consumer goods and services can be advertising media. For industrial products and services, customers are exposed to sales representatives, dealers, and printed materials. In a marketplace, possible considerations about purchasing decisions from a customer may include acquiring information about certain brands reinforced by advertising and design, word of mouth from family members and friends, displays in stores (through merchandising and point of purchase), catalogs, promotional materials, and many other sources (Webster Jr, 1999).

In ensuring their survival, businesses have to be adaptive in their approach and every marketing and advertising effort is to ensure that potential consumers be made aware of the existence of a product, service, or message. Marketers need to also ensure that a product, the company or the message make a favorable impression on the consumer. It is important to note that awareness itself does not always produce desirable results. Differentiation is important for a company to distinguish itself from its competition, as Curry (1999) puts it because through continued differentiation from competitors can lead to an expanded market.

Designers and marketers carefully build consumers' confidence by educating them over time to make sound judgments about their products or services. If marketers over-promise, they can jeopardize their campaigns or products by creating expectations that cannot be met. Therefore, they need to be consistent with their ability to deliver superior products or services. Even if they are able to do so, one superior product may be inferior to another customer. It is also important to draw distinctions that products and services cannot be marketed in the same way for there is a service component for every product sold.

It becomes crucial for graphic designers and marketers to carefully target their market by using direct communications at specific individuals rather than anonymous consumers in a mass and competitive market. The value of a product must be inherent in the product itself to make the promise sound and most importantly, to avoid over-promising. Marketers and advertisers adeptly position a message to be inculcated into their target audiences' mind by establishing a product as a distinct image or brand. In a limited sense, the first impression of a company's image is sometimes based upon one's first glance over a business card or a Yellow Pages advertisement. In a broader sense, beyond the product, no matter how well it is designed and marketed, the customer's expectations include all aspects of their interactions with the company, its personnel, the product, and the promise itself.

Glaser (1995) wrote that because businesses now come to accept the truth that "good design is [also] good business" (p. 253), businesses would remove designs from the hands of designers and to place them in the hands of the marketing departments. The use of design as a marketing tool, according to him is when commerce has triumphed over culture; materiality over spirituality, so to speak. Mok (1996) offered a more pragmatic view by stating that every business that understands the importance of providing their customers access to information knows that good design is also good business.

Whether it is market- or product-driven, companies forge a collaborative relationship between design and business as it provides an avenue for competitive advantage (Peters, 1996). A well-targeted communication design can successfully convey and enhance the value, differentiating, for example, a 80¢ product to a $80 product. He writes that "design is arguably the number one antidote to the commoditization of products and services" (p. 16).

Relationships breed expectations. Companies will see their best profit opportunities in exploring their customer base and building a long-term relationship with their customers. This is because the antiquated view of marketing that focuses on the next sale is being replaced by one that centers on the customer as a long-term business asset (Webster, Jr, 1999). It is viewed as a more effective and profitable method to treat customers as principal business assets and to rely on marketing alliances to broaden their offerings.

Technology is forcing designers to reinvent themselves. Keedy (1994) stated that today's graphic designers think of themselves as producers of work that express their place in contemporary culture, not just plain marketer's hired hands. Clients are not just commissioners of work but they are part of a larger cultural context that engages the designer and the client in a real world; therefore, they are both dependent on each other. Creative services employed in the marketplace at large have no value except in relationship to a client. In most cases, graphic design is commissioned because someone had something to communicate. The relationship between a designer and the client is reciprocal and interdependent. A designer's involvement is to provide expertise and guidance. Ideas conceived are meant to be sold to a client.

The main objective of every marketing, advertising, and design program is not simply to "solve the problem" through an aesthetically-pleasing advertisement or design that masks an inferior product or to portray a shady company's image. The task should be to "delight" the customer by exceeding their expectations and to build trust and relationship by instilling values in them. Successfully executed, consumers will develop "brand equity" (Webster, Jr, 1999, p. 128) and loyalty by believing in the values of the products. The idea is to build an ongoing relationship in which buyers become interdependent on the product or services. The optimum solution to a company's survival is to align itself with the strategy of marketing and graphic design in achieving the desired results.

Market-driven businesses always find markets by figuring out what is desired and then striving to produce the goods or serves. Whichever products supplied is dependant upon the consumer's demand. While in the product-driven arena, businesses create an artificial demand through advertising, marketing, and packaging in the hope of creating a new, long need for the product. Simply put, marketers and advertisers have to convince consumers to believe their message. An example of this is when marketers equate efficiency with computer software and hardware in image and word processing, desktop publishing, and spreadsheets that caused millions of people worldwide to believe in the need for computer technology. This line of thought makes possible the idea that this "one-way" communication lies in the hands of the sender, not the receiver.

However, by demanding businesses to do certain things effectively and efficiently, customers are unwittingly defining the business. Because of ecological awareness, informed, sophisticated, cautious, moral- and value-conscious consumers expect manufacturers or resellers to assist in the recycling and disposal of wastes. As a result, manifestations of designs must now reflect the additional costs of responsible product manufacturing, usage, and disposal. Although retailing is likely to remain local, regional, and national in scope, global retailers are likely to be responsive to such awareness.

The marketplace evolves under changing demographics, politics, economics, technology, and so forth, along with the competitiveness, divisional, hierarchical, and bureaucratic nature of business. When times are rough for businesses, such as the slow-growth markets of the 1990s, retaining present customers is better than gathering new ones (Webster, Jr., 1994). Besides, not all customers are valuable to a business. As these factors change, the role of marketing which they employ changes as well. The old marketing concept of stimulating demand for what the factories could produce is suicidal to a modern business because of the changing marketplace conditions (Webster, Jr, 1994). The ability to increase sales and profitability, stay ahead of competitors, and grow market share are also important to the survival of the company.

By understanding the targeted audience and by using tactics such as positioning, segmentation, and differentiation, businesses have a better chance of outdoing their competitors (Mello, 2002). The fundamental idea of market segmentation is to break a large market into smaller pieces, consistent of customers who are similar to one another in ways that are important to the marketer. The categories chosen for market segmentation can be demographic (i.e., age, income, occupation, family status, type or place or residence) or psychographic (i.e., self-concept, life-style, risk aversion, buying decision process). The latter is harder to develop because it is difficult to observe and measure unless they can be related to more observable attributes such as age and occupation (Webster, Jr).

The trick is simple: provide customers with a product or service that fills a specific need in the marketplace better than competing solutions. It may sound easy but there are many factors that can influence a successful marketing campaign such as the following factors: budgets, market share, growth rate, profitability, shareholder value, or any other measurement of business success (Mello, 2002).

The widespread use of the Internet has increased the global exchange of data. This form of revolutionary communication has created a need to conduct business that includes instant accessible information exchange through a virtual world. The Internet has also created a tremendous opportunity for reaffirming the needs for graphic design. Because the Internet is dynamic and constantly evolving, the watchword is to proceed with care. In order to understand what drives our technological impetus, Rossman (1998) suggested that the role of technology in supporting globalization lies in our corporate culture where the multinational corporations and consumerism thrive in a global economy. The numbers of media choices create unparalleled challenges for everyone working with computer technologies.

Because of the Internet, it is possible to reach a mass targeted audience or to create a one-to-one communication. The speed of the computing medium's advancement pushes everyone into unknown territories. A global customer learns very quickly about the wide range of choices in events, news, fashions, economic developments, and more through modern telecommunications technology.

The first task for graphic designers is to determine when and how to work on a strategic partnership with marketers whose principal driving message is to enhance profitability and a sustainable competitive advantage. From a graphic designer's perspective, the driving message is how to communicate effectively and to overcome other factors such as budget, technical, and production concerns. The ability to communicate is important, not just to articulate an idea, but also to clarify the developmental phases especially when large projects or long-term projects are involved.

Whether design and marketing strategies are possible under a system of market-driven and profit-directed world of capitalism, it is obvious that the role of communication and design begins with its deployment and lasts in its effects, changing the public's knowledge, attitudes, and behavior. Each field requires talents and skills but they must have a working understanding of each other to be truly effective in a collaborative effort. Designs in its entirety have two purposes. The first part is the expression of the client or designer and the second purpose is about creation of a response in the viewer. Together they add up to form communication. The supportive purpose of design in communication is to enhance the flow of information to its readers, not just merely adding aesthetical qualities. In order to communicate the intended message, the design must be effective and producible, to say the least. Exercising good judgments in practical matters are wise choices but understanding the factors that will eventually influence the final design are even more important.

The graphic design standards and procedures learned in the class and the realities expected in the real world may seem like conflicting agendas but they are necessary components in the design process. In a classroom that mimics a real world situation, educators train their students to perform. The environment is indicative of a marketplace in which they are expected to perform as designers. This encourages students to experience the results or decisions that would be possible in a simulated reality. Educators make students aware of the relevancy of a market-driven framework in fulfilling their assignments. In the syllabus for ART 3350-391, the objective aspires students "to effectively communicate the 'image' of a company, product or service [and] to accurately identify a target market through visual conceptual development [and] to become familiar with business procedures."

Courses provide students with the opportunities to understand the relationship of design to culture and the society it serves both in theoretical and practical aspects. In the syllabus for ART 4356-390, the content reads "each student will be assigned different client/target markets and several problems to solve. … Alternative materials, positioning and marketing as they relate to the environment will be explored." The role of the graphic designer is not just to arouse curiosity in its targeted audience, but also to use design as a device to fulfill a functional aspect of a problem or situation. The role of design is to address its messages to specific people, fill specific needs or interests, and help to achieve specific goals.

In a market-driven society, graphic designers function with the awareness that their design options and solutions are compelled by circumstantial force of the marketplace. More importantly, they communicate their designs by attempting to "educate" its audience through messages, products, or services that intend to change the perception and status quo of an audience. This goal is synonymous with the syllabus outlined in ART 4381-390 which reads: "We create change in the world by using advertising and graphic design to present important ideas, to raise awareness, to stimulate thought. Our focus will be on communicating issues that concern you and many others, issues of global and local significance. We'll work on subjects such as pollution, justice, the importance of art in the world, voting, sexual stereotyping, etc., to create breakthrough campaigns that can make a difference."

Graphic designers manipulate the relationship between the audience and the message or artifact based on the interaction between tools, processes, and materials, usages and needs of that society. For this, designers must be conscious of his or her social and moral responsibilities. The role of the graphic designer is not just to arouse curiosity in its targeted audience, but also to use design as a device to fulfill a functional aspect of a problem or situation. The role of design is to address its messages to specific people, fill specific needs or interests, and help to achieve specific goals.

Graphic design process framework

Designers place great emphasis of visual exploration in ideation because it is considered to be an essential part of the design process (Purcell & Gero, 1998; Vermaas, 1995). Other domains such as architecture and engineering also share similar criteria in using sketching in initial stages and further developments that lead to solving problems (A.T. Purcell et al., 1998; Verstijnen et al., 1998). Sketching materializes the content of an image and is importantly linked to the formation of images.

Because it can be perceived in different ways, sketching can be reinterpreted and this creates many opportunities for explorations. It is also an important tool for understanding and discovering design paradigms. Design paradigms can act as powerful tools for creating

44

new designs since they encourage interactivity, negotiation, and communication between art directors other designers in a design studio as well as designers and their clients. By exploring new paradigms and applying learned paradigms, designers learn what works and what does not. It also allows one to function optimally.

Oldach (1995) recommended that various free-flowing and relatively unstructured forms of idea representation during the ideation process needs to be recorded; either by doodling, sketching, jotting, scribbling or drawing. The New York Times art review columnist, Michael Kimmelman (2002) pointed out the importance of sketching:

> If a doodler is an actual artist, the doodle may hasten to consciousness some qualitative thought, spark a bigger idea, which can be developed elsewhere, more formally, in directions far removed from the source. I imagine almost all artists doodle, perhaps absent-mindedly, in the way that pianists tap fingers or photographers frame pictures of what they're seeing through an imagined lens. They can't help it. Doodling is a tic of the trade. … it is a necessary step in the creative act, a requirement of an imagination responding to the found object, the printed image, the random sight and the Proustian Madeleine. (p. B35)

The first thing before the design process can even begin is to gather information by establishing the objectives of the client or the purpose of the project. It is not to be confused with the outcomes, which is the result of analysis. The prime task of graphic designers, and, indeed, of writers too, is to communicate understandably. It is easy to look at information, but information is frequently not so easy to organize. It is important for graphic designers to separate between credible and conjectural information. Giving abstract concepts, issues, and problems a tangible form requires an understanding driven by the objectives, parameters and facts surrounding the problem. Focusing on solution-based information may limit the solution itself. This is because not all the solutions proposed may solve the problem. In order to uncover the real problem, designers need to address the real needs and to create value-based solutions to those needs.

The process of creativity in the graphic design process can begin during a phone conversation with the client or in the shower but ultimately it starts with idea generation, referred to as ideation. It is interpreted as the ability to conceive a plan for a particular purpose or effect. A designer can draw upon knowledge gained over experience, education, and empirical data. At this stage, designers usually explore several ideas which may not be of immediate resolution. There is always more than one solution to a problem and exploration is the key. Realistically, methodical and exhaustive process in design is limited to available materials within an organizational structure that involve the client and the designer. This suggests that the process is subject to change during the course of the design direction with many ongoing internal and external factors, some controllable to a certain degree and some not.

Knowing these drawbacks from the start allows the designer to have a higher percentage of control in the creative process. This can be achieved by defining the objectives realistically at the outset. From a well-developed objective, a list of visual categories can be developed that translates abstract ideas into tangible results that mean something to the audience. Several categories such as mandatory format, techniques, production parameters, issues affecting the audience, usage and longevity, budget and schedule are design frameworks that form the paradigm for explaining how things work and problems are solved. By considering these problems ahead of time, they also become the solutions for designers during this early stage of the design process.

Since a designer develops the vehicle to deliver the message, i.e., the design, he or she must be able to predict and maximize the audience's desired response. According to Oldach (1995), a successful designer controls his or her creative process by making sure that the clients' objectives are translated into the work. The designer should have a vision that is well presented where the clients can perceive and most importantly, approve.

In the world of business and commerce, clients who commission professional graphic design services are often guided by many immediate concerns and problems. They are compelled to solve problems quickly, painlessly, and inexpensively. By the time the service of a graphic designer or a design firm is needed, they may already have a set of unwritten laws and unreal expectations. They may try to "play designer" by deciding on format, graphics, and paper before the beginning of a design process. This happens because the client is not aware of other approaches and it is easier for them to deal with and confront a known problem in the same way that has been dealt with before. They may not have enough understanding of what design is.

Whether the decision is good or bad, rational or irrational, clients are the ultimate decision maker since they are the one who not only "pay the bills" but those who also evaluate, judge, and approve the final design. It is possible that they bring their prejudices, tastes and experiences into their decisions. Therefore, an open communication with the client and client education are both important because if they do not believe in the designer's

46

ideas, it will not get produced. Furthermore, involvement from the client in the process gives the decision makers a sense of responsibility and ownership.

Once the objectives are established with a client, a designer moves on to the next step: implementation. From penciled or color marker thumbnails to cut-and-pasted sketches or computer sketches, ideation is done to capture thoughts in pure and raw forms and they are not concerned with stylistic concerns. It provides the opportunity to explore, experiment, and manipulate ideas without the fear of failure. They are unpredictable, rendered rough, raw, and ambiguous to leave rooms for explorations.

As a form of discovery and negotiation from the designer's mind made visible without the influence of logistical and mechanical constraints that may influence their creativity, sketching is usually done in black and white rather than color to allow the designer to focus on developing concepts. This form of thought externalization allows generalizations of possible relations between underlying abstract entities and inferences from these representations using appropriate, efficient strategies to materialize.

Although it is personal and usually not seen by clients until a later stage, sketching provides an early form of cognitive interpretation of the creator's mind. We may make intelligent guesses as to what the sketches mean but often, they do not reveal the totality of what was in the mind but every sketch supports the structure of ideas, thoughts, and principles. Perhaps the most important inference in ideation is that sketching is associated with activities that involve reinterpretation or emergence of new ways of thinking and drawing. This model of working provides insights into the reinterpretation of images and synthesis of forms.

In Goldschmidt's study (as cited in A.T. Purcell & J.S. Gero, 1998), she argues that we use long-term memory that has relevant conceptual knowledge and knowledge previously analyzed and experienced to create images that are relevant to specific problems that we are trying to address. In this instance, sketching can act as an external memory to trigger thoughts in one's mind and it can be identified as critical aspects of the reasoning and problem solving process while other forms of external memory aids include reference books and other written materials. The ideation process of drawing (sketching, doodling, jotting, or scribbling) serves the function of allowing new ways of interpreting an idea.

Knowledge that can be accessed via imagery is different to those obtained via words. Therefore, problem solving using imagery based knowledge may appear to be unusually difficult in verbal cognitive processes. If designers are visually oriented people as A.

47

T.Purcell and J. S. Gero (1998) contended, then visual drawings are the best way to explore their "visuo-spatial cognitive resources" (p. 409). The inability of words to sustain ambiguity and uncertainty which is important to ideation, an early phase of design that requires relaxation of rules, may as well be one of the many reasons why designers do not employ words in conceptualizing ideas. Imagery seems more flexible than words in sustaining multiple meanings.

Because ideation can take form on a piece of paper or on the screen, technical expertise is critical for ideation to happen, especially with the latter when software and hardware knowledge are involved. Different software tools can influence the interpretation and translation of thumbnail sketches on the computer. A pencil sketch is very different compared to one done with color markers or computers. The computer is a unique tool because it can evaluate the result before production. Because of its high quality output, sketches from a computer output look finished and professional. When sketching on the computer, sketching is subject to the availability of tools and filters, which are capable of exploration and interactivity. These may assist designers in sketching, jotting, scribbling or drawing. Regardless of the tools and media, visualizing abstract thoughts is a critical aspect in developing a sound design.

The task of designers is to visualize abstract thoughts and to translate them into ideas or information comprehendible and usable to others. The relationship between idea generation and imagery production is primarily concerned with the question of functionality and aesthetic. Imagery is not seen as essential to creativity but rather the insights that appear to be supportive of maximizing the conditions for reinterpretations. Much like the process of communication, sketching is refined to meet a host of operative and artistic criteria.

Because of these factors, adjustments must be made accordingly. That is not to suggest that constraints are the straightjacket on the activities of graphic design. By getting ideas down on paper, designers are forced to learn how to be analytical, organized, and disciplined. As more people look at the sketches, they are able to add new perspective and interpretation to the sketches. The end result comes after continual refinements either from building on initial sketches or spinning off from the initial sketch.

An important process in initial idea generation is brainstorming. The purpose of brainstorming is to generate ideas and develop ideas for creative solutions by testing the boundaries of what seems possible. It is a freewheeling creative process for generating ideas. Several minds working together can be more productive and creative than a single mind. All it requires, in the most basic form is a chalkboard, some writing instruments, and a group of willing participants.

Compared to sketching, brainstorming is a group project and the purpose is to generate as many ideas as possible. Hence, quantity, not quality, is the key requirement of these sessions and they can last anywhere from two-hour sessions to a whole day or even a week of brainstorming. It is important to have clear goals for the sessions to be effective. Involvement from the participants is important and to prevent their minds from wondering, Mello (2002) suggests that facilitators give participants things such as Silly Putty and Koosh balls to keep their minds focused creative, yet not consumed. It may seem diverting but she contents that they can add to the team spirit and get their creative juices to flow. Criticism, refining, and testing of ideas should be introduced only after the brainstorming session. Because brainstorming can lead the designer to an unforeseen path, some of the ideas explored may bear little resemblance to the original. It is up to the designer's discretion to objectively, logically, and systematically align those ideas with the objectives.

By introducing a wide range of known solutions onto an unfamiliar problem, we can expand and then apply to new problems (Wake, 2000). The core of graphic design within the market-driven, service-oriented, client-specific, and situation-influenced factors is to present information. If the designer is striving to educate and inform the audience about a product, company, or service, the design solution can be hierarchical and information-based which reflects a neutral and stolid look and feel. If the goal is to persuade and influence the audience's thinking and to convert behavioral potentials into actions, the design approach can be more emotional and subjective. Generating attitude changes in a targeted audience and solving difficult design problems require excellent human intellectual resources and implementation of budgets for media space and time. Because a successful design addresses the needs of the client and the audience, its content must be favorably grounded in effective communication objectives and design criteria.

It is an inadvisable practice for designers to skip the brainstorming process and to directly design on the computer because the design produced will lack substance in terms of ideas (Oldach, 1995). Any designer can only draw strength from their limited experience and knowledge but by mixing, refining, and incorporating many ideas from various resources and people, many solutions can be generated instead. The design solution should not be based on the imitation of the latest trends and techniques but an eventual solution reached between the designer and the client. This explains why for the most part graphic designers have to function as a team in a service-oriented profession.

After ideas are generated through brainstorming, it is time to put them together. During this phase of design, a project gains its look and feel when the visual concept is made clear and tangible. And while they may not provide the final solution, they are necessary for the process as they lay grounds for suggestions, improvements, evaluations, and eventually approval. Any refined ideas are an evolution from earlier idea and they are within the parameters set by the clients' objectives.

Later stage involves the presentation of a comprehensive, or *comp* which indicates the size, color, appearance or manifestation of what the final artifact will look like. Depending on the project, a *comp,* shortened for composition is described as a form of mock-up or prototype. It can be a simple color marker layout to an elaborate resemblance of the final artifact. Typically, there are three categories for mock-ups or prototypes: acceptable, not acceptable, and acceptable with changes (Craig & Bevington, 1989). Because clients are involved in the project as well as creative directors, art directors, senior designer, copywriter, illustrator, and so forth, every risks, constraints and criteria that they help to create will remain intact throughout the process to ensure the success of a project.

Design must be meaningful. It is common for designers to have the final mock-up criticized by non-designers but if the designer cannot give a rational explanation for the design, this creates a problem for the client who is asked to accept on faith a design with unclear concepts. Presentation for the client reveals how effective the solution is and how competent the designer is. Ideally, each party can stay open to all points of view and be willing to work together to obtain a strong and effective design solution and thus avoid decisions made based on political or egotistical reasons. When we consider the number of people involved in an average job, it is not surprising that the design processes is unremitting and abound with human deliberations. Fundamentally, understanding a project's purpose provides a framework for defining the problem it is meant to solve.

The design process is iterative especially in a client-oriented marketplace stimulated by consumer and end-user demands, competitiveness, and other socio-economic, cultural, technological, or logistical concerns. These parameters may limit creative freedom but it is more appropriate to view them as a platform within which we are free to take calculated risks. Risk implies that we step outside the boundaries that we consider safe and predictable.

Graphic design is a business involving smallest to largest constituents that require them to make significant capital investments in equipment, personnel, and facilities. These "assets" need to be managed effectively as a fair return on investments and it is also important to assure a company's or one's survival. The nature of the design process is part art and part management, which means that even the most creative and knowledgeable individuals have to deal with an outside world. The most innovative and effective solutions become a wasted effort if the client cannot be persuaded to produce it. Designers who wish to be successful must believe that their solutions they recommend are the best ones possible given the time and budget constraints under the circumstances which they have to work. They know that a practical approach is to organize around what works best, not necessarily what they might prefer.

Using different approaches, techniques, and tools to execute their works, graphic designers must: (a) recognize the fundamental structure of the problem in relevant theoretical and conceptual knowledge, (b) use multiple skills to generate representations to aid in ascertaining the solution, and (c) conclude and produce results from these manifestations using suitable techniques.

Creativity framework

Creativity is an interesting topic and a vast literature spanning from many disciplines. It has become a catch phrase that means different things to different people. As a matter of fact, it is not applied to just people, it is also applied to processes, and products (Barron & Harrington, 1981). The term "creativity" is usually used to signify activities value in the intellectual sphere of human experience that result in the production of novelty, implying a departure from what is conventionally attainable by producing something beyond any available categories (Wiesner, 1967). Because of its broad applications, creativity can be found at all levels of ability in any settings. It seems that creativity may manifest itself in a variety of ways. The complexity and sophistication of human creativity could be understood more befittingly if I investigate it from more than one perspective.

Creativity may be approached from an artistic phenomenon but discussions of creativity are also prominent in the marketplace with creative people being seen as a vital resource needed to battle competition for market shares. While sociopolitical leaders may demand creativity to improve our society, corporate executives may view creative behaviors as those that lead to innovations in maintaining company success.

For my purpose, creativity is defined as leading to tangible products of some permanence or the capacity to get ideas that can solve a problem. Although creativity has a general applicability, it has a greater influential power when the emphasis is shifted from the individual creator to the larger context of their creations. Historically, the desire to solve problems due to our shortcomings has produced some startling inventions.

Different cultures differ in their conceptions about creativity. Eastern cultures view creativity as a process of individual growth or self-actualization. For example, creativity in Hinduism is seen as spiritual expression rather than innovation or problem solving (Starko, 2001). In recent decades postmodernists have critiqued the notion of genius for its patriarchal and Eurocentric linkages. The product-oriented, originality-based phenomenon emphasized in our society is a Western orientation (Fehr, personal communication, November 28, 2001).

When asked to give examples of genius, people often offer figures such as da Vinci, Newton, Mozart, and Einstein. To her credit, Marie Curie occasionally makes the list as a rare exception. Despite what has just been presented, it is important not to conceptualize creativity as something for a small group of gifted people. Acknowledging the fact that learning environments can be rife with Eurocentric and patriarchal linkages, developing interest in making connections between learning and everyday living become a device in understanding personality traits from different learners.

In forming a model of creativity, Rothenberg (as cited in Couger, 1995) categorized creativity into three factors: (a) creative person, (b) creative process, and (c) creative products. Realizing that the person-process-product model is incomplete because it fails to address environmental factors and their effects on creativity, Mel Rhodes added the fourth component, *press*, which refers to the relationship between human beings and their environments. According to Couger (1995), *press* is a term derived from the field of education that "refers to the relationship between human beings and their environment" (p. 3). With the new component, the Four-Ps Model of Creativity is born: person, process, product and press. In graphic design, solutions to design problems involve collective efforts and interactions between all these four areas and this model serves as a method in which the ideation process is measured in this study.

Graphic designers make up the *person* in the field who create in the tradition of their *presses (or environment)* and without the *process* of art and design, it would be impossible to create the *product* (which can also include service or message). From the designer's point of view, every internal and external factor can determine the outcome of the solution and from the clients' standpoint the solution has to be perceived in actuality as it cannot be guessed at. This means that artistic and effective problem-solving involves real risk-taking and not hypothetical risk-taking.

Several researchers concluded that creative products need to have a close relationship to reality (Bruner, 1962; Motamedi, 1982; Sappington & Farrar, 1982). In evaluating a design, Oldach (1995) recommended striking a balance between realism and creativity. By being realistic, one can refrain from producing the most bizarre and inconceivable ideas and by being creative, the designer can push the envelope, take risk, and freshly competitive in approach. By overemphasizing either aspect, the designer shall either loose sight of the main objective or risk an unacceptable innovation.

As society and technology evolve, it becomes increasingly difficult to master one or more domain of knowledge. However, creativity still requires knowledge base in some domain and without knowledge of the conventions of art and design and technological skills, it would be difficult to be a successful graphic designer. Since graphic design is a form of applied art not a science and highly influenced by internal and external constraints of the design process, there is no objective criterion to measure the results other than the fact that it has to meet the requirements to be produced.

When we speak of the "artistic preference" we tacitly admit that this refers to a subjective commodity, very much in the beholder's eye. Style preference is highly a matter of subjective choice—what one finds aesthetical pleasing and effective may be deemed tasteless and ineffective but what is important in communicating a visual idea is that it expresses the designer's ideas or the sender's message.

Creativity is a mindset driven by commitment and passion. The emotional and intuitive appeal of a new idea, concept, or product can make it "creative" in a philosophic or artistic sense but in order for one to be considered creative, several traits are discussed. According to studies conducted by Dellas and Gaier (1970), Motamedi (1982), Runco (1989), and Treffinger, Isaksen, and Firestein (1983), creativity does seem to be related to certain personality characteristics.

Creative people generally display the following personal characteristics: intelligent, capable of sustaining hard work, seek changes and adventure, impulsive, non-conformity, and sometimes undisciplined, although they are perfectly capable of highly disciplined behavior when they pursue a goal. Although these traits may show rebelliousness, arrogance,

53

and self-centeredness, creative students may be considered difficult to handle in the classroom. They also readily accept new ideas, challenge rules and authorities on occasion, prefer loose and flexible planning, and may be withdrawn or talkative.

Innate abilities aside, creativity also involves a thorough knowledge of one's field; a talent which involves combinations of sensory, motor, and intellectual capacities, expenditure of great effort in reaching the end product and finally the element of opportunity (Cropley, 1992). Without a favorable and advantageous circumstance, it is difficult to be creatively productive. Besides intellectual skills in solving problems, creative thinking requires diligent hard work, motivation, courage, a sense of recognition, and other similar factors (Cropley, 1992). For creativity to flourish there must be encouragement and stimulation of imaginative and unconventional environment. This is particularly true in problem-solving activities where one explores uninhibited ideas and concepts, exercises capability to reconsider and explore ideas in direct contradiction to accepted facts.

According to Lawson and Ming Loke (1997), designers typically develop an understanding of both the problem and the solution together. In the earliest stages of design, a designer must address several fundamental questions. These questions arise whether the design is for buildings, clothing, toys, furniture, annual reports, or bridges. If creativity is interpreted as problem-solving, several questions must be posed. Who are the customers? For whom the design is for? What is the problem that it tries to address? When is it due? Is there a prior solution and if there is, how did it fail? How much is the budget? Such questions suggest that designs produced must be clearly understood, self-explanatory, unambiguous and precise in the search for the answers.

Designers, painters, sculptors, poets, writers, musicians, and other artisan in the creative field have frequently discussed creativity and would argue that creativity involves skills or abilities (Brand, 2001). They see it as a medium for enhancing the environment, communication and self-expression, or as a way of understanding and coping with unknown areas. According to Brand (2001), creativity rarely involves totally new or original ideas; instead most creative work is an effective integration of existing information. This shows that artisans build their ideas on past accomplishments and creativity is rare, if not incremental.

More importantly, Brand (2001) added that creativity needs an audience to appreciate and validate its usefulness. Ideas that are far too ahead of their time are often ignored or even criticized. To overcome this, Brand (2001) suggested using metaphors and analogies during the creative process to facilitate in integrating abstract ideas into understandable and existing knowledge structures. According to Simons (2001), we learn and communicate ideas by using metaphors, analogies, and similes. Our mind is a dynamic muscle that is capable of incorporating new experiences.

According to Lawson and Ming Loke (1997), the way the human mind understands concepts is through physical interactions and experiences with the external world accumulated over time. Metaphors are helpful in communicating the most basic concept to complex technical systems. We can draw pictures, create analogies, construct metaphors, or tell stories and then share them. They help our brains in making connections with new and unfamiliar information with concepts, patterns, or ideas that we already recognize. Deep and abstract concepts which cannot be understood through physical interactions and experiences are made clear through the use of one or more metaphors.

Creative design requires a process and this process involves discussions and interactions in various forms, visuals, verbal, nonverbal, concrete or even intuitionally-based. Another method of turning a conceptual thought or an idea into a tangible piece of creative communication is intuition. Working on a subconscious level, intuition plays a big part in the development of an idea into a finished product. A designer should not be afraid to follow intuition since it is composed of our experience and knowledge.

Another driving force is passion which according to Oldach (1995) will drive one to search for the perfect solution to a problem. His advice is that we should follow our intuitions while keeping an eye on the objective. If we mindlessly treat every design project as another task and commodity, we relegate our minds to the perfunctory and sedentary job of a factory worker whose creativity is never an issue on an assembly line. Elaborating this approach, it is possible to subscribe to the axiom that without creativity, the role of graphic designers can be relegated to any person who can easily point and click their way through a computer program because after all computer will do most of the work including the thinking. However, defining intuition as a process is difficult but in our subconscious, unconscious, or preconscious levels, we are preoccupied with causal relationship between understanding and analysis (Papanek, 1984). This is because as human beings, we are constantly looking for ways to understand ourselves and the environment which we live in.

Creative ideas can possibly emerge from the process of giving meaning and making interpretation. One way of encouraging creativity is to assert that every idea is a possible solution, no matter how silly or impossible they may seem especially during the process of ideation. This is also when creativity comes into play when visual representations that support and enhance the design are employed. The process of creating is complex with many factors influencing its success or failure.

Designers could be driven by fad and techniques, clients may be pressured by economic concerns and politics and computers can be driven by technology. We may try to understand our complex and ever-changing existence with underlying structures that are often conscious and subconscious by putting an order to it but graphic design is a conscious and intuitive effort to create and communicate meaningful order. "Design is the conscious and intuitive effort to impose meaningful order" wrote Papanek (1984, p. 4). Being conscious requires one to be intellectual, cerebral, research-oriented and analytical while the intuitive part is the sensing and feeling part that we all have.

According to Sawahata (1999), creative designers respond to new stimulus, introduce the elements of surprise, solve specific problem to reach targeted goals and they enthusiastically grow and gain energy as the process moves them forward. Sternberg (1998) presented a similar model. They agree that traits such as the ability to adapt to special circumstances, recognize opportunities, find order in chaos, bridge broad categories, cope with new information, recognize possibilities and cross boundaries are traits of a creative person.

On the educational forefront, identifying and facilitating creativity lies in the hands of parents, administrators and educators. Our school curriculum is still practicing what Cropley (1992) defined as "closed content" (p. 20). What students learn are specified by other people as programs, lesson plans, exercises, projects, and the like that are written in advance. It seems that excessive dependence on external sources of evaluation and excessive conformity to conventions may be deemed anti-creative.

Psychological processes, motivational, and emotional factors are necessary for effectiveness in dealing with the external world. Cropley (1992) also suggested that combinations of knowledge, accurate observation, good memory and logical thinking (usually regarded as aspects of intelligence), inventiveness, unusual associations, fantasy (usually seen as aspects of creativity), inner drive, capacity for being enthused or turned on and flexibility (motivational properties of an individual) as traits necessary for identifying creativity. A simple exercise for spurring creativity, according to Simons (2001) is to reject the first three things that first came to our mind. That is not to say that first few ideas are bad but he encourages us to push our selves to take the extra step in coming up with ideas that may even surprise ourselves.

In an interview with historian Philip B. Meggs, designer Saul Bass agreed that computers are responsive and efficient but "the basic notion still has to come out of someone's head" (Meggs, 1990, p. 72). Therefore, long after the accessibility of desktop computers, design educators are still encouraging students to explore ideas until the appropriate time of execution in the computer. The computer as a tool and media is best in aiding us to create new ideas.

Creative solutions require a designer to pave uncharted territories and for clients to make decisions that may not be met with universal acceptance. It is impossible to exclude the clients from the creative process because they are the information source. Although an individual can be creative in isolation but in the field of design, a message, product, or service is intended for a specific audience. Although creative individuals can flourish in different periods, being creative is more than a personal insight as it is also co-created by domains. Naturally, one will be productive if his orher knowledge is relevant in the subject matter.

The phrase "thinking outside the box" has become a cliché. But by stepping outside of the box, we can then begin to envision solutions. It allows one's thoughts to roam freely without any constrains imposed by ritualistic, conventional or other traditionally known impositions. Exploring alternatives lead to more ways of generating ideas and solutions. In her research, Mello (2002) discovered that another important factor in accessing the solution is to develop the intangible portion of a product such as those that involve partnerships and relationships, in addition to the core product itself.

Arguably, creativity is a matter of viewing a problem in varying perspectives. The solutions can be random or systematic, a confluence of different ideas or a combination of the two, depending on the circumstances and scope surrounding a project. Fostering creativity is more likely, in the event of a classroom setting to emphasize differences as opposed to homogeneity. The latter suggests an authoritarian style of classroom management and a narrow sense of equality.

However, it is more promising to think of it in terms of fulfillment of a student's aspirations and values, rather than a standardized pattern of management. Supposedly, educational systems can contribute to the student development by recognizing and encouraging many ways of thinking. Differing vocational fulfillment and a broader range of personal development can prepare students to enter a real-world with a much wider range of jobs that offer challenge, income, and social status.

Because completion of the design process can depend on computer technology, human creativity in the human-computer combination becomes questionable. This is true especially when universities are not capable of providing all students with practical skills which they need for the rest of their lives because which vocationally relevant skills needed for the future may not be known at present. Many aspects of graphic design education are visually-based and solving problems in graphic design means usually conceiving in two-dimensions, but computer technology can create three-dimensional representation that may influence the design process.

The combination can produce a body of accomplished work quickly and efficiently. In many cases the initial design ideas are transformed and reinvigorated into fresh and unpredictable creative outcomes from direct manipulation in the computer. While the mathematical precision of computer is excellent for problem solving, it is a fallacy to think that highly trained individuals in computer skills can solve a problem. Sometimes the best ideas will emerge from one's mind making unexpected connections.

Creativity, in its imaginative and expressive forms, cannot be found in the style or techniques employed. Rather, it is found in the combinations of how effectively the problem is solved and the objectives are achieved. Given the unpredictable nature of the economy and technology, a clear and a focused set of objectives which encompasses the core message of a company, its goods and services, and purpose in articulating a company's vision is important in this age of digital media. Creative vantage point develops from a clear comprehension of what needs to be communicated. The clearer the message, the more effective the results would be.

Whether we think of creativity as novelty, innovation, progressiveness, conceptual and technical expression, or problem-solving, creativity as whole is probably the single most important factor in determining excellence. Creativity is part of who we are and it determines what we can become, when to act, where we can go and how we can function. Through design, creativity leads to the discovery in deciphering the meaning of communication through explorations and discovery.

CHAPTER III

METHODOLOGY

Subjects of the study

There are a total of 173 undergraduate students from 14 graphic design classes in the spring semester of 2002. In completing their assignments, students give visual forms to ideas, or in other words, a visual translation of a concept to production of mock-ups or materialization of their ideas into a final form. These assignments, with the course numbers as outlined in table 3.1, depend on their specificity as outlined in the syllabi assigned by course instructors. Depending on the course, the assignments usually refer to problem-specific and goal-oriented projects.

Table 3.1. Listing of course, course number, and number of student enrollment.

No.	Course	Course number	Student enrollment
1	Packaging	ART 4356-390	13
2	Portfolio	ART 4352-390	12
3	Portfolio	ART 4352-391	7
4	Symbols Design	ART 3350-390	16
5	Symbols Design	ART 3350-391	14
6	Typography	ART 3351-390	15
7	Typography	ART 3351-391	13
8	Type & Image	ART 3352-390	7
9	Type & Image	ART 3352-391	10
10	Public & Social Service Design	ART 4381-390	18
11	Systems Design	ART 3352-392	10
12	Systems Design	ART 3352-393	9
13	Publication Design	ART 4352-392	14
14	Publication Design	ART 4352-393	15

All subjects involved in the sampling are volunteers. Anonymity is protected throughout the research. Because subjects are mostly seniors and juniors in an undergraduate program, there are no minors involved. Nonetheless, minimum requirements of Human Subjects Committee charged with protecting the rights of individuals are observed.

Appendix A shows a copy of the approved human subject form. Research subjects have sufficient information to make informed decisions about participating in a study and they are able to withdraw without penalty from a study at any point. Other considerations include unnecessary risks to a research subject must be prevented and benefits to the subject or society must outweigh any potential risks. Students are requested to participate in order to understand how technology can influence their creativity in their design process.

The following criteria were used to select students who participated in the study:

1. Computer knowledge is a must since they are being evaluated on their expertise and skills in executing their project using computer technology.

2. All students are undergraduate majors in graphic design with senior or junior statuses in a university setting. Because of the course requirements, there are no freshmen or sophomores in the study.

3. In studying a developmental or evolving process, it is important to keep the research subjects' location accessible. Initially, these decisions are also dependant upon available resources, research goals, time, and energy.

Variables and their definitions

Although I can gather and analyze empirical data associated with each possible variable for predictions, varied conditions caused by technological and societal change is uncontrollable. This is because behaviors of people in complex and varying factors are hard to measure (Frascara, 1997).

A *construct*, is an abstract concept that expresses the idea behind a set of particulars. Any event, category, behavior, or attribute with different values that expresses a construct is a *variable* (McMillan & Schumacher, 1997). During initial data analysis, the identification of *properties* and *dimensional locations* in data can form the basis for making relationships between categories and subcategories both in open and axial coding. The four identifiable variables are: (a) *causal conditions*, (b) *context* and *intervening conditions*, (c) *action/interaction strategies*, and (d) *consequences*.

Independent variables are matters that affect the situation. *Independent variables* such as the participants' age, weight, social status, and socio-economic status cannot be manipulated but by identifying the research subjects by their gender in the questionnaire, I created an "assigned" or "attribute variables" (McMillan & Schumacher, 1997, p. 315). This is intended to aid in the generalizability aspect in measuring whether the data collected from all participants in this sample are applicable to members of the opposite sex under study.

Dependent variables determine the things that I seek to measure, or in other words, the question that I seek to answer as presented in the purpose of the study in Chapter I. Four *dependent variables* are included in this study: (a) student cognition on thought processes, (b) student assessment of the design processes, (c) student assessment of proficiency on technical issues, and (d) individual notions of self-concept, achievement, performance, and aptitude. Manipulation in this context means that I am able to use the information to decide and control specific treatment or condition for each group of subjects.

Since my research is about generating an understanding of a process in which there are actions and interactions among people and machinery pertinent to a topic, I can isolate and identify these actions and interactions. The research problem is the impact of computer technology in undergraduates' creativity. Thus, the central phenomenon is whether using computers can stifle or enhance creativity in the ideation process. Creswell (2002) recommended framing the phenomenon as a form of process with "sequence of activities, actions by people, and interactions among people" (p. 448). Viewing these variables as categories or themes, I can then start the process of coding or labeling these variables. In developing a category, it must first be viewed in terms of its *properties*, which can then be *dimensionalized* (Strauss & Corbin, 1990, p. 69).

Properties and *dimensions* are important because they make up the basis for forming relationships between categories and subcategories. In providing an example, let us take a look at the category of "computer technology." Its properties include: people, process, and material. Each of these properties can be dimensionalized: profiles of people using the computer technology; how and what they use the computer for; and materials and the different kinds of software and hardware involved. By giving these variables profiles, they can be grouped to form a pattern for identification.

Procedures

The hypotheses for this study state that change is inevitable due to socio-economic factors which situate both the field of graphic design and its education to respond to the marketplace. Contextualized within service-oriented and market-driven contexts, the field has the ability to affect opinions and actions within the collaborative efforts between the triumvirates of graphic design: the designer, the client, and the audience.

Most hypotheses and concepts form the basis to generate a theory from data where they are being systematically worked out in relation to the data during the course of the research. On the other hand, the key concept in data collection is to gather information that can assist in developing a theory such as the participants who have experienced the process that I am studying by linking their perceptions to suggest new concepts. The concepts are grounded because these abstractions are built from observations rather than deduced from prior theories.

In the first phase, *open coding*, initial categories of information collected from the questionnaires are being studied by segmenting the information into categories and subcategories. The aim of open coding is to discover, name, and categorize phenomena, and to develop categories in terms of their properties and dimensions. The purpose is to elaborate a concept or develop a model based on the understanding of a concept from a participants' view of their social realities. Open coding breaks down the data and the process allows me to identify some categories, their properties, and dimensional locations. Like organizing pieces of a puzzle, *open coding* provides data to uncover as many potentially relevant categories with their properties and dimensions. The sampling is open to provide opportunity to gather the most relevant data about the phenomenon under scrutiny. The idea is to generate as many categories as possible.

A reasonable number of ten categories may suffice (Creswell, 2002), although it depends on the extent of my database and the complexity of the process. I sample data that are indicative of theoretically relevant concepts through persons, sites, and documents useful in generating a theory. The sampling continues until no new or relevant data seem to emerge from a category, all paradigms elements are verified, and the relationships between categories are established and validated. Only by then, the theory will be conceptually adequate if the *theoretical saturation* of categories is achieved (Strauss & Corbin, 1990, p. 168). During open coding, being able to differentiate between consistency (i.e., systematic gathering of relevant data about categories) and discoveries (bringing to light new categories, properties and dimensions) is important.

Open coding is followed by *axial coding*. The focus is to relate more specifically to categories and subcategories that were revealed during open coding. In this stage, one open coding is "centralized" to explore for a *core phenomenon* by relating other categories to it. The categories are related by validating relationships between *causal conditions* (factors that influence the core phenomenon), *action/interaction strategies* (actions taken in response to the core phenomenon), *contextual and intervening conditions* (specific and general situational factors that influence the strategies), and *consequences* (outcomes from using the strategies). During the process of axial coding, a basis is developed for the next step, *selective coding*.

Selective coding involves the process of selecting the core category and to systematically relate it other categories, to validate the relationships between them, and to fill in categories that need further refinement and development. The task at hand is to take the categories in their rough forms with all its properties and dimensions as well the relationship between them and to develop them into a conceptual and comprehensible theory.

The final theory is limited by the categories, their properties and dimensions, and relationships that exit in the actual data collected. It is important to stress that the end result of the theory development is conceptual as it represents abstractions of incidents, events, happenings; hence, the samplings of data are concerned with *representativeness of concepts* (Strauss & Corbin, 1990, p. 191). They are not specifically about people, incidents or events, but rather an analysis of categories that exists or is being created by the constituents in this particular research.

Figure 3.1 is a sample of visual representation of the procedures discussed. Notice that one open coding category is identified and used as the core phenomenon. In axial coding, other variables such as *causal conditions, action/interaction strategies, context, intervening conditions*, and *consequences* are related to it.

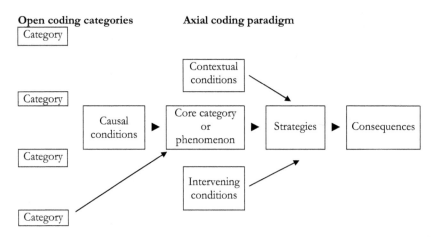

Figure 3.1 Open coding to axial coding paradigm

Instrument

This section discusses the tools, i.e., the instruments for measuring or documenting my data. The word *instrument* is used here to refer to the means of measuring my study, which in this case, would be the survey questionnaire. Because of the small samples, *purposeful sampling* is logical especially if the research is studied in depth in the hopes of yielding many insights about the topic. Information obtained from a small group can increase the utility of information gathering without the need to generalize to a larger population (McMillan & Schumacher, 1997).

In order to maximize opportunities for verifying data and relationships between categories and filling in poorly developed categories, Strauss and Corbin (1990) developed *discriminate sampling* (p. 187) where the researcher purposefully chooses a site, person, or documents that will allow him/her to return to the site for any necessary verification of data. By selectively choosing the site with unlimited access and people to study, I hope to sample information that is likely to contribute knowledge and data about the phenomena.

In encoding data, the exact words of participants are used to capture the essence of their reflective responses. Because words are written by participants, meanings may be ascribed to them. I am concerned with the possibilities that participants may choose to respond negatively regardless of the content of the question, guessing their responses, or to sacrifice speed for accuracy in reporting their responses. Using forced choice questions is conceivable but I prefer open-ended questionnaires because they are not restrained by definite limits or structure and they are interpretive in nature, allowing for flexibility in decoding the responses.

Testing is another crucial part during selective coding. Although it is not a form of statistical format, testing is done by constantly comparing hypotheses against the reality (the data) for modifications and retesting. As I deductively propose relationships of properties and dimensions when working with data during the coding procedures, I will also verify what I have deduced against the data. This reciprocal action and reaction between proposing and checking "ground" the theory. The systematically validated relationships between categories can be explicated and tested further but it is important to keep in mind that each condition under which a phenomenon exist is different.

Should a new test be required, the methodology can be replicated but the situations where categorical concepts develop due to different conditions may vary and affect the interpretation of data. When conditions undergo change, the theoretical formulation that works in the first place needs to be changed to meet new conditions. Therefore, in order to verify the test, it is necessary to take into consideration the different conditions in which the phenomenon exists and to make room for alterations and modifications.

Design of the study

This is a qualitative single-site case study and the purpose is to understand one phenomenon: the impact of computer technology on the design process of ideation in undergraduate graphic design students. As students' early conceptual sketches evolve from ideation into further refinements, the sampling and data for this study become incremental, exploratory and discovery-oriented. This is because the method is sensitive to individuals in their natural settings, works in practice, and it may unveil complexities found in the process. This inductive analysis provides insight into how computers alter the way university-level design students think.

The step-by-step procedure is rigorous as it provides a systematic way of approaching and analyzing data. The idea behind this research is to develop a theory "grounded" in the data rather than use one borrowed from the social sciences literature. The method is ideal because the theory is derived from the data, and can be extracted, which explains the importance of the results. The knowledge gained can lead to alternative methods of teaching using technology. It also allows me to generate an understanding of a process related to a substantive topic.

In this study, students typically begin their assignments by developing their concepts (ideation) with the simple technique of sketching either by using some writing instruments or direct computer sketches. Eventually, they employ computers to materialize their concepts into a finalized representation of idea called a *comp*. Because computers are used in the project at different stages, definitely towards the end to either conceive or produce their design concepts, I am convinced that their creativity is impacted one way or the other. Although various methods such as observations, conversations, interview, public records, journals, and even my own personal reflections could be used, perhaps the best approach for my research is to capture the reflections of the participants in their own words in a self-administered questionnaire.

The questionnaire is designed to solicit participants into revealing the "hidden data" for formulation of a theory. There are ten major questions with sub questions and they are reduced in size and are presented in their entirety in appendix C. The original questionnaire is printed on both sides on an 11" x 17" paper. The reduction in size is necessary to fit the format into the appendix section. The horizontal tabloid format (11" x 17") is folded into two and that allows for the creation of four pages that measure 8.5" in width and 11" in height.

This format is chosen so that all the four pages do not have to be copied onto two pieces of letter-sized paper (8.5" x 11") to avoid misplacement of pages. All the ten questions are laid out on the inside three pages on the inside spread and the last page is on the back. Should a research subject decide not to participate in the study; they are not exposed to the questions inside because all that is exposed is just the front with introduction and instructions for the research.

The questions are developed based on the following four aspects:

1. The complete thought and design processes from initial concept development to visual manifestation.

2. The influence of computer on students' conception and production processes, i.e. their creativity in the design process.

3. Fulfilling the instructor's course objective. The analysis of data collected from each class is assessed separately where different levels, different project objectives are considered.

4. Because classrooms are conducted to mirror a real-world situation, this aspect is included because it reflects the external conditions of working with instructors who take on the persona of a client that graphic designers face in a real-world situation. Educators take on a role that mimics the characteristics and expected behaviors of a client because of the iterative process of design. This process is subjective to revisions, evaluations, and approvals. However, because the reality and criteria in a classroom may be different in comparison to a market-driven capitalistic environment, educators are inadvertently involved in authoritative and facilitative roles in a classroom.

There are ten questions in the study:

1. Do you sketch* with pencil and paper during the early phase of your design process? If you do, please explain how it can be beneficial to your work.

66

If you don't, please explain how it is not beneficial to your work.

If you don't sketch with pencil and paper, do you use the computer to sketch instead?

If you use the computer to sketch, please explain how the computer is beneficial.

*Sketching is defined as a rough or tentative drawing representing the ideas often made as a preliminary study in a design.

2. Depending on which medium you are comfortable with, how does sketching either by pencil and paper or the computer influence your design process?

3. As you go through the process of searching for a solution and alternative designs are generated, do you rely on your intuition or common sense? Please explain.

4. Do you discover anything new while working on your computer in terms of idea generation? Please describe.

5. Which area do you find yourself worrying about more: the early idea generation aspects or the later production (mock-up, software knowledge, technical information, presentation) aspects?

6. Briefly list and describe each step involved in solving your design project from the beginning to finish. Indicate any tools, artifacts, or devices that are important at each step.

7. Do you think computer technology is maximizing or minimizing (enhancing or impeding) your creativity? In other words, what are the pros and cons of using a computer to execute your project?

8. How do you find your initial concepts in relation to your end result? In other words, does your final solution match your initial sketches or ideas? Please explain how it does or how it does not.

9. In relation to question #8, what factors influenced or changed your initial sketches or ideas?

10. Do you feel prepared to enter the field of graphic design? Please explain why you are and why you are not.

While writing the questions, I take into consideration the pacing of questions to create excitement for the students while answering the questions. There are four dependent variables of the design processes, thought processes, technical issues and individual notions within the ten questions. For purposes of a brief description, questions three, four, five, and seven deal with student cognition on thought processes; questions one, two, eight, and nine are about their assessment of the design processes; question six is about proficiency on technical issues and finally individual notions of self-concept, achievement, performance, and aptitude are on question ten. Table 3.2 shows an itemization of dependent variables with *properties* and *dimensions* for open coding.

Table 3.2. Listing of dependent variables with properties and dimensions

Question	Dependent variables	Properties and Dimensions of the questions
1	Design processes	Methods, Skills, Visuals, Form-making
2	Design processes	Methods, Choice
3	Thought processes	Perception, Cognitive skills, Experience
4	Thought processes	Discovery, Cognitive skills
5	Thought processes	Choice, Decision-making
6	Technical issues	Technical, Methods, Presentation skills
7	Thought processes	Cognitive skills
8	Design processes	Aesthetics, Comparison
9	Design processes	External factors
10	Individual notions	Evaluation, Performance, Achievement, Aptitude, Reasoning

The questionnaire is a self-administered survey handed to the instructors of the class with an accompanying letter to explain the purpose, objective and the rights of participants. I purposely choose an open-ended and self-administered questionnaire for the following reasons:

1. The possibility of interviewer bias is eliminated because participants are insulated from the expectations of the interviewer,
2. They allow for privacy in answering questions which reduces the likelihood of response bias,
3. The results can be obtained more quickly, and
4. They allow for a large number to be surveyed in a shorter time.

Collaboratively working with course design educators, the questionnaires were distributed during class sessions and the data collection commenced from mid through late April of 2002. Each course instructor is given an instructional sheet on how to distribute, collect, and proctor the questionnaire.

The subject is selected from a defined population. By the end of April 2002, I had received all envelopes with subjects' responses except for ART 4352-391. The total number of responses is 68 reported by 36 male and 32 female participants. Table 3.3 reports information about the number of students enrolled, the number of male and female students, the total number of participants, and codes assigned to the course for coding purposes.

Table 3.3. Course number, number of students enrolled, number of respondents, and assigned codes.

No.	Course Number	Students enrolled	Number of males	Number of females	Total	Assigned codes
1	ART 4356-390	13	1	0	1	PAC-390
2	ART 4352-390	12	3	4	7	POR-390
3	ART 4352-391	7	0	0	0	POR-391
4	ART 3350-390	16	7	3	10	SYM-390
5	ART 3350-391	14	0	1	1	SYM-391
6	ART 3351-390	15	2	1	3	TYP-390
7	ART 3351-391	13	6	6	12	TYP-391
8	ART 3352-390	7	4	3	7	TYI-390
9	ART 3352-391	10	1	1	2	TYI-391
10	ART 4381-390	18	4	10	14	PSS-390
11	ART 3352-392	10	5	3	8	SYS-392
12	ART 3352-393	9	2	0	2	SYS-393
13	ART 4352-392	14	1	0	1	PUB-392
14	ART 4352-393	15	0	0	0	PUB-393

The research subjects are fully aware of the nature and objective of the research as they are presented with a cover that fully explains the research before they turn the page over to reveal the first question. Because some students may have participated in the same survey in another class, the instructors are asked to make sure that participants do not repeat the survey. From a pilot study conducted in the spring of 2002, research subjects require anywhere from 20-30 minutes to respond to all the ten questionnaires. After the students are done, the instructors would collect and place the responses into an envelope provided. They will then seal it and place it in my mailbox.

Treatment of data

The initial interests for this study are based on concepts derived from literature and experience. Generating a theory that explains the impact of computer technology on the ideation process in design is supported by literature review and further supported by the questionnaire, designed to solicit responses from student participants who are involved in the process. They are purposefully sampled because they could provide information for the generation of a theory that reflects the perception and the reality of their experiences as they use computer technology in the process.

By deciding where the data will be collected, when the data will be collected, how the data will be collected, I am able to proceed deductively in verifying the hypotheses based on the sampling of theoretically relevant concepts. Theoretical sampling is cumulative because a reciprocal interaction between data collection and analysis takes place which increases the relationships between them as I generate as many categories as possible during the axial coding process. Because of that, some categories sampled could also arrive inductively and the best way to confront the situation is to always challenge the concepts and perspectives (Strauss & Corbin, 1990).

My experience as a graphic design instructor has given me some "sensitivity" which enables me to draw insights from my professional experiences. While there may be a number of sources for theoretical sensitivity, it can be derived from literature where the researcher is "sensitized" as well as one's own experience.

CHAPTER IV
RESULTS OF THE STUDY

This chapter explains the data analysis using systematic procedures developed by Strauss and Corbin (1990). It describes the sequences and processes, with the provision of options for action, and with the identification of factors, connections, interactions and their use in the development of a theory. It lays the framework for paralleling my hypotheses and makes recommendations for the field, educators, and students in the next chapter. The results from this study are meant to paint a more realistic description of a design process that takes place in undergraduate students when computer technology is involved. The resulting theoretical formulation not only can be used to explain that reality but it can also provide a framework for future action.

Data analysis

After the data was collected, it was determined that three factors influenced the final sample. First of all, the same student may have registered in different classes. Secondly, absenteeism during the distribution of questionnaires may have caused the number of respondents to deflate and finally, some may have abstained for whatever reasons from participating in the research questionnaire.

The study is "grounded" in the questionnaire data of 68 undergraduate students. To consider the question of whether computers have the ability to encourage or diminish the user's creativity, those features which identify the thought process in ideation must first be identified. In the following section, identified by subheadings of Question #1 through Question #10, selected judicious responses from some respondents who provide the framework for the open coding, axial coding, and selective coding processes are discussed. The method used to analyze the data involves identifying a *central phenomenon*. In this study, "technology develops new applications" emerges as the central phenomenon.

Contributors are indicated by their gender (M for male and F for female) followed by an assigned number to indicate their positions in the survey and the assigned code for the class they are enrolled in, for example, F-3, PSS-390. If both respondents of the same gender from the same class are quoted, their position numbers will be repeated and followed by the class number, for example, F-1, F-2, PSS 390). *In vivo codes*, which are the exact words of respondents, are used whenever quoted in the following paragraphs.

71

Question #1

Do you sketch* with pencil and paper during the early phase of your design process? If you do, please explain how it can be beneficial to your work. If you don't, please explain how it is not beneficial to your work. If you don't sketch with pencil and paper, do you use the computer to sketch instead? If you use the computer to sketch, please explain how the computer is beneficial. *Sketching is defined as a rough or tentative drawing representing the ideas often made as a preliminary study in a design.

Sketching, or "seriation," as one student recalls it (F-1, TYI-390), provides ambiguity and uncertainty necessary for interpretation and exploration. Depending on technique and preference, "[s]ketching is a quick way to express your ideas and seems to build the more you do it. It can become very clean or stay rough and [sic] depending on what you're working on" (M-1, TYI-391). The act of sketching with pencil, pen, or ink on paper helps students in getting their ideas onto a tangible format that is capable for sustaining multiple meanings during the brainstorming process. Another respondent writes that sketching gets her "in the mode to design more than anything" (F-1, SYS-392).

For 91% of them (62 out of 68), sketching with pencil and paper saves them a lot of time as they go through a formative period of visual investigation by producing a number of quick and small interpretations. It becomes an inspirational lead that takes them into a computer at a later stage as reported in this response: "Yes, sketching with pen and paper is quicker than the computer in most cases and allows me to visualize ideas and how well they work before translating the drawings on the computer" (M-1, SYM-391). One respondent describes that sketching "... allows for trial & error so you learn what works & what doesn't" (F-6, TYP-391). Sketching with pencil and paper seems mandatory because one cannot produce a successful piece of design without giving consideration to the composition: "I sketch with pencil, it benefits my work because it helps set the project up for preliminary problems. I can resolve some problems before I even get to the computer" (F-1, TYP-390).

In a similar response, another respondent writes, "Sketching is a quick way of finding out if an idea is worth expanding on. Drawing is easier with a hand than a computer any way [sic] unless you have a computer drawing pad" (M-4, TYP-391). Sketching is also facilitative for the reason described by the following respondent: "It helps with the production of ideas and also makes it easier to put those ideas into the computer" (M-5, TYP-391). Sketching can also record ideas. According to one respondent, "Sketching helps get ideas out of my head quickly before I forget them. It is easier to translate from head to paper to computer,

72

than straight from head to computer because technological aspects are sometimes distracting" (F-3, TYP-391). Another respondent agrees, using sketching for notation purposes as well as for "not forget[ting] some different ideas that [are] formulated … These sketches are very rough and usually make sense to me" (F-2, TYI-390).

Quantity not quality in sketching is key in getting many ideas recorded. Most respondents seem to understand the importance of explorations during the initial stage. However, the "old fashioned" method of sketching with pencil is also credited for allowing the respondent to "create work that is more original" (F-5, TYP-391). The simplicity of sketching with pencil and paper in comparison to the computer is appealing to many, particularly to one respondent who writes that "… the computer has to be managed and requires a process to create even the simplest of images, but with paper and a pencil, you are able to lay out plans in a quick manner that has a personal interpretation and allows continuous re-verification of the image" (M-2, SYS-392).

More importantly, sketching can be described as a form of trajectory or, as one describes it, as "a direction to take or a framework to start from" (M-1, TYP-390) where students can often rely on initial sketches to inspire them for newer ideas. As indicated in the following response, "… it helps generate ideas and put my thoughts on paper quickly, so I can get multiple ideas out of just one quick sketch" (F-2, TYP-391).

Conversely, a respondent who used to sketch with a computer now discover that it is generally faster and more accurate to first sketch with pencil and paper even though their first choice of sketching is on the computer. "I used to 'sketch' using the computer but now I've learned that it is generally faster and more accurate to what I invision [sic] in my head now that I know how to use the computer," remarked one respondent (M-3, POR-390). Surprisingly, a respondent reveals that a mistake with a pencil can also lead to other good ideas as described by the following comment: "I believe it is beneficial to the idea process. What can be a mistake with a pencil can lead to another good idea, plus it helps me to quickly sketch my idea while brainstorming for quantity of solutions (M-1, TYP-391).

The accumulative or "additive" (F-3, TYI-390) nature of sketching also allows them to build on initial doodles or sketches and to expand and organize as they progress. She writes, "Concept for me comes to me while I work on the computer. It is an additive process - I like to add & take away quickly" (F-3, TYI-390). As their responses indicate, the unstructured and free forms of sketching facilitate in helping them to work out possible problems before they work on the computer, saving both time and effort. Sketching is

73

facilitative as indicated in the following response: "When I am ready to move to the computer I am more focused and able achieve a better design" (M-2, PSS-390).

The computer requires operational and know-how even to create the simplest of images. This probably explains why the lack of sophistication in sketching means students can explore freely, away from the constraints of computer software interface and restraints of hardware limitations. One respondent indicates, "I sketch with pencil & paper. It helps me get ideas & work out possible problems before going to the computer. Once I get on the computer, I find it harder to see things" (F-3, PSS-390). In concurrence, another respondent adds, "I always prefer to sketch out my work because then I am only limited by my imagination. When try to use the computer for sketches, I find that I am confined by the tools and my work tends to lack individuality or serious ingenuity" (M-4, PSS-390). However, in the sequential stages of design, computers are used to refine ideas and because of the superior visualization capabilities, effects from the computer can be perceived as a superficial surface treatment.

Believing that there is something wrong with computer usage during the initial ideation phase, one student makes a conscious effort to write that "I personally use sketches first. I feel it gives me a direction & a stranger thought process than the computer does. The comp. [sic] may be faster @ [sic] generating ideas/sketches, but I think the theory & conceptualization of the project gets pushed aside. Sketching helps me organize a more all around thought process" (M-4, TYI-390).

Feeling restrained by the computer but liberated by sketching, this respondent writes, "I feel limited from what the computer will allow me to do. Its [sic] beneficial to my work because in these steps I need the full freedom & open creativity" (M-3, TYI-390). Another student expresses the following: "I feel that sketching out ideas with pencil/paper gives me a nice change (being more tactile) from the world of computer generated imagery. Pencil/pen also seems to be more flexible" (M-6, TYP-391).

As for 4% (3 out of 68) of the respondents who choose to solely sketch with the computer, tools that are part of the software are helpful. One respondent credits the computer with providing the ability of "seeing the fonts on the computer help [sic] with differentiation and positioning" (F-2, TYP-391, quoted from question #4). Another respondent adds that "[w]hen sketching out fonts and considering colors, I use the computer b/c [sic] it speeds up the process" (F-1, POR-390). Another respondent reports that as his sketching skills on the computer progresses, he finds himself spending more time sketching

74

on the computer but not for conceptual developments. Here is his comment: "I use [sic] to sketch all the time, as my skills progressed on the computer, I find myself using the computer more. I use it to get more of the design decisions out of the way, but not the concept" (M-1, PUB-392). Whether on the computer or with pencil and paper, sketching is the first step in generating ideas.

Question #2

Depending on which medium you are comfortable with, how does sketching either by pencil and paper or the computer influence your design process?

For some, the benefits of sketching on the computer are clear because of the "different components" in a computer, one respondent becomes creatively inspired as opposed to "staring a blank piece of paper" (F-2, SYS-392). Similarly, another respondent writes that when sketching "with [the] computer they are visually stronger" (M-2, TYP-390). Reluctant to move out of her established parameters, one student candidly admits that her instructor "pressures" her to create a sheer quantity of 30 – 50 thumbnails for a project and she feels that it is a waste of her time especially when she could be more productive with the computer. She remarks that "[m]y ideas further develop once on the computer & I can do so much more there that I never go back to sketching for that project" (F-3, SYS-392). It perplexes her why such abundance in experimentation is necessary at this initial stage when she would eventually revert to the first few initial sketches.

Oppositely, another student reports that "I notice when I sketch first on paper, there are less formal design concerns later and my ideas are usually more varied and creative than when I start on the computer" (F-1, POR-390). Sketching with pencil and paper, one writes, "By sketching as part of my process, I am able to try anything. The more I do the better off I am. It allows me to get my mind flowing, to get to those ideas which will work, not just settling for an 'ok' idea" (F-6, TYP-391). Another facilitative benefit of sketching with pencil and paper that can influence the design process is described in the following comment, "It makes my comp. [sic] work more organized (wasting less time)" (M-4, TYI-390).

One respondent describes sketching with pencil a "more natural" process when compared to the computer which is "more confining" in the following comment: "Pencil is easier for me to use. It is more natural. I've been sketching forever where the computer is more confining" (M-1, TYI-391). Another respondent writes, "Using pencil seems to lend itself to more linear designs. Especially with type. It also lends itself to a more 'organic' feel" (M-6, TYP-391). "When sketching, my design is free to roam and do whatever I want, with the computer as a supplemental tool, whereas sketches on the computer allow the programs to dictate my design and direction. Making it look generic and uncreative," remarks one respondent (M-4, PSS-390). The same conviction is shared by this respondent who writes that "I can get more ideas out more quickly w/ [sic] pencil & paper. The computer limits my idea generation" (F-5, PSS-390).

It is important to have a well-developed idea because without it, the later stage cannot ensue as reflected in this response: "Paper sketch allows me to figure out basic design solutions before getting caught up on the computer, where one can easily get distracted and focus too much on 'perfecting' before a successful design has been worked out" (F-8, PSS-390). In another instance, the computer seems to reverse the design process by bringing the final production to the initial stage as indicated by one respondent who writes, "I feel like I always start on my 'final' design the first time I start designing on the computer" (F-4, PSS-390). She represents only 9% (3 out of 32) of female students who would sketch with a computer in the initial stage compared to 8% (3 out of 36) of male students in the study.

Most of them feel that sketching by pencil and paper provide "a good groundwork" and "the overall quality of the final piece will be enhance by using sketches" (F-1, TYI-391) but most importantly, sketching is viewed as a fast way to express their ideas. Another describes sketching as "blueprint," in the following remark: "I feel that pen & paper provide a blueprint. If I go immediately to the computer, I often get stuck and lazy" (F-1, PSS-390). Rather than trying to make the sketches "perfect," the imperfection allows one respondent to treat sketching as a trajectory and she writes, "I am less inclined to feel obligated to finish a piece if I sketch in pencil, which is good, because then I have more freedom to branch off into different directions, paying less attention to the initial stages looking 'perfect'" (F-2, TYI-390).

Equally important, the following statement reinforces the importance of sketching because its loose format allows for creativity: "I think sketching allows more creativity. You don't have to think about margines [sic], rules, leading, kerning, ect [sic]. You can just design" (F-3, PSS-390). A respondent even goes as far as saying that he could always revisit his thumbnail sketches for other possible layouts usage by writing the following statement: "I can always go back to my thumbnails and use other sketches for layouts" (M-4, SYS-392). For that particular student, it is as though sketched ideas can lie dormant for future usage. This conviction is strengthened by a student who remarks that the pencil medium influences his design process by "… making everything more different which a computer makes everything the same" (M-2, TYP-391). The room for "difference" is important for exploration purposes.

Question #3

As you go through the process of searching for a solution and alternative designs are generated, do you rely on your intuition or common sense? Please explain.

Commonsensibly and intuitively, two people cannot perceive things in exactly the same way; therefore, the ideation processes between two people are always different (Belvin, 1997). Ideas that take shape in a form can be developed from a number of sources. We relate perceptual imagery to real things that exist or did exist and survive in our memory. By incorporating our intuitive understanding of one's situation, feelings, and motives into designs, we have the ability to transform empathy and understanding into serviceable and marketable forms.

If ideas are conceived intuitively, then 31% (11 out of 36) of male respondents and 41% (13 out of 3) of female respondents would use this kind of "gut instinct" (F-1, SYS-392) to guide them in the design process. A respondent writes, "I'm the type of person that goes by a 'gut reaction.' If I like the way something looks on paper or on a computer screen, I have a tendency to want to leave it that way" (M-6, TYP-391). One respondent writes that he uses his intuition "… because most of the time my common sense fails me" (M-3, TYP-391).

Alternatively, a respondent who combines his common sense for developing theoretical concepts while relying on intuition for his artistic development (M-4, TYI-390) makes up 56% (20 out of 36) of male respondents compared to 50% (16 out of 32) of their female counterparts who use both common sense and intuition for guiding them in decision-making. Succinctly described by one student: "Intuition tells me what … I can do, and common sense tells me whether or not it will work" (M-5, TYP-391).

Respondents are using their common sense in deciding on matters that affect them on a broader scale and intuition on a more personal level as outlined by a few respondents: "Common sense helps you with the obvious and the obvious can be good in design it helps people understand your design. Through intuition however I come up with ideas that are more complex & subtle and this can be good too" (M-7, SYM-390). Another respondent clearly summarizes her intuitive and commonsensible awareness: "Both compliment my

77

work because intuition gives a personal feel where as common sense is more based off knowledge of the public" (F-1, TYP-390).

Realizing that designs are meant for the public who may understand common sense better than intuition, a few respondents choose common sense over intuition because the general public relates to common sense more positively, as the following comment indicates: "… it seems design is meant to be viewed by non artists and designers, so it should be read easily and common sense lend itself to that" (M-1, SYS-392).

Some respondents are trying to put themselves in the viewers' or clients' position. "What may be obvious to you or other designers may not be obvious to the average viewer. You must put yourself in the viewer's place" cautions this respondent (F-1, TYI-391) and according to one respondent, "I find myself worrying more about the later production aspects because that is what the professor or client sees" (M-5, TYP-391, quoted in question #5).

Following the same line of thought, this respondent emphasizes the influence of a client over his design process: "A little bit of both. As a designer, there must be an intuitive ability to decide where things should go, often only later to find out that if your decision was in-line with some obscure rule of design, but there must always be a reason for choice. A client & a client's needs should dictate how design is done, whether or not it is appropriate, and other such matters" (M-4, PSS-390). Similarly, another respondent writes that he relies on intuition "… because you have to know the target audience and do research to know more about them. This helps you formulate ideas, needs, and stategies [sic] which develop the idea. Common sense is not a factor. Some ideas have to break away from the norm to catch the viewers [sic] eye" (M-3, PSS-390).

Contrarily, another respondent documents that he uses just his "[c]ommon sense [because] as designers we are creating artwork that is to be understood by the general public. The general public understands common sense, but not necessarily intuition" (M-5, SYM-390). Likewise, one writes, "Commen [sic] sense is always factor because things have to be logical (there has to be a reason for what you do)" (M-4, TYP-391). Some respondents are concerned with what the public thinks and opted to use common sense to help them figure out their uncertainties as reported by this respondent: "I work on ideas that catch my eye, but I also think about how the public would see it" (F-3, SYM-390). In this research, only 6% (2 out of 32) of female students would use solely only their common sense when compared to 14% (5 out of 36) of male students.

Succinctly describing the combination of intuition and common sense to form ideas, one respondent writes, "Intuition is my common sense. They go hand in hand & influence each other" (M-1, PSS-390). Another respondent adds that "common sense is a big part of intuition" (F-3, SYS-392). "Intuition tells me what I can do, and common sense tells me whether or not it will work" according to this respondent (M-5, TYP-391). "Both - if I intuitively like one solution better but it is not logical enough for an audience to understand, then I will go with the commen [sic] sense idea" writes this respondent who carefully balances between her intuition and common sense (F-3, TYP-391).

Combining intuition and "synesthesia" which is a condition in which one type of stimulation evokes the sensation of another is described as one of the many techniques used by one respondent. She writes, "My design is based mostly on intuition and the concept behind synesthesia. Good designs are often stimulated by some inherent quality - after this is when I begin to think more formally (layout/precision, etc)" (F-2, TYI-390).

Question #4

Do you discover anything new while working on your computer in terms of idea generation? Please describe.

91% (62 out of 68) of all respondents report that they discover something new while working on the computer but the dependencies are more or less in the ways of using the computer as tools of automation, accuracy, expediency, presentation, execution, and implementation. As an example, one respondent reports that "I put in what I thought up in paper. It is just a more cleaner [sic] and modified version" (F-7 PSS-390). Another respondent adds that "... normally when I use the computer it is to make a finished product of something I have drawn" (M-2, SYM-390).

According to one respondent, "The computer helps when you want to explore compositional changes" (M-3, POR-390) while another respondent adds that "[i]t is also nice to know that with a simple command, ⌘Z, a mistake can be 'undone.' This makes the sense of freedom w/out [sic] messing up and getting stuck ..." (F-2, TYI-390). Similarly, another respondent asserts that "... you do not have to redraw every time you have a change you want to make" (M-5, TYP-391).

Images are conveyed electronically, enhancing the ability to experiment once displayed on the screen. In other words, the initial design ideas are transformed and reinvigorated into fresh and unpredictable creative outcomes from direct manipulation in the computer as evident in this particular quote: "When it comes to layout, I can generate many ideas very quickly and options that would normally take longer to do by hand, and when doing photo adjustments, there are happy accidents..." (M-4, PSS-390).

A respondent notes that the sketching process helps mainly in the preliminary process in terms of visualizing ideas, it is also helpful in figuring out problems before moving sketched ideas into a computer. She writes, "... ideas on paper may not work out on the computer. You have to trouble shoot & try other ways to present the idea in a way that the computer can execute it the most" (F-4, POR-390).

Despite whatever approaches they take and regardless of how they use the computer, some made discoveries while toiling with tools within the computer software and report them as "happy accidents" (F-1, F-2, TYI-390; M-3, M-4, PSS-390; F-7, PSS-390, quoted in question #7). Similarly, "beneficial 'accidents'" (F-3, SYS-392) or "happy mistakes" (F-6, PSS-390) are also described as discoveries made unexpectedly while using software programs to execute their projects.

One respondent even suggests that mistakes are encouraged because it can lead to more ideas that can be discovered on the computer. According to him, "As you learn more about programs you can develope [sic] mistake[s] that really push other ideas" (M-3, PSS-390). Similarly, another respondent documents that "[b]eneficial 'accidents' are more likely to happen @ [sic] the computer - those 'accidents' usually result in better idea generation" (F-3, SYS-392). One respondent agrees and reports that "many times a mistake will spark an idea, or can see something in the design during developement [sic] on the computer that can spark ideas also" (M-3, SYM-390).

Other similar comments include: "Changing a small detail that easily can inspire new ideas. A slight change might remind me of something I had not thought of before" (F-3, TYP-391); "... often times an idea is generated through a slight change on the computer (F-6, TYP-391) and "[m]any times a mistake will spark an idea, or can see something in the design during developement [sic] on the computer that can spark ideas also" (M-3, SYM-390).

The same reason probably prompted the following response: "... when I'm working on the computer, new ideas usually come to me. Actually seeing the layout on screen can give you ideas that you haven't had before. Strengths & weaknesses of layout can be more clearly seen" (F-1, TYI-391). One respondent folksily writes that "... one mistake can lead to the 'oops ... wait, that kinda looks neat' factor. Plus I can manipulate objects text and ideas easier and faster, plus use the tools that the programs provide for new ideas" (M-1, TYP-391).

The serendipitous role of accident in the design process while on a computer seems to trigger an "a-ha" moment for some while others are glad that they are able to do "variations" (F-5, PSS-390) or "compositional changes" (M-3, POR-390) on the computer. According to one respondent, "… a computer can generate looks and effects not easily created by hand" (M-2, SYS-393) and "… the computer teaches you everyday. By playing with it on an everyday basis you experiment constantly" (M-1, PUB-392).

Sketching with pencil and paper may not produce the same result as facilitated by sketching on the computer with all its "bells and whistles." One respondent writes, "Sometimes, when you are working with a program and you see how a filter or tool affects a drawing that can be useful in coming up with ideas …" (M-7, SYM-390) while another reports that "[i]t is easier to manipulate the designs once they are on the computer" (M-4, SYM-390). "Yes, because with all the different tools available, ideas keep popping into my head for different solutions" argues this respondent (F-3, SYM-390). "The computer gives ease to additive & deconstructive elements. It allows you to play & always reverse back to where you started. Various filters also give ideas that you might have never considered" asserts this respondent (F-3, TYI-390).

The benefit of paper is surpassed by the computer because according to this respondent: "Going from paper to computer is a great change. You can manipulate images on the computer and you can't do that on paper" (M-4, SYS-392) while another respondent adds that, "… sometimes the gradient tool or blending is generated into my ideas" (M-1, SYM-390). More accolades come from another respondent who claims that the computer helps her to come up with new ways to improve an idea: "The computer allows me to nail down details … I get a basic idea on paper and the computer is where the idea comes alive" (F-3, PSS-390).

The computer becomes a practical outlet for creative expressions, liberating the computer user from manual adeptness or having constraints of previous experience. However, depending on the nature of the project, craft-like functions to produce a mock-up (prototype) is still a requirement towards the final stage of the design process. This prompted some respondents to lament that computer technology is removing the tactile and crafty side of design. One respondent writes that "… some level of hand skill and 'man made' quality is taken from the idea" (F-2, SYM-390). Similarly, another respondent cautions that "... more often then not, idea generation must come before you get on the computer" (M-4, PSS-390).

One respondent warns that "... it is not always wise to take ideas from the computer. It heads you in new ways that you might not want to go" (M-5, SYM-390). Similarly, "every now & then I'll do something by accident & it will take my design in a completely different direction" (F-4, TYP-391). Notice that "new ways" and "different direction" suggest the discovery aspects of using the computer. Another respondent purposely renders her sketches with fewer details in pencil because it is easier to do the same on the computer. She writes that "I find myself making my sketches less accurate especially w/ [sic] geometric shapes b/c [sic] I know I could just easily do it on the computer" (F-5, TYP-391).

It is worth paying attention to a response that states that the computer is excellent in producing a finished product. When it comes to editing imageries, the computer is just as helpful in contributing to creativity as one respondent who writes, "Sometimes certain things that the computer can do turn out nice even though I may not have thought of it in pencil roughs" (M-2, TYP-391).

Within the same line of thought, the computer is described as helping one respondent to take some of his ideas further (M-1, TYI-390) or "to the next level" (F-3, POR-390). Concurring to the same idea, another student reports that the computer allows him to "... see things in a whole new light [and] see things that you have never seen before [and to] implement them" (M-1, POR-390). In generating ideas on the computer, one respondent writes that "[i]t's easier to go through several ideas at a time by clicking" (F-9, PSS-390).

As a tool, computers can be used to perform, simplify, or support a task. One respondent writes that "there are many processes it is hard to visualize w/out [sic] a computer. Filters are a good example (Photoshop). Sometimes to help get an idea moving more I run through the filters to see what it can stimulate visually" (M-4, TYI-390). According to a few respondents, technology has transformed the creative process especially in the areas of visualization for exploring layout with elements of typefaces, colors, forms, and images which are handled better by computers. One respondent writes that "... there are a lot of things [with] typography that can be achieved through the computer more easily than the paper ..." (F-3, POR-390).

Type becomes invigorated when it is integrated with other graphic elements including shape, texture, and illustrative forms. The computer's beneficial features prompted another respondent to write that he "… can add, subtract, multiply, or divide to anything that you have created which in turn expands your ideas" (M-3, TYP-391).

In terms of the benefits of using the computer, another respondent writes, "… placement & type choice particularly b/c [sic] free hand sketches cannot have the precision & capability the computer has. Color choice as well - Pantone helps…" (F-1, TYP-391). One respondent acknowledges that she benefits more from the interaction with people because according to her, "… more ideas are gained by interaction throughout the process w/ [sic] teachers & peers" (F-1, SYS-392).

Question #5

Which area do you find yourself worrying about more: the early idea generation aspects or the later production (mock-up, software knowledge, technical information, presentation) aspects?

To an experienced designer, the process of ideation or development can be natural and spontaneous but for a novice student designer, it may be a daunting task. According to this respondent, the challenge lies in "[i]dea generation due to the fact that this is where the process starts [and] it is more difficult [in] coming up [with] the idea that works, is unique, complete[ly] executable is more difficult" (F-4, POR-390). Similarly, "[a]nything can be made to look pretty, but if the idea sucks, the final piece will suck" (F-1, POR-390).

Another respondent agrees and adds, "The hardest part is getting started. The early idea generation can take a while to develope [sic], but once the idea is discovered it becomes easier to try in different ways and finish up in all stages" (M-6, SYM-390). Succinctly described is the following comment: "Once an idea gets formulated the rest falls into place" (M-1, TYI-390) while another respondent writes that "its [sic] making them into effective designs that are hard" (M-1, PSS-390). "The early idea generation aspect is a "foundation [that] needs to be laid out first" emphasizes this respondent (M-2, TYI-390).

50% (18 out of 68) of male respondents and 44% (14 out of 32) find the idea generation aspect as the most challenging part of the process because it is difficult to think of original and unique ideas reflected in this comments: "A good foundation is always the toughest to find" (M-4, TYP-391). Both the early idea generation and the later production aspects are important because a great idea could be destroyed by poor production as emphasized in the following response: "If you have a great idea though it can be destroyed by poor print production, mock-ups, etc." (F-3, POR-390).

When it comes to confronting the production side of design, the following statement describes one respondent's "worst fear," "I am always worrying about program version problems, paper problems, weird printer colors, font output problems ect [sic] It is so frustrating to be finished but not able to get into a hard copy form" (F-3, PSS-390). One respondent writes, "The late production I think is more important. After all that is what everyone sees, so I think I worry about how it will look and how I can get the computer to do what I am hoping for" (M-3, SYM-390).

Similarly, another respondent replies that "[p]roduction is a concern because it takes a lot of concentration to present everything cleanly, and without any smudges. Getting everything to print out right is another big problem" (M-1, SYM-391). 42% (15 out of 36) of male respondents and 38% (12 out of 32) raise concerns specifically regarding later production in graphic design while 8% (3 out of 36) of male respondents and 13% (4 out of 32) worry about both idea generation and later production. Collectively, 59% (40 out of 68) of respondents are concerned about idea generation while 53% (36 out of 68) are worried about later production. According to the respondents, finding an elusive and effective solution seems harder.

Lacking the confidence in computer knowledge, this respondent writes, "It [sic] most situations I get more anxious about taking my ideas to the computer. The amount of things to do & you can use in the software & my knowledge of that causes some intimidation" (F-6, TYP-391). Another respondent documents that the production stage is "… more time consuming" because "… one wants it to be perfect for presentation" (F-8, PSS-390). Therefore, the later production stage is equally, if not, more important for some respondents because this is the stage where ideas are realized into tangible and visual formats.

For one respondent, the idea generation is not a concern but because of its importance, later production becomes pale in comparison. She writes that "… if early ideas are not present then the whole process WILL LAG [sic] and production is not even a worry - idea generation is" (F-1, SYS-392). After all, for an idea to be producible within a marketplace context, the likes and dislikes of graphic designers are waged against influences such as age, education, advertising, ethnic background, and income of their audience despite the fact that designers meticulously consider theme, style, symbolism, and other forms of visuals.

Question #6

Briefly list and describe each step involved in solving your design project from the beginning to finish. Indicate any tools, artifacts, or devices that are important at each step.

Throughout the compositional stages, all respondents in this study sketch one way or the other using varying media. In order to sketch, ideas must first be conceived. This is the first step where they visualize conceptually and then they visually and tangibly realize their concepts. They have ideas and they must choose a medium in which to express them but before they do, some form of research is involved as one respondent chronicles that "… a designer must know their client/topic. Ignorant design is useless design" (M-4, PSS-390).

Perhaps for validation purposes, one respondent writes, "Throughout this process have others look at it to gain a different perspective than yours (M-1, TYP-391). Similarly, another respondent writes that some level of research is necessary during the initial stage of design: "First, I research, see what I need to know about the client or the anticipated design" (F-6, TYP-391) and so is the following reply: "… knowledge of the client and their service/nature of business helps a lot in the way of idea generation" (M-1, SYM-391).

In reality, a graphic designer may have to rail against the client's indifference and ignorance of aesthetic over profitability to come up with a solution that functions midway between satisfying the client and the designer. Adaptation and compromises during the design process come as no surprise, which further explains the iterative nature of design. Muddling through, learning by trial and error, or simply picking the brains of instructors, peers, other non-designer friends seem to be the norm during this phase.

As indicated in question #1, 91% (62 out of 68) of them solely choose non-technological devices such as pencil and paper to sketch to their hearts' content while only 4% (3 out of 68) work directly on a computer to plot out design ideas, make changes until the composition falls into place. Students approach their projects with their own choices for interpretations. Most of them prefer a looser and more exploratory method of describing form through traditional media such as pencil and paper while others adopt a calculated and mathematical route to sketching by using the computer. According to one respondent, "I start with small pencil sketches. I then refine and enlarge the sketches. Then, I use my pen to add value ranges. If I like the design, I will attempt to put it on the computer" (M-5, SYM-390).

The main purpose of exploratory drawing is to discover their personal expressions through the images they are creating. There seems to be two kinds of "roughs" (or initial ideas) that are reported in this section. The first kind is the pencil and paper thumbnail as reported by the following respondent: "I usually begin with pencil sketches, critic those & choose a few of the best roughs. From there I will do a tighter ink version, then put on [the] computer w/ [sic] refinements on the ink drawing. Then refine the computer rough & usually finish from there" (M-6, SYM-390). The second kind of rough is generated from the computer directly.

As for the tools used, one resourceful respondent combines both traditional and technological tools in his design process. First, he makes a few quick sketches with pencil and by combining methods from traditional medium such as tracing paper and x-acto knives, he manages to simplify his initial ideation process. Later in the process, he scans his sketches into the computer and along the process a digital camera is used to "edit and create" (M-1, TYP-390). Similarly, a respondent replies that "I start by creating small rough thumbnails and then refine the best thumbnails before put[ting] them in the computer. I will usually do several versions once on the computer and then pick one and refine it more until I am pleased with the final comp" (M-4, SYM-390).

Respondents who choose to sketch with the computer present different reasons but it is apparent that the electronic media is chosen for facilitative reasons. It is obvious that computer-generated roughs are more refined compared to pencil roughs. According to one respondent, "Now that I more fully understand the computer, I can use the sketch as a 'template' for the design" (M-3, POR-390, quoted from question #2). Similarly, another respondent adds that the "[c]omputer helps more because trying different options is much less time consuming. You can more easily compare very similar ideas to make decisions" (F-3, TYP-391, quoted from question #2).

During the brainstorming sessions, one respondents documents that thoughts take place "during the rough sketching of ideas. Next comes choosing two or three, designs that have potential and refining the rough sketches …" (M-5, TYP-391). Anything from "write down things that come to mind - relative & arbitrary" (F-3, TYI-390) to "word associations" and "mind map" (F-6, PSS-390) for idea generation is how some respondents list their initial steps involved in their design projects.

There are benefits from sketching because for one respondent, "When the projects are faster I find myself refering [sic] back to the pencil & paper for association list" (F-9, PSS-390). For another respondent, it is from many idea generations of thumbnails on pen and paper that leads to the "lists of related words, ideas, formulation of a concept & translation to thumbnails" (F-8, PSS-390).

At a later stage, some respondents, depending on the project, would scan their initial pencil-and-paper or pen-and-ink sketches into the computer via a scanning device. In describing the necessary tools that are important in the design process, one respondent writes, "Pencil, paper, computers are all important when making a design" (M-2, TYP-391). Graphics were scanned in via a scanner attached to a computer system and engagement with the hardware is characterized by an obsession with the image manipulation provided by the software package. For one respondent, after ideas are conceived, usually during rough sketching of ideas, he chooses two or three potential designs, puts the images into the computer, scans and redraws them with Adobe Illustrator as "computer roughs." After several stages of refinement, they are printed and mounted (M-5, TYP-391).

Refinement is an essential part which exists in both of these stages regardless of the medium they use. One respondent who describes his idea about design refinement mentions that it is a "… process of retooling and eliminating ideas and finding the one that is the best" (M-4, PSS-390). Experimentation with medium is also an important aspect for one respondent who writes, "I use the scanner, collage, digital camera, paint, etc. whatever seems appropriate. … the photocopy machine is one of my favorite " (F-1, TYI-390).

One respondent reports that "… the computer provides ways of doing things that you could not do without it. Easy manipulation and color change, screening back. I think all of those tools and more can produce ideas" (M-1, TYI-391). According to one respondent, "I find it is much easier to explore color options & reversals on the computer. Specific copy to headline sizes are also easier to work on the computer. Therefore I do often explore totally new ideas once I have moved onto the computer" (F-8, PSS-390, quoted from question #4).

If a printer is used in conjunction with it, the finished product is always visually pleasing and professional looking. Different printers offer differing qualities, measured by the number of dots per inch (dpi). However, because of the inherent difference in the two media, initially conceived ideas may not work on the computer, adding a layer of complexity to the design process. One respondent describes that "[p]rinting is a bit of a problem sometimes - matching screen color to the different printers in the lab" (F-1, TYI-390). In terms of the software used, the most mentioned software in particular order includes

Photoshop, Illustrator and Quark" (F-8, PSS-390; F-3, SYM-390; M-5, TYP-391; M-1, PSS-390).

Depending on projects assigned and certain specific requirements for the class from the instructors, the general steps involved in design projects from the beginning to finish can be broken into basically eight steps: (a) accepting the project, (b) analyzing and researching for ideas, (c) identify problems and clarify objectives; (d) conceptualizing and visualizing ideas into various forms and shapes through sketches, (e) brainstorming which involves refining available ideas and/or develop alternative ideas; (f) approval for suggested improvement and usually at this age the computer is utilized; (g) production of prototype; and (h) presentation of ideas.

The end of these eight steps do not cover the production aspects which include the areas of trouble-shooting problematic computer files to ensure that files are producible into a mock-up, and in a real world situation, getting the approval of a client, and finally getting the files produced.

Question #7

Do you think computer technology is maximizing or minimizing (enhancing or impeding) your creativity? In other words, what are the pros and cons of using a computer to execute your project?

When asked if computer technology is maximizing or minimizing (enhancing or impeding) their creativity or what are the pros and cons of using a computer to execute their projects, 50% (16 out of 32) female respondents answered maximizing as opposed to 69% (25 out of 36) of male respondents. Forty-four percent (16 out of 68) of all respondents think that computer technology can both maximize and minimize their creativity. The computer is deemed as an expediency tool as it speeds up the design process while others think that it is helpful in terms of cleaning things up and making things appear more professional as replied by the following remarks: "It makes the work look cleaner and more professional" (M-1, PAC-390). Acknowledging the same opinion, one respondent replies that "I believe that a computer helps to maximize my creativity because of the ability to change things quickly and the neatness of the final product" (M-5, TYP-391).

However, some respondents think that the computer is more than just another tool. According to one, "I feel it maximizes … [because] some things come to me on the computer that I haven't thought of before" (M-1, TYP-390). Another writes that the computer is capable of aiding her "very rough drawing style … [and] the computer helps [to] refine [her] hand drawn designs" (F-3, TYP-391).

The computer allows its users to visualize their work even before they begin as documented by this respondent who writes that it "allow[s] you to see your work before you begin" (F-4, TYP-391). The computer "allow[s] the designer to work in a virtual field" (M-1, TYI-390) and " … in some instances it does improve creativity by the happy mistakes" (F-7, PSS-390). Similarly, another respondent writes, "I think the computer maximizes my creativity because so many things happen there that cannot happen w/ [sic] other mediums [sic]" (F-3, SYS-392). One respondent who is a web designer credits the computer for helping him to "review new sites … [so that he can] analyze the competitors" (M-4, TYI-390).

Sixty-seven percent (40 out of 68) of all the respondents surveyed think that computer technology maximizes their creativity mostly in utilitarian purposes. Some best and most popular features reported include the abilities to scan images or sketches into the computer for further refinement and explorations. In one reply, a respondent writes, "I use it as a tool for refinement" (M-4, SYM-390) [and it] "… is maximizing, because you can do so much more with it … Pros: clean images, various tools, easy to experiment" (F-3, SYM-390).

Following the majority who use the computer in later stages during design process development, a respondent writes that once he passes the "exploration' phase" the computer enhances the "final stage." He can make various compositional variations because "… the computer enhances the "final" stages in that you can change colors, papers, and composition w/ [sic] copy" (M-3, POR-390). Along the same line of thought, one respondent replies that "I think the computer aides because it is easier to visualize the design in a more final appearance throughout the process enabling the designer to see design flaws & successes easier. It is also easier to see how alterations will affect the design" (F-8, PSS-390).

Some still think that the "physical work [of] collage, sketch, etc. cannot be totally abandoned [because] a combination of the two must be used" (F-1, TYI-391) and another respondent writes that the computer "… can become a 'crutch' for many people." He adds that "[a]lthough helpful with imagery [it] still cannot replace ALL ASPECTS [sic] of handmade imagery" (M-6, TYP-391). This opinion is seconded by the following remark: "[The computer d]iminishes the art for hand design" (M-3, PSS-390) while another respondent thinks that a combination of manual and computer skills is useful: "I think every good designer knows the importance of art, and texture, and actual hands on feel that you can't get w/ [sic] a computer, but good designer use both to push design" (M-2, SYS-393).

Another respondent thinks that the computer can help those who are not skilled at drawing: "It helps maximize time used on projects, as well as help out the designer in the process if he/she aren't [sic] the best at using their hands. It also helps us to do things that you just can't do anywhere else but on the computer" (M-6, SYM-390). "Computer technology maximizes my work because I can do things on the computer that can not be done by hand" is another benefit documented by one respondent (F-1, TYP-390). Particularly poignant is the following remark, "I am not able to draw as well as I see things in my head. The computer allows me to 'cheat' & cover up my lack of drawing skills" (M-1, PSS-390).

Optimism in computer technology usage is also foreshadowed by one respondent who raises the concern of having difficulty in keeping up with new software upgrades: "The computer has the ability to maximize my work but since there is always new software coming out it is hard to keep up with" (M-4, SYS-392). Another student expresses his concerns about the cost involved in maintaining computer technology, "… the problem is that in a town like Lubbock it is hard to find buisness [sic] including Tech that has updated software, its [sic] great when its [sic] available, but its [sic] not unless you have 10,000 grand to spend for your home equipment" (M-1, PUB-392).

A respondent expresses his discontent with the computer equipment: "A con might be when the computer freezes or the printer won't work" (M-5, TYP-391). Similarly, another respondent reports that "[s]ometimes though there are computer problems that hold me back whether it is lack of knowledge or computer gliches [sic] (F-3, TYP-391) while another warns that the computer can minimize one's creativity "… as long as one remembers the computer is only a tool and cannot design for you" (M-1, SYS-392). One respondent shares his concern in the following comment: "I feel that people are relying less and less on artistic and drawing skills. With computer we're getting closer for any John Doe to be able to do what we do" (M-4, TYP-391).

Another writes, "For me, the computer should never be part of the creativity. It helps to clean things up and make drawings look more professional, nothing more" (M-5, SYM-390). The same notion is repeated by another respondent, "I guess because it is just another tool. The pencil & paper will never be replaced by the computer. But to depend totally on the computer is impending [sic] creativity" (M-7, SYM-390). "If you jump onto the computer too soon, you tend to generate fewer ideas, and therefore you may miss a solution to the problem that would work better" (M-1, SYM-391) warns this respondent. According to one respondent, the "infinite options" of computer technology can also become its disabling features with "almost too many options" (F-2, TYI-390).

Related to these observations, another respondent laments that "… while the computer allows for quick, easy explorations & a broader range of ideas, it makes it easier for the designer just to use a few filters & crazy type & say they're done" (F-3, TYI-390). According to one respondent, computer technology has created monotony in the outcome of design: "For some reason a lot of graphic works come out looking the same or a lot alike" (F-1, TYP-391). Similarly, another respondent expresses that "I think slowly my creativity is diminishing. Things off the computer start to all look the same. Nothing is new any more [sic], at least if you are drawing it, it has a diff. [sic] feel" (F-9, PSS-390).

Anyone can use a computer and reliance on other skills may be necessary as stressed by the following response: "I don't use any "special new features" when designing. I try to rely on type & design characteristics because anyone can use filters etc. and create something that has been seen before" (F-6, PSS-390). One warns that "… technology can minimize your creativity if you don't know how to use it (M-3, SYS-392). Succinctly described by one respondent, the computer is "unreliable," "too technical," and "limiting to [the] capability of [a] CPU" (M-2, TYI-390).

Because all respondents use computers in executing their projects, some respondents feel that the lack of computer software and technical knowledge can impede their creativity. One respondent writes, "I would say it was hindering my creativity because I had limited knowledge of how to use many programs" (F-5, TYP-391). Another respondent acknowledges that those with software knowledge and technical competency can outperform those without: "… it's really hard to keep up with the software or even the point that someone's who's [sic] idea isn't as strong as yours can make theirs work through the program" (F-6, TYP-391). Computer technology appears to be at least as much the problem as the solution.

Question #8

How do you find your initial concepts in relation to your end result? In other words, does your final solution match your initial sketches or ideas? Please explain how it does or how it does not.

Forty-six percent (31 out of 68) find that their initial concepts bear close resemblance to their end results but because of the iterative nature in the process of design, the rough and unrefined appearance of their early sketches are refined, altered, and changed. This experience is reflected in one respondent who writes that "… [o]ften an idea continues to evolve as you are forced to address specific issues and concerns" (F-1, POR-390) while another finds that her design always changes because "[u]sually my initial sketches are vague and only hint to a concept. My initial concept usually does not match the end result because there is such an evolution during the different stages between" (F-2, TYI-390).

Another respondent reports that "[t]he end results look close to the original but I usually have to change small things to get the look I want" (M-4, SYM-390). "The concept usually matches, but almost never do the sketches match identically. The concept has just been pushed farther on the computer" adds another respondent (F-3, POR-390). Similarly, another respondent adds that "… sketches show very rough examples and just hints to the final design" (M-1, TYP-391).

On the contrary, "… there have [sic] been a few times where I think a rough has been superior visually or by layout" (M-6, TYP-391). For some, "It depends, half of the time my finished result will look almost identical to my first drawings, sometimes they will change a little but still retain most of the same forms, but sometimes the initial idea and the finished project looking nothing alike and all they share was an idea" (M-4, TYP-391). According to one respondent, "Sometimes my drawn elements are better than my finish product" (F-1, TYP-390). Because "… things happen along the whole process - parts are removed, things are added - sometimes ideas are remodeled. There is so much on the comp that the original idea can develope [sic] far more than it would have w/o [sic] a computer" (M-3, TYI-390) writes one respondent.

This conviction is shared by another respondent who replies, "My final solution never matches my initial sketches. All initial sketches are done by hand, but when I go to the computer, they always change" (F-4, PSS-390). For one, it is the refined thumbnails that bear closer resemblance to the final design: "Once I develop a concept, those stronger thumbs are more closely related to the final" (F-5, PSS-390). The iterative process plays an important part in the design process according to this response: "As the design process proceeds, new ideas are generated changing the original concept" (F-7, PSS-390). "From sketches to computer my ideas grow, concepts strengthen, and at the end I have a much better solution that what I started with" (F-3, SYS-392) replies one respondent.

"Yes my final solution does match my initial idea, but improved" writes one respondent (F-7, PSS-390). The final solution is a tangible and vivid visual in some sort of mounted piece or prototype of a 3-dimensional mock-up. Conversely, for those who choose to sketch with a computer, they report that conceptually and visually, both are rather similar. One respondent gives an example of an assignment that is not likely to change much from an initial concept to the end result: "In well planned areas like logo design the output matches the initial idea" (M-4, TYI-390). However, "through exploration you can often find a better solution" (F-3, TYI-390). For one respondent, a well thought idea is important because the "[f]inal is always a serious more [sic] of the original idea, but the original idea is the seed" (M-3, PSS-390).

For one, technology comes with severe repercussions as expressed by the following remarks: "… heavy dependency on the computer to help generate my design and a tendency to forget the power of real design (or design done hand) would tend to produce results far below the quality expressed in my thumbnails" (M-4, PSS-390). This is due to the fact that they are experimenting with the tools within the software program that will eventually be used by those who prefer to use the computer at an earlier stage. As for this respondent, "[g]enerally things (concepts) don't change often. But type and layout often get modified based on critiques" (F-1, PSS-390).

Question #9

In relation to question #8, what factors influenced or changed your initial sketches or ideas?

Opening their projects for suggestions to non-designers to view and criticize their works is a good reality check because in the real world, designers' works are subject to criticism from clients that may not be designers themselves. For one respondent, "Input of fellow students, teachers, & friends who are not designers help a great deal. I take everyone's opinion seriously. This helps me break out of I'm in a rut & see the project from someone else's point of view" (F-1, TYI-391). One respondent confesses: "I like to take my work to people and friends that aren't in design or art and see what they think and listen to any ideas they may have" (M-4, TYP-391).

Voluntarily or not, during brainstorming and critiquing, sketched ideas from students are openly analyzed and commented upon. Because initial ideas are likely to change, one respondent describes that his design process involves "… [a] variety of media used and how much critiquing & criticism has gone into the work" (M-6, TYP-391).

Some respondents cite the computer as having the ability to change their ideas because of the tools provided in the software: "As I get it on to the computer, I know there are things that I can do on the computer that I couldn't dream of doing by hand. I am more skilled on the computer than by hand" (M-1, TYP-391). Likewise, "[m]ost of the time accidents on a program change my idea" (M-3, SYM-390).

One respondent even credits the computer's ease of use as contributive to making discoveries in design ideas: "I find that by combining programs, almost any idea can be translated to computer. Actually the computers [sic] ease of change in design has often left [sic] to design changes that were unexpected & successful changes" (F-8, PSS-390). According to one respondent, not having a good knowledge base in the software used can be debilitating: "My lack of knowledge of ways I can use different computer programs & the time it takes me to figure out how to do what I want to" (F-5, TYP-391).

Functionality is an issue for some respondents who raise their concerns about the usability of design: "The factor I most consider are the useability [sic] of the design" (M-5, SYM-390). Another respondent describes the same concern as "… the strength of the ideas, the practicality of it, the practicality of elements within the design (lines, shapes, colors, ect [sic]), and the overall concept of the work" (M-5, TYP-391). As discussed, there are many factors that can change their initial sketches or ideas. For one respondent, it is about catering to the needs of different professors. In his words: "This is really simple. You design for what the professor wants, his or her tastes. The problem is every prof [sic] has different tastes. What might be genius to one might be total crap to another. Catch 22" (M-1, PUB-392).

What the respondent expresses is a form of negotiation and compromise that is achieved between the designer and the client in a real world situation. Apparently this respondent is getting a reflected dosage of reality in dealing with his professor who has assumed the persona of a client. Reacting to criticism, one respondent writes, "Seeing the way others react to it. It is all about societies view as to how well it works" (M-3, PSS-390). Effective communication design means that one has to first understand the intent of the message or the core of the problem, and then to work on a solution or its look. According to one respondent, the following three principles can influence his initial sketches or ideas:

"How well the idea comes across, How good the idea is in the first place, [and] How well the idea solves the problem" (M-1, SYM-391).

Computer technology is capable of influencing students' initial ideas according to one respondent who replies that it is "[t]he way that the type usually works. [It] changes because my sketches of type usually work differently than the actual layout on the computer" (F-3, POR-390). Similarly, one writes, "The computer does change the idea because of the tools involved" (M-1, TYI-391). One respondent writes that "[m]ost of the time accidents on a program change my idea" (M-3, SYM-390). In terms of hardware, one respondent credits a mouse pen as a better piece of equipment because she "… can control a pen mouse like a pencil" (F-1, TYP-390).

One respondent laments about his dependency on the computer for ideation: "The factor that has most directly influenced my design is having too much dependency on the computer to realize my design. Despite proper research and thumbnail/idea generation, if you go to the computer solely depending on it to produce your design, forgeting [sic] hand made design on things created by hand, and abandoning our artistic skills, then the end design, I have found, suffers detrimentally from the original concepts/sketches" (M-4, PSS-390).

One respondent emphasizes that "[t]he only thing that might influence a change is mass production limitations" (M-3, POR-390). Even latent ideas are capable of influencing a design as reported by the following respondent: "ideas that come up later" (F-3, SYM-390). Spur-of-the-moment is another element that could possible influence or change an initial sketch or idea (M-2, TYI-390). However, keeping one's "eyes open" to "daily experiences [and] everything in this world" is just as influential in changing the respondent's initial sketches or ideas (F-2, POR-390). Another reported influence on initial sketches or ideas include: "… other designers work in magazines" (F-6, PSS-390). Other issues such as "… Changing negative space, composition, tweaking little things to make a better design, etc." can also influence the design (M-7, SYM-390). This respondent reports that "… noticing something minor that could be changed such as type or color" could influence the final solution (M-3, TYP-391).

Question #10

Do you feel prepared to enter the field of graphic design? Please explain why you are and why you are not.

Sooner or later, respondents will enter the marketplace whether they are ready or not. In this study, some students have such low self-concepts that 61% (22 out of 36) of all male and 31% (10 out of 32) female respondents feel prepared to enter the field. It is alarming to notice the difference between male and female respondents. Ten percent (7 out of 68) of all respondents are not sure if they are ready for the field. They cite various reasons for their insecurities. Some notable concerns are practical and technical knowledge of later production surrounding production and the interpersonal business side of design such as "working with actual clients" (F-1, TYI-391).

The same concern is reflected by this respondent who writes, "I don't really know how to deal w/ [sic] a client" (F-1, SYM-390). Another cites not being creative enough to become successful in his a field that is vastly diversified: "I feel prepared to enter certain areas of graphic design partly because I think I can do it and partly because I am just ready to move to the next step. I am worried that I am not good enough or creative enough to become successful" (M-3, SYM-390). Definition of terms for "design" in chapter I outlines the different areas of profession in graphic design.

Most student designers are well-versed in their artistic training and stylistic appreciations but few of them receive any formal education in the phases of their studies that involve interpersonal skills, bookkeeping, accounting, insurance coverage, legal structures, and other management and operation agendas. Yet, they are expected to help their clients weave through a process called design, which includes subjective aesthetic choices and the complicated nature of human behavioral patterns.

One respondent who feels that he is not ready to enter the field of graphic design because he has to learn more before leaving for the real world: "I don't feel I am ready just yet because I have not learned all of what the university offers to teach me, but I am confidant [sic] that when I am finished I will be well prepared to enter the field of graphic design" (M-5, TYP-391). One respondent succinctly describes that "technically [she] need[s] to learn more" (F-1, TYP-391) while another student expresses, "I do think that more computer design classes would have been beneficial but not always necessary" (F-2, TYP-391). Another respondent writes that she is overwhelmed that "… there is so much more to the field than a good idea or concept" (F-4, TYP-391). In what appears to be a timid response, a respondent writes, "I still feel afraid of the computer. There are many terms that I don't know & I feel the tool keeps changing & I can't seem to catch up" (F-5, TYP-391).

Another respondent writes, "Yes and no. I need to learn more about the programs, but my ideas are usually pretty good" (F-3, SYM-390).

One can be prepared but may not necessarily get the job due to scarcity of jobs and the competitive nature of job employments. According to one respondent, "I feel prepared to do the job but not get the job. Aparently [sic] work is scarce for us, and thats [sic] heart breaking when you love design" (M-1, PUB-392). Another concerned respondent writes, "I don't know of even a few companies that are currently hiring" (M-1, SYM-391) while another respondent adds that "…the economy for graphic designers is real poor right now" (M-1, PAC-390).

Some of them raise concerns about not having enough knowledge about printing and other technical issues related to end production of graphic design. "From the business end and printing (as in print shops) I feel like their [sic] is a lot yet to learn" writes one respondent (F-1, PSS-390). Like wise, another respondent confesses that "I feel prepared design wise, but not company wise. I don't feel I know enough about collecting for output, sending to press, etc." (F-3, PSS-390).

More confident notes come from those who had been through some internship programs, freelance jobs, or prior employment: "I do feel prepared to enter the field, especially since I had done 2 internships in addition to several free-lance jobs while still in school. However I am planning to attend grad school to further my design experience in a non-constricting environment" (F-8, PSS-390). According to one respondent, "I don't think I'm prepared yet. I don't feel that I have enough experience working with actual clients. I am confident, however, that my remaining classes and an internship or two will equip me with the tools I need for this field" (F-1, TYI-391). Like wise, one respondent acknowledges that internships can help prepare him for the field: "Business wise, no. But my internships & freelance jobs are changing that" (M-4, TYI-390).

Part of graphic design is knowing how to run a design business or to function in a design business environment. Some respondents are concerned about the lack of business knowledge in their present curriculum as reflected in this response: "I am still unclear how a firm would work, maybe, an internship will make me feel more comfortable" (F-1, TYP-390). Although prepared to enter the field of graphic design, one respondent expresses, "… I would of [sic] liked more exposure to the business/marketing side of design" (M-1, PSS-390). Respondents seem to emphasize that the current design education curriculum is disproportionately high on the subjectivity of aesthetics and usability of technologies while disproportionately low on the analytical nature of running a business efficiently and profitably.

Students credit their design classes that are taught by instructors and professors who are also designers in the field. They are being taught by graphic designers who not only assimilate technological factors and skills into their teachings but they also bring professional experience into classrooms. One student writes, "Yes, I have had every experienced teachers that are very knowledgable [sic] in the field prepare me in my portfolio class" (M-3, POR-390). However, there is one respondent who claims that "the teachers spoon-feed us design ideas and teach us to use other's ideas altered to fit our own" (M-2, SYS-392). One respondent credits her experience and an Associate degree: "I have already done graphic design on a lower level successfully and have an Associate degree in it. I feel very prepared" (F-3, SYS-392).

Another confident respondent writes, "I feel I've been here long enough & learned enough to do well. My design skills are good & I'm open to learning more. The world of design is always changing & you have to know how to constintly [sic] learn" (M-6, SYM-390). A boost of confidence comes from the following respondent, who despite of competition, writes, "Yes even though there is a lot of competition and closeness in the skill of my peers, everyone has their own approach and style. I feel I have what I will need when I make place in the world" (M-1, TYP-390).

Showing intense feeling, this respondent documents the following response, "Yes because the faith in me to achieve my ultimate goal 'being happy in life' designing in the real world - I know my client will be happy with my work. If not - I will work harder, until I bleed damn it!" (M-2, TYP-390). There may be various reasons for their insecurities and helplessness, but dedication, education, practice, and training are important requirements for anyone to excel.

<u>Open coding</u>

Using a paradigm model as shown in Table 4.1, saturation of data into *properties* and *dimensions* for categorizing purposes in open coding can be observed in the following table. The information generated is derived from data collected in Appendix D which shows verbatim reports from all 68 respondents who responded to all the questions. These responses became the groundwork for identifying conceptual categories or properties from the data gathered which is translated in Table 4.1. Conceptual categories or properties in appendix D are labeled as "keywords." The appendix also identifies the respondents' gender, the classes they report from, the code assigned to them as well as the keywords used in coding their responses for this study. During this stage, many properties and dimensions may overlap and the idea is to generate as many categories as possible for the ensuing step, axial coding.

Table 4.1. Open coding categories of the roles and impacts of computer technology usage on creativity in the ideation process compiled from data collected

Category	Properties	Dimensions
Contribution		
	Automate	- A tool for actualizing ideas
		- Acts as a transitional medium from rough sketches to later refinement stages
		- Offers calculated and mathematical alternatives compared to traditional media (pencil, paper, pen, color markers, etc.
		- Provide functional and exploratory tools to aid in design creations
		- Effects through software filters
		- Preparatory work frees us to focus on other tasks
		- Features within computer software allow for mistakes and explorations
		- Easier to create continuity and consistency in design formats
		- Software interface offers order, logic, orientation, and format standardization
		- Cross-media/format interactivity
		- Modularity of periphery connections
	Visualize	- Superior visualization capabilities create visual stimuli
		- Simulated three-dimensional visuals allow instant feedbacks for evaluations
		- Enhancement to rough sketches
	Produce	- Image/graphics manipulation, typography, page layout, writing, drawing
		- Flexibility in digital format allows files to be saved, produced, reproduced, transferred, and transported.

Table 4.1. cont.

Category	Properties	Dimensions
Transformation		
	Facilitate	- Getting ideas down swiftly leads to more ideas/sketches - Quantitative experimentation of ideas - Induce generative and corrective natures in the design process - Explorations/variations/refinements
	Inspire	- Experimentation of something previously untried of - Serendipitous discoveries such as "Beneficial" or "happy" accidents" trigger inspirational leads - Design solutions - Lay the foundations for more ideas to follow
	Stimulate	- New interpretations of design ideas/concepts - Exchanging of ideas during brainstorming - Learning/mastering of computer software knowledge - Induce problem-solving and problem-finding skills
	Discover	- Creativity in design ideas - New ideas/Concepts through explorations - Problem-solving/Problem-finding - Solution to design problems - Extrapolations of meanings in design - Self concept
	Liberate	- Expediting tasks/Saves time - Control over production - Alternative/Substitute for artistic and manual skills
	Enhance	- Performance: technological expertise, competence, flexibility - Aptitude: Resourcefulness, reasoning, decision-making, responsiveness, achievement, confidence - Self-direction: Decision-making, risk-taking, performance, assertiveness, motivation
	Improve	- Knowledge/Methods

- Add aesthetical values to design
- Design solutions

Category	Properties	Dimensions
Implication		
	Computer technology	- Democratizes the design process
		- Users become passive receptor while working on the computer; lacking interaction with peers/no constructive criticism
		- Requires constant computer software and hardware upgrades
		- Computer software creates conventions
		- Predictability features of software creates monotony
		- Rapid technical and knowledge obsolescence
		- May bring about plagiarism through online materials
		- Connectivity of multiple peripherals allow new possibilities of interactions and information-gathering
		- Technology capabilities limited to computer software and hardware
		- Software/Hardware/Platform issues and maintenance/troubleshooting
	Visualization	- Creates immediate gratification that may discourage further explorations
		- Visuals are mechanistic in appearance, predictable, programmed, and monotonous
		- Lacking tactile depth/personal style
		- Allows analysis of strengths and weaknesses of layout in design

Category	Properties	Dimensions
Challenge		
	Situational factors	- Constraints such as course objectives, goals, instructor's expectations
		- Manmade mistakes
		- Equipment and media failure
		- Solutions that must meet practical, effective, feasible, suitable, and appropriateness criteria
		- Requires software knowledge and hardware technical ability
		- Constant technology up keeping and diagnosis

	- Requires user to have requisite knowledge or minimal competence with computer software and hardware
Adventurousness	- May create a state of dependency
	- Personalization of style
	- Creates a knowledge-based class
	- Lacking interpersonal skills/dehumanizing
	- May abandon or become unwilling to experiment with own visual materials
	- Users may settle for easy solutions
	- Willingness to take risk is limited to software and hardware restrictions

Based on the responses from the questionnaires, I analyzed the information and identified four major categories during the open coding session:

1. *Contribution* is a category identified as the advantages that are afforded by the computer technology. Three different areas are identified where computer technology allow its users to automate, visualize, and produce. This area focuses on the computer's format and the opportunities afforded by computer technology.

2. *Transformation* indicates the influence and impact of computer technology on its users. Identified for obvious beneficial changes that, as a result from using the computer technology, users are able to vary, improve, visualize, automate, and liberate them in their various areas when using the computer. This category focuses on the user's advantageous gains from using computer technology.

3. *Implication* is something that logically or naturally follows from an action or condition from using computer technology and in this section, the negative influence and impact of technology are explored and finally,

4. *Challenges* faced by computer users in other situational factors that influence the design process are explored.

Selection of one open coding category

As responses from each question in the questionnaire are carefully reviewed, concepts or themes with similar *properties* and *dimensions* are grouped together. Not only are the categories grouped together, properties of the categories are also examined. This selection is based on several factors such as its relationship to other categories, its frequencies of occurrence, quick and easy saturation and a clear implication for developing a theory (Creswell, 2002). For example, in the "transformation" category, properties from "inspire" are combined with "discover," so are "enhance" and "inspire." The consideration for linkage is based on two aspects: similarity and relevance. The latter aspect, relevance, is given a heavier consideration to make sure that saturation of data is reached. Saturation means that the categories are arranged and rearranged or when there is no new or relevant data that can emerge for grouping in terms of their properties and dimensions.

Continuous discoveries are made as categories emerge through analysis in the four identified major categories (contribution, transformation, implication, and challenge), forming a categorical structure for me to derive a core phenomenon for the next step, the axial coding. During the open coding process, subcategories (dimensions and properties) are linked to the identified four categories for saturation of data.

Core phenomenon

The final selection of one open coding category is "centralized." In the next step, axial coding, "technology develops new applications" is identified as the core phenomenon. In axial coding, all other variables (causal conditions, contextual and intervening conditions, action/interaction strategies, and consequences) are linked to the core phenomenon. Once the diagram is formed in axial coding, saturation of data is checked both in open and axial coding, the third step of selective coding which allows the formation of theory takes place.

According to Strauss and Corbin (as cited in Creswell, 2002), identification of a central or core phenomenon consists of the following six points:

1. It must be central; that is all other major categories can be related to it.
2. It must appear frequently in the data. This means that within all or almost all cases, there are indicators pointing to that concept.
3. The explanation that evolves by relating the categories is logical and consistent. This is no forcing of data.
4. The name or phrase used to describe the central category should be sufficiently abstract.
5. As the concept is refined, the theory grows in depth and explanatory power.
6. When conditions vary, the explanation still holds, although the way in which a phenomenon is expressed might look somewhat different. (p. 452)

Because computer technology in this case study is identified to have a contributive factor which is an advantageous aspect as well as a disadvantaged factor, both major categories are carefully paralleled and matched for saturation. Both "contribution" and "transformation" categories are combined for further data saturation since they both cover areas that are afforded by computer technology. Likewise, the "implication" and "challenge" categories are also combined for saturation.

In order to understand the impact of computer usage on creativity in the ideation process, four dependent variables in the study include the students' knowledge on thought processes, their assessment of the design processes, assessment of proficiency on technical issues and their notions of self-concept, achievement, performance and aptitude. The name or phrase used to describe the central category is sufficiently abstract in a way that it openly relates to other major categories such as contribution, transformation, implication and challenge. Technology develops new applications in many ways. In order to describe the multifaceted influence of computing technology, the word "develop" is unrestrainedly used in making correlations to the development of a core phenomenon. There are several powerful principles at work that are consolidated here.

The first principle is that student designers are using computer technology for a particular purpose which is a part of the fulfillment of their projects. They are able to develop and expand their creative capacities during the design process when computing medium is involved. The computer aids in the explorations and development of their design ideas by improving the quality of their initial sketches into a tangible format. For some, the computer medium is even capable of replacing or alternating their manual skills by letting them discover new interpretations and expressions of ideas with technological tools.

Computers are capable of influencing the behavior of the user by developing the following areas. Users are able to develop their aptitude, performance, and knowledge using computers. On the other hand, it can become more complex and obsolete so they acquire the role of a constant learner. By knowing how to operate the tool of the trade, the computer not only adds detail and fullness by elaborating and transforming their design ideas but it also provides order, orientation, standardization, and instant feedback for evaluations. The flexibility in digital format with functional and exploratory tools within the software and the modularity of peripheral connections develop a continued dependency on technology. This in turn develops a knowledge-based class that constantly upgrade and upkeep their software, hardware and operating platforms.

<u>Axial coding</u>

Axial coding integrates the data broken down during the open coding back in new ways to form connections between a category and its subcategories. Categories are organized into a visual model as represented in Figure 4.1. By plugging specific factors, events, actions, and consequences from the open coding into variables or matters that affect the situation described as *causal conditions, context and intervening conditions, action/interaction strategies*, and *strategies*, I can determine if the categories are saturated but more importantly, it becomes the underpinning structure for theory generation in the preceding step of selective coding.

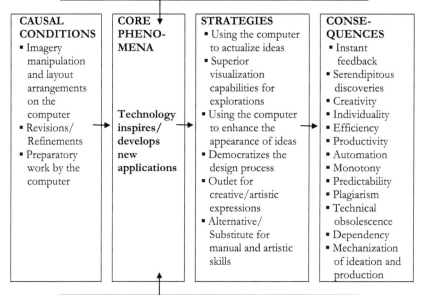

CONTEXTS
- Factors such as feedbacks, requirements, and course objectives
- Equipment (hardware and software) limitations
- Users are required to have at least minimal technical knowledge to operate tools and other features within computer software

CAUSAL CONDITIONS	CORE PHENO-MENA	STRATEGIES	CONSE-QUENCES
- Imagery manipulation and layout arrangements on the computer - Revisions/ Refinements - Preparatory work by the computer	Technology inspires/ develops new applications	- Using the computer to actualize ideas - Superior visualization capabilities for explorations - Using the computer to enhance the appearance of ideas - Democratizes the design process - Outlet for creative/artistic expressions - Alternative/ Substitute for manual and artistic skills	- Instant feedback - Serendipitous discoveries - Creativity - Individuality - Efficiency - Productivity - Automation - Monotony - Predictability - Plagiarism - Technical obsolescence - Dependency - Mechanization of ideation and production

INTERVENING CONDITIONS
- Computer technology demands constant upgrade and up-keeping
- Iterative, generative, and corrective natures of the design process
- Early idea generation and final production concerns
- Solutions must meet practical, effective, feasible, suitable, and appropriate criteria
- Conventions, traditions, convenience, efficiency, and expediency affect the final result
- The possibility of equipment and media failure

Figure 4.1. Axial coding diagram showing context, intervening conditions, causal conditions, phenomena, action/interactions strategies, and consequences

Causal conditions

There are several ways the computer is utilized by respondents as documented in the questionnaires. For the most part, it has been used as facilitating and actualizing tools, allowing the students to execute various tasks, ranging from ideation to production.

Computer software with "filters" such as those with built in image manipulation, graphics, and page layout programs allow them to experiment with various explorations, revisions, and implementations. Having accepted this premise, it is indisputable that typesetting processes and desktop publishing capabilities make the computer a favorite choice for graphic designers. The computer can do preparatory work which frees us to focus on other tasks.

The result can be immediately visualized on the screen before the production stage. The design can be modified to correct any flaws that were revealed after a comp is produced. This is, in essence, the iterative nature of the design process. With the computer, they explore the "undo," "save as," "duplicate," and "revert" commands, something a manual hands-on or traditional media are incapable of doing. Reliance on computer technology is understandable because of the opportunities that new technologies make possible. Production becomes more automated as old skills of production and analog methods are turning into digital methods. Not only can mistakes on the computer can be reverted with a mouse click, automotive features such as "copy," "cut," and "paste" allow for time-saving and control over production where users can easily repeat redundant features that would be time-consuming with traditional media.

According to Dix, Finlay, Abowd and Beale (1998), computers allow for rapid feedback and such direct manipulation allows users to explore without severe penalties thanks to its graphics-based systems. With "what you see is what you get" (WYISWYG), technology enables visualization of the final product before it is even produced. Educators' theoretical and students' intuitive sketches can be fed into computers to generate outcomes that allow instant feedback (Tsai, personal communication, October 23, 2001) and evaluation with a few mouse-clicks. Students should be encouraged to try something different and they must not be penalized when they make mistakes. The computer is making this statement a reality. Computers with the undo, save as, or repeat features are great for experimentation.

With these benefits, technology fosters self-direction, experimentation, multiple solutions, and original ideas. This flexibility permits reproduction and distribution on CD-ROM, DVD-ROM, video or the Internet. It also increases the originator's ability to duplicate and transport work with ease. Other indirect incentive factors include visual stimuli, responsiveness, competence, confidence, assertiveness, flexibility afforded by technological effectiveness.

Compared to the not-so-sophisticated medium, traditional media like pencil and paper are great for users to generate ideas quickly. Besides giving forms to their ideas, they can visualize them in a rough way how things will look and see problems that lie ahead. Traditional tools are limited in comparison to computer technology. As an alternative and/or substitute for manual skills, computers are great for those who sing praises about being liberated from not having any prerequisite knowledge of art creation, or needing to rely on manual skills or handcrafts. Technological advancements will continue to streamline the design process.

In ideation, anything imaginable is possible but not always permissible. Design is about organization of parts into a coherent order through selection and elimination. Students go through a series of decisions of elimination and refinements until the design is finished and presented. Refinement and revisions at their best is about perfection of ideas. In the process of making things right, students generatively add or correctively remove components in their sketches. This further strengthens the notion that the iterative process of design is subjected to repetitive, cyclical, and refinement routines with obligatory approval-seeking from either the clients or the instructor.

The striking visual display on the computer screen is a great indicator of how things are likely to appear, enabling most of the students to credit the computer as helpful in making their ideas appear orderly and precise in procedure. Not only that, they are given an instant feedback. As a result, their ideas appear professionally refined. The computer can optimize the performance of its users who through the iterative process of selection and elimination transform information into meaningful work. Student graphic designers use of the computer acts as a transitional medium to refine their ideas from rough sketches to refined versions.

During the stage of ideation when computers are utilized, the unfinished design exploration looks finished and as a result, clients may assume that it is finished or at worse, the designer is immediately gratified and stops to explore because of its finished look. Instructors and professors are quick to catch these flaws and as they continue to push their students to produce more, they help to dispel the danger that lies in many student designers who point and click on their indispensable tool as a substitute for their thinking. That is one reason why the computer is received with mixed blessings.

Contexts

Contexts are specific contextual properties that pertain to core phenomenon or in other words, specific constraints leading to the development of an event. External factors

such as trends, constraints from course objectives, project deadlines, instructor's
expectations, and knowledge and equipment limitations may restrict the outcome of a design
project. Designers facing their design project with these shortcomings in mind may not be a
bad thing after all. The iterative nature of the design process requires the student to
constantly alter, adapt, change, revise, and renew their design explorations. While the
computer is helpful in the revision stages, it is not immune to antagonistic interests. Routine
evaluative responses from peers and instructor are unavoidable.
Knowing what the deficiencies are can help the designer to avoid making any mistakes
because effective solutions must meet practical, feasible, suitable, and appropriate criteria.

It is impossible to be a graphic designer who is capable of performing in all the
various available media. The technical demands alone are forcing designers to be committed
to specific areas in the field in order to stay marketable as a specialized expert (Boylston,
2001). In order to use the computer, one must have several kinds of skills–a requisite skill
and minimal competence within computer software in the areas of image-editing and
manipulation, graphics, and layout. Designers need to have knowledge to operate the
computer, use the software installed, and to eliminate or settle problems associated with
computer usage. Different software programs offer different capabilities for performing
functions in art and design but the intricacies of the machine can stand in the way of
expression, particularly when the users are not familiar with the program. On the other
hand, as he or she learns the technical aspects of a software program, the learner can identify
the features and possibilities of using the medium. The designers' abilities to manipulate the
design or sketches on a computer are limited to the technical knowledge acquired as well as
hardware and software invested.

The immediate technical skills needed to practice the new technology may overwhelm
students but the reality may be that the dependency on computer technology will persist due
to its facilitating capabilities, especially towards the final stage of production. Like any piece
of tool, equipment is subject to failure and it is just another price to pay in order to benefit
from the computer's facilitating capabilities.

Intervening conditions

Generic properties that pertain to core phenomenon are known as the intervening
conditions. One way to conceptualize intervening conditions is to consider them as broader
constraints. In this study, students create projects that utilize their thinking skills as well as

computing competency. Within the process of creation, they go through two stages: early idea generation and the final production. The solutions offered must meet practical, effective, feasible, suitable, and appropriate criteria set forth by several factors such as the iterative, generative, and corrective natures of the design process.

As we realize and resolve every problem, it becomes a valuable learning experience for all of us in overcoming conventional conformance that is created by computer. By using various combinations within the software, students are able to come up with various ideas. However, the initial same tools within computer software could be combined and used in various ways by other students. Therefore, computer software makes it possible for anyone to reproduce the same image. The flexibility of the format is also capable of producing ideas that appear to be mechanistic, predictable or monotonous. Predictability and repeatability are essential from a productivity standpoint but from a visual representation and a conceptual standpoint, it becomes a "sell out cheap thrill," not to mention the possibility of liable repercussions.

According to Becker (as cited in Johnson, 1995), conventions dictate the materials that designers or artists use. Whether we are conscious or not, accommodations of "taste, fashion, tradition, convention, convenience, efficiency, and expediency" dictate the final outcome of design (Spencer, 1964). Conventions created by the tools they use, traditions that govern the field, convenience that expedites issues of efficiency, and expediency all combine to affect the final result. However, after mastering the techniques of a computer program and understanding the conventions, designers may strive to transcend the program. The predictability of the software may force the designer to break the rules of the convention (Johnson, 1995). And this is a good phenomenon for stimulating creativity in graphic designers.

Action/Interaction strategies

In spite of these constraints, many students report positive outcomes from using the computer. Their perception of how data and the contents that the data represent are transferred to the computing medium, displayed on a screen. Everything seen and used in a computing environment must relate to the systems in which it operates which explain why using the technology requires knowledge. As we are aware of it, using the computer to actualize one's idea requires technical competency or minimal understanding of how to operate the computer system.

Because the computer enhances the appearance of ideas, some students choose to sketch on the computer. They admit that they still have to print their ideas. This is because in actualizing their ideas, the sophistication of a computer screen is no comparison to a tangible format, such as a printout, which is easier to work with. They are required to bring a tangible format into the class during brainstorming sessions, where ideas are pinned up on the wall. More importantly, digital media lack tactile depth and we have a limited understanding of the way it actually is when areas or visuals are represented two-dimensionally on a colorful and simulated screen. In comparison to the print medium, we can tangibly feel its format and construct its structure, especially in projects that call for three-dimensionality.

The visual nature of a computer interface serves to capture and retain the attention of the user which partly explains the captivating enticement a user has when he or she passively inputs data into his or her computer while the computer actively receives it by acknowledging it through a screen. The lack of human social interaction created by computer technology can dehumanize the design process. Users become passive receptors while working alone on the computer. Fortunately, brainstorming sessions and the interactivity between peers, instructors and students provide the needed motivation for creative input and output. From the effectiveness and simplicity standpoints of sketching with non-technological devices, the research data show that students will continue to record information and ideas on paper despite the availability and popularity of computers. Print is still an excellent material in creating kinesthetic experiences in comparison to a simulated computer screen.

The ubiquitous computer is now available to the mass public. The same software utilized by a graphic designer can be installed and used by the public. In a sense, the design process is democratized. Technology is becoming more available and easier to learn. This places the opportunities in the hands of many non-designers. Laptop computers facilitate portability while the pervasiveness of technology in design curriculum and the availability of personal desktop computers are forcing students to invest in learning software and new media opportunities in comparison to learning manual skills (Sebastian, 2001). Such an observation is made clear by a few respondents who equate the ability to do manual skills as complimentary to computing skills while another student finds it liberating for not needing to know the manual aspects. What one lacks in manual skill is compensated with computing knowledge. It seems as though latency in art can be fulfilled with technology in aiding the growth and potential of its users.

Consequences

Although a number of educators, theorists, and designers expressed their negative views about how disturbing and perplexing change is in technology, participants in this study interactively use and combine the different tools afforded by the computer software and hardware to explore different ideas that arouse creativity in their designs.

While it is arguable that students have a sense of empowerment where they are being able to do more than they could with traditional media, it is unquestionable that computers that integrate sound, images, text, and animation can make discoveries through design more interesting. Serendipitous discoveries are reported as "happy accidents" by respondents who make discoveries afforded by the tools, filters, and a slew of connectivity to multiple maneuverable gizmos.

With the same equipment, users also explore, refine, and produce their ideas into a realized and tangible creation. As a result, users are emboldened to experiment in a computing environment. Audiences respond to new styles, symbols, and contents and most relationships between person and object begin with appearance especially in product and visual designs. That is a compelling reason for making sure that visualization of ideas is optimized but it is not the first reason. The three-dimensional display capability of computing technologies combined with the connectivity of multiple peripherals allows sophisticated new possibilities of explorations, automation, creativity, individuality, efficiency, productivity, and even personal liberations.

All of these sound too alluring not to allocate some financial resources for maintaining software upgrades and hardware up keeping as well as facing technical and knowledge obsolescence. In order to keep their wheels of productivity from breaking down, users must make sure that the computer technology used is of the latest or at least comparatively new version in order to exploit the features offered by computer software manufacturers. Failure to keep up with technology will cause other problems such as file incompatibility and other printing errors. This puts the users in a vicious cycle of constant dependency on technology as well as the demand of upgrade and up-keeping.

Synthesizing visual information can be abstracted from found or available images. With the advent of the Internet, while limited just by speed of connection and browser capabilities, one concern is that when they realize that they could incorporate images from existing web sites for layout purposes, they may became unwilling to experiment with their own visual materials, which were abandoned in favor of materials found online.

Researchers have indicated that some students are anxious that this might be interpreted as plagiarism (Cunningham & Rivett, 1999). Appropriating ideas is dubious at all times but blatant mimicry of concepts is not acceptable though they are not as easily traceable as copying a picture or style. Therefore, students that emulate or plagiarize ideas do so at their own risk of being discovered but they should be more cautious in using their computer software to execute ideas that may look otherwise too similar to an already produced idea somewhere by someone.

Selective coding

The third set of coding procedures is selective coding. This is where categories are integrated to form a theory by developing a story that connected the categories. By integrating the categories along the dimensional level to form a theory, validating their relationship, and filling in any categories that may need further development, selecting coding allows an evolving theory to finally become a solid one (Strauss & Corbin, 1990).

As I interact with the data, I become more insightful. To generate an understanding of whether technology can enhance or stifle creativity in the respondents, I linked their perceptions to suggest new concepts which form the categories for this section. Because the theory is grounded in the data, the theory is "illuminated" by data reflectively drawn from different individuals. However, it is difficult to evaluate exactly the extent that technological influences have on them, but one thing is clear: computer technology has "developed" new ways of applications by its users.

Theory generation

For this study, I would like to present my findings in a narrative form. To the extent to which I attempt to understand the impacts of computer technology usage on creativity in the ideation process, the better will be the likelihood of my own arriving at design pedagogy.

Throughout the open, axial, and selective coding, my understanding about the phenomenon that I am studying becomes more obvious as I develop small theoretical frameworks in creating concepts and their relationships. A theory as abstract explanations or understanding of a process about a substantive topic is not a grand theory because it does

113

not have wide applicability or scope. I expect additional empirical research and evidence that would influence the field of graphic design to happen even as this theory generation phase is taking place. The theory presented here is not permanently fixed, especially when dealing with the ever-changing technology.

Defining the creative process within a field which is constantly changing due to technological advancements and the demands of the marketplace of graphic design is like describing an unfinished painting. Determining if the students' creativity is compromised in using technology is another layer of difficulty added to this research. To elucidate this problem, more research is necessary but for the current research, I identify key areas that shape the field by looking into three theoretical frames: marketplace, the graphic design process, and creativity.

In order to generate a theory, I want to first exclude the influence of technology and to place the act or activities of design within the faculty of the user itself.

Validation of theory

The theory generated must be able to explain what happened, set the framework for predicting what will happen and explain what is currently happening in the area of inquiry. The formulation of a theoretical discourse is meant to describe this particular study and it is by no means self-referential. Responses recorded by participants on the questionnaire are reflective thinking that dealt with interpretation of their reality. It is always helpful to evaluate theoretical possibilities in light of their function in an actual application.

According to Blauvelt (1998), the practice of graphic design is historically and generally thought of as the means of production and this line of thought restricts the field to rejecting theory because the field is entrenched in materiality of the real world of industrialization and capitalism. After all, theory with its abstract nature is characterized as independent to the design process, too vague, and philosophically abstract to be practical for graphic designers. It is also seen as interruptive to a designer's perceptive insight and thus can be limiting to the designer's creative imagination. By introducing theories in design pedagogy and to the field of graphic design itself, educators, students, and practitioners can benefit by understanding the underlying factors that constantly evolve under the ever-changing natures of economy, demography, geography, technology, politic, and society.

The process of coding data can occur during data collection to determine what data to collect next. Creswell (2002) considered the validation of theory an active part of the

114

process of research. Glaser (1978) added that it is important that "a theory must be readily modifiable" (p. 4). This is inevitable because of the possibilities of developing more categories that are generated directly from the changing notion of data. Triangulation of data takes place between the information gathered and the emerging categories. This is also replicated during the open and axial coding phases. Questions that relate to the categories are posed as well as returning to the data to reexamine the categories. After a theory is developed, I validate the process by comparing it with existing processes found in the literatures by Strauss, Corbin, and Creswell.

Criteria for evaluating theory

My hypotheses form the basis for generation of theory but because data yields information, it is interesting to witness how things eventually fall into place for the theory to emerge. By engaging in the process of data gathering, sorting them into categories, collecting additional information, and comparing them with new information for emerging categories known as *constant comparative procedure,* I can obtain frameworks for generating a theory about the influences of computer usage on idea formation in graphic design students. It is a form of inductive procedure whereby specificity to broad analysis of data and asking questions about the data is engaged. During this process, Creswell recommended that constant comparing of "indicators to indicators, codes to codes, and categories to categories [in order] to eliminate redundancy and to develop evidence for categories" (p. 451).

When evaluating the theory, the following four checklists must be marked:

1. Is there any obvious connection or fit between the categories and the raw data?
2. Is the theory useful as a conceptual explanation for the process being studied? In other words, does it work?
3. Does the theory provide a relevant explanation of actual problems and a basic process?
4. Can the theory be modified as conditions change or further data are gathered?

When evaluating the process of research, the following six checklists must be marked:

1. Is a theoretical model developed or generated? Is the intent of this model to conceptualize a process, an action, or an interaction?
2. Is there a central phenomenon (or core category) specified at the heart of this model?
3. Does the model emerge through phases of coding? (e.g. from initial code to more theoretically oriented codes, or from open coding, to axial coding, to selective coding)

115

4. Does the researcher attempt to interrelate the categories? (e.g., propositions, discussion, a model or diagram)
5. Does the researcher gather extensive data so as to develop a detailed conceptual theory well saturated in the data?
6. Does the study show that the researcher validated the evolving theory by comparing it to data, examining how the theory supports or refutes existing theories in the literature, or checking the theory with participants? (Creswell, 2002, pp. 458-459)

Procedure used in generating the theory

In order to discover a theory, one is required to generate conceptual categories or properties from evidence. The evidence from the category is used to illustrate the concept as done so in open coding and axial coding. According to Glaser and Strauss, (1967), the "concept itself will not change … [but] their meanings [are] respecified at times because other theoretical and research purposes have evolved (p. 23). In other words, because the research is qualitative in nature and is dependent on contexts assigned, the word may take on a new meaning. Because of this awareness, in vivo codes, which are direct quotes from the respondents are used in the hopes of attaining the closest meaning to their reflective reporting. Testing is important and it is built into each step of the process by constantly comparing hypotheses against the data, making modifications, and testing again for possible variations.

There are two analytic procedures during the coding process. The first choice is to make comparisons and the other is asking questions. Since there can be many forms of emergence from data collected, Glaser (1978) introduced "refit" and "emergent fit" at the initial stage (p. 4). Many categories may emerge and some may have more relevance than the other and it is important to refit them into the research. Once I have identified particular phenomena in my data, the process of grouping them is done to reduce the number of labels which I have to work with.

Assessment of the theory

There can never be enough theories to cover all of the areas that are possibly and potentially outlined in this research. A case in point is the expanding possibilities afforded by computer technology. The field of graphic design is constantly being redefined internally and reshaped externally by most obviously the technical know-how of personal computers.

By verifying my hypotheses against the information generated from the data, I am able to validate the theory. In presenting the findings, the four hypotheses are paralleled with the findings to substantiate the theory.

The first hypothesis indicates that the field of graphic design in the marketplace at large has no meaning or value except in relation to a client. Graphic design is about communicating ideas and since all of its communicative modes, verbal and nonverbal, are capable of manipulating, persuading, transforming, and educating the public, the role of technology in graphic design does not end in its deployment, but rather in its effect which is iteratively approved and produced. We are aware that design has consequences because the message and effects created are capable of influencing its intended audience within a marketplace. In that venue, design is worthy of appreciation only when it functions as a commodity, ruling out the claims for esoteric appreciations.

As graphic designers entertain the broadening definitions of design and marketplace, their creative roles become engaged in entrepreneurial actions as they withstand the changing definitions of the marketplace as well as the society and culture which it serves whether they like it or not. This argument creates an interesting scenario: creativity in achieving the most effective solution is strongly motivated by the demands of the market, which forms my second hypothesis.

The computer can create synergy between the mind and the potentiality of technology, as asserted in my third hypothesis. Respondents in the study have access to the same technology that professional graphic designers use. However, being aware of the procedures, tools, materials, sets of values, the purpose and goal of the communicative nature of design, the designer becomes capable of defining and achieving an acceptable design solution.

According to the respondents, many factors combine to affect their ideation process, ranging from the media used during the initial stages of the design process to suggestions from instructors and peers during idea formation to final selection of materials for presentation. Besides software conventions and traditions and biases within the field, they also have to contend with equipment limitations and failures. Finally, a proposed solution has to be acceptable or validated in the construct in which it exists to be considered effective.

Therefore, creativity may be compromised because the respondents have to function within certain parameters which may dictate their creative thinking process. But as a tool, the computer aids in the areas of automation, accuracy, expediency, presentation, execution, implementation, and even maximization of the respondents' creativity. My fourth hypothesis states that new ideas can be created when human minds are combined with technology. According to the study, all of them use the computer in one way or the other and for various projects and reasons, the computer is not only a facilitative and productive device, it is also a medium for discovery.

This is because computers as a medium can alter our working environment in facilitating users in thinking more critically to reorganize, develop, and extend their ability. Fifty-nine percent (40 out of 68) of respondents in the study solely equate the experience on the computer as "maximizing." In this context, they mean that the computer is capable of rendering images and ideas to become visible, expanding their knowledge, aiding in the conception of ideas, improving the quality of their designs, influencing their design process, and probably, the most important factor, to producing results.

CHAPTER V

CONCLUSIONS

Interpretation of results

In this chapter, results from the previous chapter are interpreted and summarized. Can computer technology stimulate creativity? This is one pressing question that this research is eager to discover. As indicated earlier in this chapter, the answer is yes. The main influence of computer technology on its users is that it inspires and develops new opportunities when they apply and put technology to use. There are many reasons for that answer and they are further explained in the following four subheadings in this chapter: (a) the influences of computer technology; (b) the influences of market-driven framework; (c) the model of creativity; and (d) the idea formation process.

Computers are quite useless unless we provide them with instructions but with the integration of human creativity, computers can be a mental and computational guide that can promote the aspects of human thinking. We have fears that overusing technology will result in design standardization. There will be reduced potential for uniqueness in expression but by balancing technical and cognitive knowledge, technology can be a driving force that propels students' imaginations.

It is important to stress that because of the pervasive nature of technology that changes our *modus operandi* and *modus vivendi*, we are "forced" to develop many different approaches in adapting it into our lives. Professionally, technology changes how design is practiced and how business is run. Rapid computerization of the design industry will increase pressure on clients to turn work around more quickly at lower cost.

New technologies also have considerable implications for educational practice– not only in providing new ways of delivering learning materials but also in facilitating communication among learners and changing the ways in which instructional resources might be organized and presented. Technology is not simply a tool for creativity because it can inadvertently refine our sensitivity to differences and reinforce our ability to tolerate the incommensurable. Technology has become the media in defining an ideation path that eventually will lead to a final design. Theories of creativity will change over time, but technology will continue to change at a much faster rate. In order to cope with the change, we have and will develop new ways to harness it.

The field of graphic design mirrors the practice of medicine, constantly being advanced by the latest technological inventions for human-centered implementation. It is a network of extended learning with close connections between learning institutions, the profession, and the community. The complexity of new communications combined with the diversity of society requires a broader knowledge base and more sophisticated skills.

Education has to take on a role that fosters the growth of strong personalities to cope with change, develop a new concept of self development and independence. In order to be prepared for the change, not only strategic partnerships with clients need to be fostered between the clients and the designer but also student designers need to learn about the marketplace and what drives their client's needs. We need to acquire knowledge not only of our technological and social organizations, but also of ourselves, of other people and the society in which we function. These phenomenon need to be elaborately considered when educators design and plan and conduct a lesson. Tasks and assignments should be carefully planned and directed to the course, curriculum goals and standards.

There are two imperatives in developing student attitude towards reality in the marketplace: advancement and societal responsibility. Technology in its simplest form is a device for solving human-created problems, but because technological innovations can form a mutually beneficial relationship with its users, we need to consider its implications by taking on social responsiveness. This is because all classes are influenced by technology, one way or the other. Human inventions have consequences and implications. Although we are not able to foresee the future to predict our inventions, we need to live with the choices we make because it will dictate the life we live.

The influences of computer technology

Every printed sheet, every message, every product, and just about every conceivable and producible thing around us is designed by someone. Design is not something natural, but rather something produced. This requires a combination of constructs, methods, tools, and most importantly, human beings to realize it. Graphic design is a dynamic field where methods and products are interactive and constantly changing due to the market it serves, the people it targets, and the medium it uses. Since computer technology is the *raisons d'être* tool in the field of graphic design, it has not just become the tool of the trade, but also a common ground for educator, students, and professional designers to use for broadening their design palettes. The screen, the mouse, and the keyboard are the governing media.

Because the graphic design field is constantly changing due to technological advancements and realizations of the final solution is derived from outside sources, governed by whimsical clients and the demands of the marketplace (Lasky, 1998; Lionni, 1986), the governing factor then becomes factor-driven, despite the creativity that may aid in the design process. However as demonstrated in this study, computers are able to let users make discoveries.

As a medium capable of discovery through explorations, the computer lets its users probe their minds for concepts, visualize them and combined with software capabilities, it enhances their visuals too. Technology is no longer a device as it is used as a medium of expression. In extending the domain within which we conceive and plan, we are widening the boundaries of graphic design practice by applying our input expressions and output responses through technological innovations. Media literacy of the computer becomes necessary to facilitate the development of ideas as technology becomes an integral part of the creative process in the sense that it defines what is achievable with technological peripherals and knowledge.

In a computer lab setting, the responsibility falls on the school to select the "industry standard" software, providing students with instructions to use it and giving the students time to use it. Users are locked into the product line of single manufacturer or one set of software. The software industry has great motivations to improve their sales with constant upgrades and sales pitches that determine the survival of the industry as a whole. This form of monopoly creates a state of dependency which can lead to complacency because if we become hooked on one particular software company, we are more than likely to be dictated by the "convention" and standards created by that particular software company.

Moreover, having computers in university labs does not automatically provide opportunities for students to explore creativity. The responsibility lies in the hands of educators who believe in a strong curriculum to select good software. It is important for the software to address basic concepts that will in turn enable students to learn about the creative problem-solving process (Tedeschi, personal communication, September 19, 2002). Computer software is more than drill and practice because more importantly, students must find an acceptable and practical outlet for their digital creative expressions to come through. The viable thing to do is to keep our sights on technology's possibilities because in comparison to the industry, pedagogical trends are slow catching up with the latest technology.

To mitigate the above mentioned problem, Mercedes (1996) recommended thoughtful class discussions, activities, debates along with examples about computer ethics. These issues need to be discussed in various learning environments where students are encouraged to investigate the consequences of various options in confronting issues regarding moral, legal, and ethical dilemmas.

There are reasons for adventurous and creative ideas because we are now confronting a new kind of student audience, one that has lived continually with mass media and has been desensitized by technologies. Because students are already using computer software and hardware, it may be simplistic to suggest that they will transform in accordance to the technology's requirements because technical idiosyncrasies and nuances will constantly change the way the field is taught and practiced.

This is where personalization and flexibility become valuable in mitigating the issue. Creativity in design can result from individuality in the designer. Just as there are no two people who are exactly alike, the same principle cannot be applied to computer technology especially with the abundance and availability of computer technology to the mass public. Perhaps, out of this situation, students have to reevaluate their choices for using these tools and to individualize their work by introducing personalization to it.

Over the years, the impacts from using computer technology have become sophisticated due to the advancement in technology itself, as well as our exposure to mass media. Being presented with the opportunities and challenges of technology mean that educators must be creatively flexible in solving their students' design problems. This is another situation caused by technology which inspires its users to develop new application methods. For educators, they can divide classroom operations into generative and interpretive activities. The former is defined as creating new designs during initial ideation and the latter is defined as activities that involve interpretations of existing designs.

As a facet of the design process, the computer acquires a special role in the process. According to Mok (1996), we can use the computing medium to "explore, create, work, and play outside the constraints of physical space." He further adds that space in computing medium is both "information container and a destination" (p. 113). The "destination" Mok describes can be translated as the final solution to a problem and the computer acts as an "information container" because the computer is capable of storing information without any lost in detail and the data stored can be recalled at any time.

The combined visual and manipulative factors on the computer create an opportunity for its users to make unintentional discoveries which in turn can evoke new responses and stimulate new thinking in their ideation processes. The computer is more than a tool because when it helps to make our minds work, it may therefore enhance creativity. This conclusion is further substantiated by the findings when student made serendipitous discoveries and are able to revert their design processes when using the computer.

The computer acts as a device for its users to actualize their ideas through its software interface which offers order, logic, orientation, and format standards. It is through these standards that users are able to "exploit" the computer any way they see fit: a choice of stylistic expressions or a functional tool of representations. Based on this observation, computer technology is not only a medium for expression, it is also a medium for productivity.

As Cullen (1998) reported, computers are more than tools for expediting our tasks because as a medium, it has the capacity to infiltrate and influence the society that embraces it; hence becoming a catalyst for change. As a catalyst for discovery, computers are great for a collaborative effort where ideas from our mind are actualized into reality through it. Clearly, computer programs are designed to facilitate its users in various applications. When students "exploit" the software, they are amplifying their ideas by using the tools afforded by software and respondents are able to extract more ideas for design solutions.

Even though we are required to have at least minimal knowledge in operating a computing system, the experience of using a computer can be intuitive and exploratory. Even if the user is incapable of operating the software to the fullest extent, he or she is still able to explore software created within a menu-driven interface computing environment such as those offered by Apple Macintosh and IBM-compatible computers. A physical reality that the computing medium lacks is made up by a screen environment which incorporates our metaphorical understanding of an environment that we are familiar with. With metaphor, we bring with us our own interpretation into technology and it becomes a personal experience where we are able to use the computer to tap into our creative force by immersing into an imaginative environment.

Lacking tactility and being disembodied from our physical world, we need to reconsider the interplay between virtual and physical systems and to start thinking about context versus content, especially in interactivity. For example, when a student designs an annual report for his or her class project, they are able to control the size, shape, texture, color, and quality of a print media but things are different with computer media. With a website, the appearance, features, and interactivity depends on the size of the monitor it is viewed on, the browser, the choice of typeface selected as default and so on. We can view the web from a mechanistic point of view, but it operates very much like an organic system with many infinite possibilities with interdependent relationships as it defies compartmentalization because of its own order, logic, and orientation.

Using the computer as both a developmental tool and a delivery medium may instigate dependency in its users. However, it still relies on the designer's proficiency with the tools and the medium. Although it is unclear what level of technical ability must be attained to avoid limitation of creative expression, what is clear is that when users are on the computer, the computer is at worse, a tool but at best, a device to facilitate creativity and discovery. This is because transactional communication between the computer and the user is not a linear exchange but it occurs as an ongoing process of interactivity between the designers who reflect and build on their personal knowledge as they create meanings in visuals and realizing it in its final forms.

Within the computer, we are presented with a new perspective in approaching our problem, a new approach that takes us to a new level to realize the potential that we have. Because of the benign and holistic approach that a computer system embodies, with the modularity of its periphery, we form a relationship which transcends the simplistic view that computer technology is merely a tool.

While interacting on the computer, users privately interact in an environment that facilitates discovery without the need for brainstorming, although that stage can come later in the design process. A good example is using the computer during the initial ideation process because no one is judging their design capabilities. This is characterized by many reports in Chapter IV when respondents write about making serendipitous discoveries while working on the computer. However, any good ideas must be given time to incubate and students must give themselves time and flexibility to perfect their skills and their learning strategies.

Many aspects of graphic design are visually-based and design as a visual counterpart of communication is a form of imagery rhetoric. It comes in a variety of forms and is generally non-personal in that it is targeted to a mass audience. In this day and age of computer technology, younger generations are becoming visual learners. Computer software uses icons which require visual memory such as recognizing faces and such features can help visual learners. In a culture dominated by visuals, the prospect of images and written words

124

evolving to combine in motion and sound is extremely tantalizing. The latest versions of web browsers are capable of displaying sites that contain Flash-animated pages with ease. The wide availability of high speed Internet connection takes information as a means of communication and dissemination to a higher level.

Students who benefit from the experience of utilizing technology and an understanding of the potentiality and limitations of the medium will prepare them to contrive on a broader scale. Because they know their medium, graphic designers can offer options beyond standard desktop publishing. Students trained as graphic designers are not just equipped with technical capabilities, they are also made aware of design sensibilities and the underlying values of effective communication. Yet we are still grappling with the difficult decisions of balancing between aesthetical, functional, and logistical concerns. Because of the iterative nature of the design process, recidivism, identified as a tendency to lapse into previous design choices may occur. Because of this, students tend to function in a random generate-and-test mode. This encourages more explorations and an eventual path of finalization of design.

Some argue that rules are made to be broken. With the computer all rules of legibility and readability are broken: type is stretched, condensed, colorized, and distorted, rendering in some cases, page layout designs that are totally different from the linear, step by step, and logical sequence of layout design. This implies rule-breaking and risk-taking. After all, taking risks mean experiencing a paradigm shift and facing challenge is something that we are all not naturally inclined to pick. Part of "calculated risk" in taking a risk is to know one's goal and one's audience, two important ingredients in the process of communication design. The potential of design has become even greater now that people have access to computers with software that promise new manipulation and flexibility.

The computer is a device capable of sustaining many different choices for its users. Computerized type styles are available in serif, sans serif, display, and script with a variety of choices from Roman, book, medium, light, bold, heavy, black, italic, bold, expanded, condensed, and outline. Moreover, there are a number of options on how the letters can be arranged: centered, stacked, ragged, or justified. When one is faced with a large amount of text to be fitted into the design, "copy fitting" becomes a necessity to figure out how much space the text will occupy (Swann, 2000, p. 58).

From the varying selections of computerized typefaces to efficient "grid" where type can be organized into columns in a page layout program such as QuarkXpress mentioned in the questionnaire, users are able to experiment with typestyles and layout ideas. That is not all. Computer programs like Adobe Photoshop offer filters that allow for image editing capabilities. Because of the computer's superior visualization capabilities, analysis of layout is made possible where the strengths and weaknesses are vividly displayed, allowing ideas to be created, revised, and manipulated.

When respondents use computers to help them in the ideation process, the software with its all-encompassing capacities from design to production forces every graphic design student to think, draw, manage, and produce. With this broad responsibility, although technical expertise is important to the ideation process, the essential thing to focus on here is the components of thinking and managing. Both categories imply that students have to focus on reasoning and judgment.

The influences of market-driven framework

It is important to stress that design's relationship with technology is just merely to satisfy the vulgarity of the market but worthwhile results imply the tangible end products or results that meet some social, professional, or aesthetic criterion. Since graphic design is intended for creative and communication purposes, technology as a medium and tool can become powerful combinations in creating a synthesis between the designer, client, and audience. Clients invent new products, develop new ideas, and create new messages. Graphic designers facilitate these by working with the client to send these new inventions to a targeted audience. By sharing their expertise and experience, every professional has a separate body of knowledge that can contribute to the design and marketing process.

From the market-driven lens, the field of graphic design is legitimized in a competitive commercial world where time is money and the process of design requires a deliberate, swift, and confident and assuring technique. Functioning within the constraints of efficiency and expediency, the computer is used as a tool to actualize concepts and as a hired professional, a combination of talent, experience, service, opinion, and technical skills is what clients pay for. The market's conditions change at a pace that makes it imperative for businesses to keep up and for designers to think of creative ideas that respond to these changes.

The nature of businesses is still to sell but how they send the message is changing due to the technological environment. The ever-changing product or service reflects the trends of society and the challenge as a designer is to be aware of the targeted audience and the trends in the marketplace. There is a real inherent dilemma for a professional graphic designer who in the real world is retained not to express his or her design integrities but to enhance his or her client's impersonal products, complicated process, or bamboozling message.

In reality, clients realize that the most important contribution a graphic designer can make to their business is not just to make things look better, but to help in achieving better sales and promotions. Student designers need to train themselves as a partner and a creative collaborator with their clients or their employers. Understanding the business mentality requires an important shift in attitude from a solo designer to a team player. Understanding how to work effectively with people, employing a well-conceived strategy and analytical skills in developmental phases of the work, and a high level of professionalism are key factors to forming a successful strategic partnership with a client.

As a form of visual communication that brings together artistic creation and the practical world of commerce, the field is measured by how well they offer solutions to their client's problem. Within the contexts of design and marketing, sharing goals and understanding the intended audience will lead to a more successful campaign because creativity depends on its appreciation. Success to the design is measured by the response of the targeted group.

Although the scope of a project is defined, structured, designed, and implemented are dependent upon a set of external and internal factors, the role of communication design is expanded to include its effects in transforming an existing situation into a desired one. These concerns are not limits to creativity but rather established parameters and objectives that narrow options down to a manageable level. These obstacles should not be seen as problems but rather as assets for paving the path for an idea to fall into place. I agree that part of the fun in design is to make discoveries but the discovery has to be functional, manageable, and producible in a market-driven context.

Although there are many ways technology can impact us, the ultimate concern of the graphic designer is to creatively harness technology into a productive device, aiding in the productivity of transforming ideas into reality. The proverbial "sky is the limit" does not apply to graphic design because as presented, graphic designers concern themselves with many factors that may constrict their design solutions.

However, knowing the limitations can be advantageous. The process of graphic design is iterative and exists on a continuum, ranging from the early idea generation to final production to its effect within the community it targets. These conditions or factors are shaped by a multitude of situations that exist in a competitive situation or place in which values, opinions, ideas, products, services, and messages are put forward for recognition or sale.

In making the project a reality, students learn to ideate, execute, and interpersonally communicate with people as well as dealing with the vagaries of machinery. While the students are learning the design process, they are in fact engaged in simulating a "real world" environment. It is beneficial to prepare students before they enter the field by matching bona fide "real world" expectations with what students learn in a simulated environment such as the classroom.

The model of creativity

The theoretical model in this research, the Four-Ps Model of Creativity states that graphic designers make up the *person* in the field who create in the tradition of their *presses (or environment)*. Without the *process* of art and design, it would be impossible to create the *product* (which can also include service or message). Graphic design in a market-driven context means that solutions to design problems involve collective efforts and interactions between all these four areas.

Cognitive flexibility, motivation, or an unusual and inspiring experience may occur all the time but social settings becomes a powerful determining factor in accepting or rejecting what kind of novelty gets produced. Approval implies that design ideas are determined by the judgments of others and although until the results have been placed before other peer designers, fellow educators, mass public, or discerning critics that it becomes clear if the result is accepted or rejected. This form of validation is highly dependent upon acceptance within an acceptable construct.

This leads to creativity as an interaction. If effort, persistence, and motivation are necessary for maintaining creativity as Cropley (1992) argued, then it makes sense to think of creativity as a form of mental exercise that is a direct result from a collection of extensive, diverse knowledge base rather from eccentric or serendipitous natures. Our minds are affected by prejudice, etiquette, politics, judgments, and criticisms and it is not easy to keep an open mind. An offensive or disturbing idea is not necessarily a bad idea since one of the many objectives of a design is to solicit a reaction from its audience.

128

The same idea of interactivity is something that exists in a computer environment. Computers are a benign tool but what is apparent from this study is that the utilization of computers as a tool within a market driven context creates a "guideline" for creation that directs and affects creativity. The computer consolidates many areas of ideation such as assessment, refinement, elimination, selection, and production into one environment that encourages exploration which leads to creativity. That is not to say that traditional media and method such as pencil and paper and brainstorming lack the capacity to encourage creativity but rather these media are not integrated into one environment.

An overwhelming 91% (62 out of 68) of respondents in the study report that they discover something on the computer but upon investigation, it was more or less along the lines of using technology as a facilitative tool. However, with the combination and interactions between the human mind and computer, new ideas are created. What happens here is that with the computer, the surrounding conditions such as the ability to multi-task, evaluate, expedite, and many more forces its users to interact and to bring in separate ideas that culminate into a single working environment.

The tools embedded in software are capable of developing and inspiring new applications in its users which makes it an attractive medium. Computer filters let its users analyze their sketches in a whole new way. Computer users are also able to manipulate their ideas in many different ways using the tools and filters within software applications which can contribute to the design process.

It is important to note that filters, in and of themselves, are not creative but the manipulative aspect becomes a driving force for respondents to push their ideas further. Coupled with the awareness of goals and objectives for consumption in a market-driven context, respondents are still creating something that has not existed before. Another way of looking at it would be to restate that respondents design with an objective in mind and they are making new ideas that are applicable in the marketplace.

When we speak of creativity, we often imply the ability to conceive something new, original, or different. Creativity can be an ability, knowledge, or a set of skills in solving problems and its effects are revolutionary as well as evolutionary, holistic as well as specialized. Yet there is no one-rule standard that applies to all because everyone is different and these differences can be caused by cognitive factors, personality, environmental, and social influences (Glover et al., 1989). What we need to realize here is that although

129

creativity may suggest genuineness and innovativeness, I believe that the sole purpose of graphic design is to inform, educate, and persuade.

Having said that, a creative innovation has to have an utilitarian purpose in order to function within an environment such as the market-driven framework that validates it. In the name of practicality, efficiency, and productivity in a market-driven context, creativity can best be thought of in terms of accomplishments and productions. The beauty of creation lies within the benchmark of these environments which constantly pushes the boundary for challenging old ideas. By combining new information through research, a designer can establish a basis for a creative solution.

The first task is to realize that creativity involves shifting our perspective which requires us to depart from facts, find new ways in making unusual connections, and to challenge the status quo. The latter may suggest defiance. Therefore, it is important for educators to identify traits that are associated with creativity such as willingness to take risks, innovativeness, boldness, flexibility as well as valuing different behavioral and personal traits in students. It is not an easy task because universally educators prefer their students who are "courteous and considerate of others, punctual, energetic and industrious, popular with their peers, well rounded, receptive to other people's ideas, and obedient" (Cropley, 1992, p. 19). Some aspects of social problems involving human behavior are likely to go beyond the rules and require human judgment.

We need to think of organization as a way of facilitating creativity. We need to view ourselves, the environments in which we function, and the media we use in a relatively objective lens. If ideas are better structured, central, and accessible, creative innovations are likely to happen in problem-solving. The basic problem-solving methodology involves speculative formulation of reasoning, techniques, tools, and adequate information to resolve issues and select the ultimate solution that leads to an explicit goal. The process of achieving an effective solution requires an understanding of the problem and evaluation of the technical accuracy of process and materials. The computer with its efficient, methodical, precise, and organizational capacities allows its users to organize information and vary functions that contribute to the whole and to collective functions in the design process.

Another possible approach to the notion of creativity is to view content, context, and objective as the driving force for development and implementation of future ideas. Each problem requires a unique solution and every solution requires an original approach in dealing with a multitude of factors that may work for or against it. This in itself requires creativity. What we are dealing with here is that the possibilities are endless with the notion of creativity but for every functional path a graphic designer takes, the solution posed has to be accepted not just by the designer, it must also be approved by the client or instructor and realistically producible. Although creativity itself is difficult to be structured, the procedures that facilitate creativity in the design process such as brainstorming, thumbnail sketches, research, and refinements are accessible, as reported by all the respondents who sketch for their initial ideas.

A proposed design may not always stimulate perception and imagination to an equal degree. Hence, the challenge becomes making designs that appeal to the senses and to the imagination of viewers or readers. An easy solution is to design something that is obvious or is easily available. After all, a direct solution means that it requires no guessing work. While exposure and experience allow us to relate to a design, a broader understanding of experience covers our apprehensions of feelings and emotions, beliefs, and attitudes. Communicating a design that embodies our total experience through design requires a creative imagination. It is necessary not only to create things for oneself, but also to fully enjoy the creations of others. It allows us to express ourselves by allowing thoughts and actions to occur in a more holistic manner.

When creativity is combined with knowledge, technical capacity, and experience, designers and artists can stimulate and support free play, manipulation of objects, and ideas to produce tangible products of creativity in design. As a catalyst for discovery with developmental and productivity tools, computer technology can add values for creating meanings in design. By fusing technology with personal experience and cognitive knowledge, students can transmit new discoveries into design.

The idea formation process

Most design begins with a basic organizational plan such as the preliminary sketching in the ideation process. Every student designer approaches his or her ideation processes differently. Some work in spurts while some generate a lot of ideas and hone down to a few. Students may feel overwhelmed by the possibilities and have no idea where to begin because the infinite number of potential variations in any design can be both liberating and terrifying. Those who prefer to sketch with a pencil and paper are more inclined to produce sketches that are unrefined mostly because of reasons for expediency. Because sketches can be rendered loosely or vaguely and they are usually meant for the designer only, the end result can be seen as an evolutionary stage in design where sketches evolve into a refined idea and eventually into production. The computer with additional peripherals such as scanners and printers are used to turn ideas into a tangible format.

The act of design can be analyzed as a logical process which consists of identifying the problem and working out an approach to it. However, due to elusive, cyclical, and iterative natures, the design process is subject to assessment, refinement, elimination, selection, and production. Coming up with many ideas, considering possible solutions, and finding the best possible ideas are not easy. This is because ideas can be created, destroyed, and recreated but a good idea will lay the foundation for more ideas to follow.

External factors such as usability, manufacturability, and viability are a few issues that graphic designers face when playing a formative role in a complex interdisciplinary environment where design is likely to be practiced. This is because for a project to become a reality both the external and internal factors are reciprocally needed for a design process to be complete. It is iterative in nature and these factors co-exist to validate and cancel each other out.

The iterative nature of the design process dictates that every step of the way is repeated and revisited for confirmation. Even after the selection was finalized, production constraints may alter the outcome. From the outset, the designer works out a plan and continues to explore the solution through a process that involves some logic, commonsensical and intuitive guesswork, some trial and error, and tried-and-true methods until the problem is finally solved. Even then, in order to realize and produce an idea into a tangible form, it has to be checked for practicality, effectiveness, suitability, and at times, appropriateness and the solution may be elaborated and fine-tuned.

Although every project is different, there are mainly two obvious divisions in the process of design: idea generation and later production. The combined aspects of early idea generation and later production serve not to sharpen the sensibilities of an intended audience, but also as a readily communicable device. A situation that arises in this research is when a number of respondents in the study worry about the later production process, which means that they think ahead with the end result in mind. Ideas are not always easy to express but the process of sharing a vision, making meaning, and communicating ideas are being complicated by the fact that the students are trying to solve problems.

Students who worry about the later production create an interesting approach because in their struggle to achieve the most effective solution for their design problems, the think with the final product in mind. This mode of problem finding (Starko, 2001; Wake, 2000) is probably due to the fact that by realizing that problems do exist and by thinking with the end in mind, some form of solution can be achieved; albeit the process is reversed. The design process is not just a simplistic two-phase idea generation and production stage, but within it lies many facets, obstacles, and factors that transcend the surface value of a design process.

When a designer focuses his or her energies in the later production of design and permits other factors to shape his or her work, the design process becomes a regiment, rather than characters of imperfection, ambiguity, and unpredictability that occur during the initial ideation process. When searching for a design solution, part of the exploration involves uncertainty in the process. Although by knowing the goals and objectives of a process can afford certain level of control over the design process, the uncertainty in design exploration means that a designer can freely explore an area without any restrictions. Computers are great exploratory tools and with explorations during ideation, mistakes are common. Mistakes are sometimes part of the process in discovering the right solution and it can be a good learning experience.

In borrowing the concept of divergent and convergent thinking by J. P. Guilford, I would like to extract the strength from both modes and to place them in the ideation phase by proposing the "first-divergent, then-convergent" model of thinking. In this explanation of knowledge acquisition in divergent thinking, students learn to step outside their "safety zones" and to be experimental and mindful of their surroundings. They identify as many solutions as possible in the beginning and as they develop their designs into a refined stage, they "converge" their ideas to refine them into a single best solution.

Convergent thinkers are those who "play it safe" and are afraid to take risks. These preventative measures can lead to mediocrity, but when they combine the "first-divergent" mode of thinking, they are able to become better problem-solvers. The "then-convergent" mode of thinking is ideal when ideas need to be refined, eliminated, and finalized at a later stage. If this method is to be represented visually, it can be best visualized in a diamond-like shape, or a rhombus, starting with "first-divergent" at the bottom and "then-convergent" at the top.

Once we remove the pleasure of making a design and focus on the realities of seeing the results as the market-driven framework may dictate, there is nothing to creativity but maintenance. As much control as it seems that we are able to point and click on a computer, the truth is that we cannot fully control the outcome of the design direction due to the iterative nature, the vagaries of computer machinery, and the context in which design functions. Relinquishing control is one way to enjoy the ambiguity and uncertainty in the design process.

Adaptability is key and computer technology is subconsciously and coercively providing the developmental abilities for its users to use it the way they see fit. Our ability to adapt to technological evolution is crucial because in a world of communication, every success and failure is human made. Every mistake and oversight cost extra money and time. Equipment failure, typographical errors, a mislabeled package, or delay in delivery can spell disaster. To avoid trouble, the designer should keep regular contact with the client at all phases of a project. Approval and proofing processes are also best protection against any possible errors whether in a classroom or a real world situation.

Flowing with the design process is crucial because in order to design for the marketplace, student designers need to understand that a distance is created between them and the people who presumably inhabit the market. Filling in the gap of what the consumer or targeted audience desire comes from the data supplied by the manufacturer, company, or individual. The task is to distinguish between what is fundamental to the design process and what is incidental to it. This mode of operation and thinking is helpful in reorienting the way in which we have become accustomed to design due to the iterative and elusive natures of ideation.

A design creation is an arrangement of stimuli containing linguistic and nonlinguistic symbols and these things are not independent, but they interact closely to become an object or manifestation of attention and interested contemplation. Communicating an effective message means that all stimuli must be aroused to respond to perceptive, interpretative, imaginative, cognitive, emotive, and conative natures. It is possible for a design to be visually appealing and yet unsuitable for a particular application. Award-winning or published pieces may not always make the best solutions but rather, they offer an insight into what kind of works that have been produced. In dealing with mimicry, style obsolescence in a faddish approach is possible though realistically it will be supplanted by technical obsolescence of computing media due to the advancement of technology. In recognizing this similarity, the task then becomes interpreting the message, not copying the style.

In experimentations, errors should be expected and no idea is "stupid." If students are afraid to explore, they should motivate themselves by investigating as many options as possible while on the computer because exploration during this stage is a one-to-one interaction between the user and the computer. Even though designs are subject to drifts of antagonistic interests and the field functions only within a framework that defines its existence, be it economical or apolitical, the act of designing itself is highly individual. This places the individual who uses technology as the most important factor in the equation.

Different medium changes the impression of the design. Pencils are available in a variety of grades from hard to soft with different colors, allowing for tonal control. Even the way it is sharpened will determine the kind of marks the students make. Even the papers used can influence the quality of the print. Moreover, projects do not just end when printed materials are delivered or Web sites are posted online. Another example is experimenting with colors on the computer's monitor, it is vividly inspirational but in reality, what you see is not really what you get because colors shown on color monitors rarely match when it is printed on a printer with varying resolutions.

Realizing that every assignment and every instructor's objective and requirements are different, most respondents find that their initial ideas differ from the final version because of the "evolutionary" stages in design. From constant refinements to brainstorming with peers, instructors, and even non-designer friends who offer suggestions to computer manipulation at a later stage, it is no wonder that most of their initial sketches have changed dramatically but the concepts are intact. This may be due to the fact that design is iterative, generative, and corrective. It is inevitable because materials, techniques, styles, technology, and manufacturing processes have not evolved evenly and when designers strive to put all of them together, the process becomes convoluted by financial, functional, practical, producible, and acceptability concerns.

Dealing with the issue should a design solution look good or should it work? The most popular and succinct expression from the Bauhaus leaders in Europe and from Americans sculptor Horatio Greenough and architect, Louis Sullivan, was "form follows function." (Caplan, 1982). Frank Lloyd Wright restated it as "form and function are one" (Papanek, 1984, p.6). The idea is that as long as the functional requirements are accomplished, form will follow and it will seem pleasing at the same time. Designers first need to understand how an object works, its shapes and appearances. But "form follows function" can also be interpreted to mean that if a message is well understood, then it would result in an appropriate and pleasing appearance.

Ideally, it would be a perfect match to satisfy both of them. This is no easy question because in reality, the psychological, spiritual, social, and intellectual needs of human beings are the most difficult and less profitable to satisfy because most values within that culture are frequently based on the traditions of that culture. Creative and novel solutions must be unusual yet appropriate for it to be producible. Therefore, contexts and contents are important considerations. However, it still does not provide a framework for authenticating what is published. Although technology is partly to be blamed because of the profusion and ubiquity of the same technological tool used by graphic designers, the abundance of design in a competitive real world marketplace will sort out good design from the bad design.

The comprehensive creative process in a market-driven framework requires the following steps: (a) the understanding of a market, whether real or created; (b) its potential customer needs; (c) the basic capabilities of the designer to conceive potential ideas; (d) the act of designing it, and eventually (e) deliverance to their targeted market.

The final solution remains mysterious until the final production. However, certain commonalities in the process such as understanding the process and setting clear objectives and goals can help designers to provide structures in tackling a problem. Even though solutions to the problem can be discovered through some accidental mistakes on the computer or sketching, the step-by-step process involved is a complex, collaborative and sometimes personal negotiation that involves the designer, the process, the environment, and the product.

Recommendations for educators

In view of what the strengths and limitations of computers in education are, it is interesting to note that the utilization of technology in pedagogy has many facets of inherent benefits as well as challenges. As a communal institution, ever changing and complex social, economic and political environments continuously shape the educational institution's role as providers.

Learning in a digital age requires an interdisciplinary approach and a mixture of various talents. This is because in any learning situation not everyone learns the same way and absorbs the materials similarly. In facilitating creativity in classrooms, it is important for educators to consider the cultural contexts of students' lives and to provide various channels or strategies to suit students' varied abilities and learning capabilities. The course instructor is an important person in facilitating and challenging the students to build their confidence.

Educators can be relieved of some of the labor that traditionally takes their physicality through the convenience of computer technology and focuses on making judgments that constitute a strategic ability to communicate their ideas through computing media. Educators must be able to determine the best solution in solving inefficiencies in the ideation process. In the complex and unpredictable directions of design, cognitive flexibility means that creative educators must be able to accommodate fluctuations without affecting efficiency in the classroom.

Allowing students the opportunities to be creative requires them to find and solve problems. It becomes necessary to demonstrate that problem-solving in the ideation process is contingent upon how well the information is presented or how efficient the solution is to fixing the problem. Such an initiative expands the students' horizons and emboldens them to take risks. Idea formation takes place best when students are placed in the challenging "hot seats" of problem solvers and communicators rather than the one-way street of absorbing knowledge. This is not an easy position for teachers because they have to set problems for which they may have no answers, but part of the fun is to work to find the solutions.

Students need to apply creative problem-solving techniques and instructional design process will have a more lasting effect on their professional productivity than learning how to use the latest piece of software. Although what we learn may be rendered obsolete before we have to relearn a new set of skills again, there is no doubt that extrapolation of the meaning of technology takes on more importance.

As we have seen, it is impossible to reduce the supplementary task of computers but we can use computer programs that facilitate complex cognitive skills such as problem solving and design composition in design curriculum to break the monotony in design and learning. The biggest challenge that graphic designers face is not about mastering the technical aspects of computing medium, but introducing meaning and "life" into the design process and creativity is one valuable way to do so. Design methodologies that stress the importance of skills, abilities, attitudes, values, and motives are important and creativity-facilitating educators should promote them in the classrooms.

During the ideation and brainstorming process, ideas are created, destroyed, and recreated with interventions between students' peers and the instructor. The generative aspect comprises of choosing a paradigm for application to an existing design problem and developing design concepts. The iterative nature, characterized by repetitiousness, is in and of itself to be found in the two aspects of generative and interpretive. By understanding how the design process and systems work, educators can stress the importance of articulation during brainstorming because it permits conscious and autonomous self-reflection. Specific feedback by teachers allows all students to participate, compare, identify, learn, and make improvements in their designs.

Since computer technology has moved our discourse towards metaphor, educators should encourage the use of visuals and language that conjure up compelling imagery and imagination for the appropriate audience in students. Inspiration and creativity are still important in design. A very important element in the classroom is the educators themselves. Teaching is about inspiring curious minds and recognizing raw talents, challenging them to think beyond their perceived capabilities. Especially in the field of graphic design, education is not just about preparation for practice, it is also about widening one's perspective in participating in a dynamic field where methods and products are interactive and constantly changing.

We can train students to acquire all the necessary skills for the job on the assumption that the skills acquired would be lasting throughout his or her professional life. Such an approach in design education today involving technology is altogether unrealistic without some form of post baccalaureate retraining or graduate education. Not only do we need to review what is now being taught, the aim of teaching should include enhancing the creative productivity in students. However, the fear is of educational curricula that place a strong emphasis on correct or best answers arrived through the use of logical thinking processes. This is a limited, outdated, and exceedingly biased view.

The intricacies of the computer and the software should not stand in the way of expression and thus limit the potentiality for creative thinking. The goal is therefore, to use the computer as both a tool and medium where synergy between the limits of the mind and the extreme potential of technology is combined. To facilitate this goal, educators need to define what roles graphic designers should be aware of in their human-computer interactivity and what skills need to be nurtured.

The focus must be shifted from a technically specific to a creative and conceptual development that will still be relevant after the limits of the technology have been surpassed. Therefore, clear communication is important in ensuring that the students and the educator clearly understand the purposes, goals, and objectives of the course. Communication can be in any shape from verbal, phone conversations, emails, letters, faxes, etc. With current email and Internet technologies, our communication boundaries are enhanced by one that transcends brick-and-mortar.

In training others to perform a task or learn a new procedure it becomes necessary for educators to have knowledge of the subject. This knowledge comes from studying the subject or by doing it. Paradoxically, just by studying it does not guarantee that one will be able to train someone. Learning how to swim by reading an instructional book is very different compared to a real dip in the pool. Basing the process of design on a hypothetical situation such as in classroom is an exercise in confronting and experiencing certainty in a real world situation.

Real problems must be brought to awareness through collaborative planning with companies that present a problem solving opportunity. In cases where it is applicable, internships and real-client involvement must be introduced into the classroom. This is because as the program trains and prepares students for the field, we need to realize that we must bridge the gap between what goes on in the market-place and the ivory tower. Administrators have to realize that they are preparing students for the real world and their job is to create a learning environment that best reflects that situation.

The notion of graduates entering the "real world" accentuates the fact that we commonly view academia and the corporate environment as two distinctively different and polarized groups. A basic tenet of this perception holds that the universities' educational emphasis is on theory and businesses focus on practices. The conflict between the two leads to doubt about what is being taught and what is being practiced.

One suggestion is to staff an administrative director to oversee a graphic design program. He or she is all that is needed at any university-level program to administer undergraduate studies in graphic design. As for other faculty members, part-time educators who are professional graphic designers, principals, business executives, marketing gurus, and other related professionals in the field should be hired to teach students instead of tenured professors. These professionals can bring into the classroom real world experiences and expectations which will in turn enrich the students' learning experience.

We can teach a student what to expect and how to deal or react with the marketplace, but the optimum learning experience comes from dealing with the "real thing" in a "real world." Therefore, teaching and curriculum development in classroom practices should be based on real rather than artificial problems. When the problem is real, students are forced to engage in creative activities of problem solving which require them to confront the market-driven context in effective, functional, and creative ways. The only way to be sure about the potential and effectiveness of the design is to create and test them on real users. The flaws can then be modified and this is the essence of the iterative part of design. This is where idealism meets functionalism.

Additionally, administrators and teachers need to develop learning environments that allow students to explore their creativity. A student designer who tries to solve a design problem may present the information in the most attractive and persuasive way but creativity as a form of problem-solving activity must be clearly defined in the classroom. The promotion of the ability to have aesthetic and creative experience must be balanced with problem-solving skills. Problem solving is essential because allows for imagination to take place using a functional approach as a gauge for effectiveness.

According to Johnson (1995), computer art unites many disciplines such as math, science, fine art, cultural studies, language arts, architecture and engineering. This offers an interdisciplinary opportunity for educators to create problem-solving assignments that integrates different aspects of learning. Although computer technology has become the means for creation of meaning and the interpretation of our knowledge, it is still a developing medium with new versions of software that require constant update as well as hardware that are becoming cheaper and faster in performance. That makes it flexible for educators to individualize instruction in terms of materials, learning methods and styles and cognitive approach.

Knowledge transmitted through this approach forms a core knowledge base for approaching a diverse learning environment where not all learners are attuned to "one size fits all" model of teaching. In doing so, educators need to be creative in sorting and arranging their disciplinary wisdoms in order to balance their knowledge base. This type of restructuring can create major implications for the contents in the curriculum. Computer technology has again developed a new approach for us in tackling ramifications that arise from using technology.

In determining what are the strengths and limitations of computers in student education, it behooves us to think that technology is not just a means of productivity; it has since become a means for addressing issues that can stimulate learning and thinking. As I map the trajectory of graphic design and technology, we need to train students to adapt and develop new approaches in dealing with computer technology. Promotion of conceptual and technical competence requires an evolving, adaptive and versatile educator who is a designer, communicator, and thinker. If the discipline and practice of graphic design are to survive and expand, we must improve our advocacy efforts and make connections to the greater community we serve. We must respond to the challenge of the marketplace with imagination and skill even though it may require the utmost attention to detail, technically as well aesthetically.

<u>Recommendations for students</u>

We are being presented with a piece of equipment that can present many opportunities despite a healthy dose of skepticism about the influence of computer technology. As a designer interacts with the computer system, the connection between concepts and tools are materialized. Borrowing McLuhan's popular "medium is the message" observation, the computer can be seen as an extension of our central nervous system. The computer has become a medium that allows the students to extend their conceptualization and visualization abilities. The computer transcends its own appearance as merely a sophisticated electronic device capable of displaying vivid images. The status of computer software and hardware as a commodity, or as property, or as an investment, inevitably influences the way we design.

Learning is a continuous and lifelong endeavor and in an atmosphere where sensitivity and appreciation to others are encouraged, learning should be fun, informative and holistic. Education should not be based merely on the ability to read, write, and count but rather on the human being's total experience, personal perspectives, perceptions, senses and most importantly, learning institutions need to fit their students' needs to function effectively in the real world.

In a classroom that mimics the real world, students are answerable to their instructors, much the same way that designers or freelancers are accountable to their art directors or businesses that hire them. However, I recognize that students' own learning is more important than blind respect for authority. In essence, this "exercise" reflects the factorial demands and will shape their tenacity in dealing with the real world.

As an institution that prepares graduates for transition into the marketplace, graphic design educational entities form interdependent and synergistic relationships between education and practice. This supports the view that technology is an apparent and necessary component of modern design education in a classroom that uses technology as a medium for creativity. Perhaps the most important reason for the inclusions of technology into curriculum is to create a holistic approach in addressing the need to equip graduates with the latest skills and knowledge in entering the profession. Because of that, technology can be seen as a commodity with a market value in a market-driven economy.

Since design has become increasingly accepted, democratic, and secular, students need to create designs that are responsive, reliable or desirable to the demands of the marketplace. In a free society with thriving capitalism, there is an inherent commercial opportunity for innovative companies to put their inventions in the public domain. The financial constraints of the marketplace usually call for cost-effective and restrained design.

The motives of businesses are to make money. If price is a factor in attaining creative services, student designers have to not just act as a liaison between creativity and profitability, they also have to establish a mutual bond and develop a genuine rapport. Realizing that "creativity" and "talent" are very much sought after abilities (Bowen, 1999), students need to acquire not just technical skills but also interpersonal skills. This displaces the importance of technology even though they are an important factor throughout the creative development and final production phases. By preparing a student's psyche in dealing with a real world situation, students become better prepared for the workforce.

The increasing accessibility of these technologies has created significant new opportunities for students to become producers, rather than mere consumers. The manageability of design and production may reflect a more general trend towards the computer user as a consumer and producer. One thing for sure: computers are forcing us to self-evaluate and self-modify.

Authoring packages that are used commercially are the economic and creative instruments in forming the relationships between design and innovation. If a student is technically proficient, he or she should shift to a universally creative approach that will still be relevant and continue to be one long after the limits of the technology have been surpassed. Although users have the option not to pay for the new updates, the seemingly endless possibilities for creativity, professional growth, experimentation, and self-expression using computer technology is hard to deny.

Students need to become more technologically savvy when computers are involved. When schools embrace technology, we are imposing a whole lot of expectations on students to learn, master, and apply technological skills. These rules imply the ascendancy of authority, the repetition of sameness, and the stifling of uniqueness. On the other hand, with every technical skill learned, there is capacity for art and design creations because with every technical skill learned, students can create something new and by understanding the medium's biases and limitations, we can deal with the problem better.

The ability to produce results within restraints becomes the measure of a graphic designer's professionalism. For students, the ability to produce striking and effective design solutions while they problem-solve their own sets of restraints become the yardstick for their achievements. Because requirements for software functionality depend heavily on hardware, we need to understand how an application operates. The end user is usually not concerned with the details of the components of a computer but it is important to be aware of its storage capacity and computational power. Only then can we harness the full capabilities of computer software. By delving into areas of technicality, students have the upper hand in managing the computer system and controlling to a certain degree the production aspects of their designs.

Students also need to apply creative problem-solving methods because learning how to use the latest piece of software can only result in a constant relearning of new updates when their pursuit of professional mentality and productivity suffer. By realizing the strength and weaknesses of technology, we can foster a social cohesion that strengthens the design process, clarify our values as graphic designers, and establish kinship with the community we serve. They are solutions to problems necessary for the survival of the field of graphic design.

Talents and technical skills become symbiotic functionalism as students cope with unlimited amounts of information to keep up with and new skills to develop and implement. Managing changes in methods, processes, and expectations are now part of the growing needs caused by technology. Willingness to take risks, among many other things, becomes an important goal for every designer in becoming a Renaissance man or woman—someone who is capable of a wide range of expertise. Creativity is the niche that is necessary and fundamental to the education of a designer.

Technological skills will be a large part of a design curriculum and job security in a technologically-driven sector such as graphic design is about taking control of technology. Because of our increasing usage and dependability on computer technology, we need to retrain and relearn new skills and knowledge. University graduates with multiple degrees are not immune to the impact of technology in our society. They, too have to acquire new knowledge on many occasions during their working lives.

Within the realm of society and culture, interactions between the viewers, readers, audiences, consumers and designers are reciprocal. One designs it while the other validates it by authorizing or repudiating it. In this context, we can look at how society and culture shape graphic design and vice versa. With the same perspective, the relationship between technology and creativity is reciprocal. Technology without creativity is just another tool and the former needs the latter to become useful. Technology depends on its users to unleash its power. Hence, graphic designers should manipulate technology to serve us, not the other way around.

The conclusion

Graphic design is not a self-serving activity because it contains content, context, and objective. Our interaction with the world occurs mainly through information being received and sent. When communicating these ideas, computers are used as a medium but what is discovered is that the computer is a catalyst for discovery. There are several factors that occur in the design processes that influence the outcome of their designs, but according to the respondents, they are able to make discoveries which aid in their ideation process while using computers as a medium.

The computer is no longer an artificial intelligence because it has representative aspects of actual intelligence. There are several reasons to substantiate that statement. Our capability to interpret and manipulate information is quite impressive but we are not infallible creatures. Part of our learning experience is derived through making mistakes and unlike the computer, we are also influenced by many organizational and social factors. Usually there is no single best design alternative because the designer compromises when he or she is faced with many alternatives. Because we are not perfect, computer systems are designed to reduce the likelihood of those mistakes and to minimize consequences when mistakes happen. Reversibility such as the "undo" feature and the "revert" feature which is about recoverability are some features that allow computer users to explore without severe repercussion. These two are just the many features that a computer can offer.

Computer technology as a means of augmenting human problem-solving ability is sustainable and the idea of using the computer to teach humans is not preposterous. The secret to deriving solutions to problems which aid in problem-solving is to provide the right toolkit—the computer. It is impossible nowadays to practice graphic design without involving a computer system. The roles of the computer may not be attenuated or in some cases entirely eliminated. The mediation of electronic, mechanical, and technical devices is important because graphic designers rely on them to assist in the creations of computer-generated or computer-assisted art and design projects.

The computer system is designed to meet the needs and purposes of many different kinds of users and even the input devices are varied from mouse, trackball, joystick, digitizing tablet, touch screens, keyboards, etc. Interactivity with the system can be seen as a dialog between the user and the computer through the usage of the above mentioned devices. However, the interaction with the system is primarily by sight and interactions with the computer are through input from the user. The computer system acknowledges the information provided with some sort of feedback, usually displayed on the screen but the user may also receive information when the computer makes a "beep" sound when a mistake is made or acknowledging an input.

For a dialog to take place, users have to have direct manipulation and visibility of the objects on the screen. This is because the user's design decisions are made based on interfacing and interacting with that software environment. Reciprocally, computer systems react to stimuli provided by the user and facilitate the flow of data which creates a dialog between the computer system and its users. However, the computer possesses aspects of intelligence such as memorization and massive knowledge storage capacity which can be retrieved at any time without any loss of details.

Many different computer technologies such as wireless networking, video conferencing, voice recognition, massive data storage, converge to allow computer users to interact in a number of modes such as voice and handwriting in addition to keyboard. The all-in-one aspect is alluring because when users are offered an environment where they can harness and exploit the power of computing, they are freed and become unrestrained to explore. Creativity and skill may be innate qualities in the designer or learned through experience, but the computer has the capacity to provide its users with tools that allow them to think and explore divergently and produce convergently.

Technology inspires and develops new opportunities in its users when they apply and put technology to use. What happens here is that because of its all-encompassing, all-in-one computing environment, its users are able to multi-task, explore, conceptualize, customize, manipulate, personalize, and produce in an environment that is interactive and reciprocal. It forces every graphic design student to think, draw, manage, and produce. Even when serendipitous discoveries are not made, users are able to produce end results of some sort.

Given the computing environment with developmental and productivity tools in the software, the possibilities of discovering something new are very likely. The computer is more than a medium because if it stimulates the mind, it may enhance our creativity. We need technology to make things easier for us but at the same time we also need creativity to be different and to excel, despite the content, context, and objectives of the problem we are trying to solve. However, it is my conclusion that computer technology has the capacity to inspire and develop new applicability in graphic designers.

REFERENCES

Abra, J. (1997). The movies for creative work: An inquiry with speculations about sports and religion. Cresskill, NJ: Hampton Press, Inc.

Alvey, P.A. (1991). Computer imaging and the creative process of design: An exploratory investigation. Unpublished doctoral dissertation, University of Texas, Austin.

American Institute of Graphic Arts. (n.d.). Technological thresholds in graphic design programs. Retrieved November 30, 2000, from http://www.aiga.org

The American Heritage Dictionary of the English Language (4th ed.). (2000). Boston, MA: Houghton Mifflin Company.

American Institute of Graphic Arts. (2002). Connect yourself to the design world. Expand your network. Build your career. Join AIGA. [Poster]. New York: Quinto, A & Blauvelt, A.

Ashford, J. (1994). Messing with pixels: Illustrators and their computers. Print Magazine, 158(2), 30-43.

Barron, F.X., & Harrington, D.M. (1981). Creativity, intelligence and personality. Annual Review of Psychology, 32, 439-476.

Belvin, M. E. (1977). Design through discovery (3rd edition). New York: Holt, Rinehart and Winston.

Blauvelt, A. (1998). Remaking theory, rethinking practice. In Heller, S. (Ed.), The education of a graphic designer (pp. 71-77). New York: Allworth Press.

Bonsiepe, G. (1965). Education for visual design. In Bierut, M, Helfand, J Heller, S. & Poynor, R. (Eds.), Looking closer 3: Classic writings on graphic design (pp. 161-166). New York: Allworth Press.

Boylston, S. (2001). Creative solutions for unusual projects. Cincinnati, OH: How Design Books.

Brand, J. L. (2001). The cognition of creativity. Interior & Sources, 13(3), 88 – 96.

Bruner, J.S. (1962). The conditions of creativity. In H. Gruber, G. Terrell, & M. Wertheimer (Eds.), Contemporary approaches to creative thinking (pp. 1-30). New York: Atherton.

Caplan, R. (1982). By design. New York: St. Martin's Press.

Cataldo, J. W. (1966). Graphic design and visual communication. Scranton, PA: International Textbook Co.

147

Couger, J.D. (1995). Creativity and innovation in information systems organizations. Boston: Course Technology.

Craig, J. & Bevington, W. (1989). Working with graphic designers. New York: Watson-Guptill Publications.

Creswell, J. W. (1998). Qualitative inquiry and research design: Choosing among five traditions. Thousand Oaks, CA: Sage.

Creswell, J. W. (2002). Educational research: Planning, conducting, and evaluating quantitative and qualitative research. Upper Saddle River, NJ: Merrill Prentice Hall.

Cropley, A. J. (2001). Creativity in education & learning: A guide for teachers and educators. London, UK: Kogan Page Limited.

Cropley, A. J. (1992). More ways than one: Fostering creativity. Norwood, NJ: Ablex Publishing Corporation.

Cullen, M. (1998). In Heller, S. (Ed.), Future te<a>ch. The education of a graphic designer (pp. 31-37). New York: Allworth Press.

Cunningham, H. & Rivett, M. (1999). Teaching online Issues and problems. In Sefton-Green, J (Julian). (Ed.), Young people, creativity and new technologies (pp. 120 - 137). New York & London: Routledge.

Csikszentmihalyi, M. (1996). Creativity: Flow and the psychology of discovery and invention. New York: Harper Collins.

Davis, M. (1998). How high do we set the bar for design eduation?. In Heller, S. (Ed.), The education of a graphic designer (pp. 25-30). New York: Allworth Press.

Davis, S. E. (2002). Mind of a master. ID Magazine, June 2002

Dellas, M. & Gaier, E.L. (1970). Identification of creativity: The individual. Psychological Bulletin, 73, 55-73.

Dix, A. Finlay, J., Abowd, G., & Beale, R. (1998). Human-computer interaction. (2nd ed.). Hertfordshire, UK: Prentice Hall Europe.

Foote, C. S. (2001). The creative business guide to running a graphic design business. New York: W.W. Norton & Company.

Frascara, J. (1997). User-centered graphic design: Mass communications and social change. Bristol, PA: Taylor & Francis.

Freedman, K. & Relan, A. (1992). Computer graphics, artistic production, and social processes. National Art Education Association A Journal of Issues and Research 33 (2), 98-109.

Glaser, B. G. & Strauss, A.L. (1967). The discovery of grounded theory: Strategies for qualitative research. Chicago: Aldine Publishing Co.

Glaser, B. G. (1978). Advances in the methodology of grounded theory: Theoretical sensitivity. Mill Valley, CA: The Sociology Press.

Glaser, M. (1995). Design and business: The war is over. In Heller, S. & Finamore, M. (Eds.), Design culture: An anthology of writing from the AIGA journal of graphic design (pp. 253-257). New York: Allworth Press.

Glesne, C. (1999). Becoming qualitative researchers: An introduction. New York: Addison Wesley Longman.

Glover, J. A., Ronning, R. R. & Reynolds, C.R. (Eds.). (1989). Handbook of creativity. New York: Plenum Press.

Goodwin, W., Mäkirinne-Crofts, P. & Saadat, S. (1997). Objects in transition: A spatial paradigm for creative design. Leonardo, 30, 319-325.

Gozzi, R. Jr. (1999). The power of metaphor in the age of electronic media. Cresskill, New Jersey: Hampton Press.

Hanna, R. & Barber, T. (2001). An inquiry into computers in design: Attitudes before—attitudes after. Design Studies, 22, 255-281.

Heinz-Glaeser, P. M. (1999). The integration of the computer into the art world: Positive and negative effects Unpublished master's thesis, University of Houston-Clear Lake.

Hozaki, N. (1996). What needs to be considered about creativity and media use in a group-oriented society? International Council for Educational Media, 30(2), 61-63.

Hurlburt, A. (1981). The design concept: A guide to effective graphic communication. New York: Watson-Guptill Publications.

Ilyin, N. (1994). Fabulous us: Speaking the language of exclusion. In Heller, S. & Finamore, M. (Eds.), Design culture: An anthology of writing from the AIGA journal of graphic design (pp. 116-119). New York: Allworth Press.

Johnson, M. (1995). Portrait of the computer artists: Between worlds. The Journal of Social Theory in Art Education, 15/16, 32-45.

Justice, L. (1998). The big squeeze. In Heller, S. (Ed.), The education of a graphic designer (pp. 53-55). New York: Allworth Press.

Keedy, J. (1994). Graphic design (is) now. In Heller, S. & Finamore, M. (Eds.), Design culture: An anthology of writing from the AIGA journal of graphic design (pp. 125-126). New York: Allworth Press.

Kimmelman, M. (2002, May 4). Decades of doodles help illuminate the creative process. The New York Times, p. B35.

Landa, R. (1998). Thinking creatively: New ways to unlock your visual imagination. Cincinnati, OH: North Light Books.

Lasky, J. (1998). The problem with problem solving. In Heller, S. (Ed.), The education of a graphic designer (pp. 95-97). New York: Allworth Press.

Lawson, B. & Ming Loke, S. (1997). Computers, words and pictures: Overuse of graphics in CAD software stifles creativity. Design Studies, 18, 171-183.

Leonard, R. & LeCroy, B. (1985). The instrument of the future: Computers in education. MS: University of Southern Mississippi. (ERIC Document Reproduction Service No. ED 270095)

Lionni, L. (1986). The experience of seeing. In Heller, S. & Finamore, M. (Eds.), Design culture: An anthology of writing from the AIGA journal of graphic design (pp. 116-119). New York: Allworth Press.

McCoy, K. (1998). Education in an adolescent profession. In Heller, S. (Ed.), The education of a graphic designer (pp. 3-12). New York: Allworth Press.

McMillan, J. H. & Schumacher, S. (1997). Research in education: A conceptual introduction (4th ed.) New York: Longman.

Meggs, P. B. (1990). Saul Bass on corporate identity. In Heller, S. & Finamore, M. (Eds.), Design culture: An anthology of writing from the AIGA journal of graphic design (pp. 71-77). New York: Allworth Press.

Meggs, P. B. (1998). A history of graphic design (3rd ed.). New York: John Wiley & Sons.

Mello, S. (2002). Customer-centric product definition: The key to great product development. New York: American Management Association.

Mercedes, D. (1996). Digital ethics: Computers, photographs, and the manipulation of pixels. Art Education, 49(3), 44-50.

Mills, W. (1994). Working Smarter: Computers as stimulants for human creativity. Social Science Computer Review, 12,(2) 215-230.

Mok, C. (1996) Designing business: Multiple media, multiple disciplines. Indianapolis, IN: Adobe Press.

Motamedi, K. (1982). Extending the concept of creativity. Journal of Creative Behavior, 16, 75-88.

Oldach, M. (1995). Creativity for graphic designers. Cincinnati, OH: North Light Books.

Oppenheimer, T. (1997, July). The computer delusion. Retrieved April 12, 2000, from http://www.theatlantic.com/issues/97jul/computer.htm

Papanek, V. (1984). Design for the real world – Human ecology and social change (2nd ed.). Chicago: Academy Chicago Publishers.

Papert, S. (1989). A critique of technocentrism about the school of the future. In Sendov, B. & Stanchev, I. (Eds.), Children in the information age: Opportunities for creativity, innovation and new activities. Selected papers from the second international conference Sofia, Bulgaria, 19-23 May 1987 (pp. 3-18). Oxford, England: Pergamon Press.

Peters, T. (1996). Design mindfulness. In Kao, J., The new business of design. (pp.16-44). New York: Allworth Press.

Peterson, B. L. (1996). Using design basics to get creative results. Cincinnatti, OH: North Light Books.

Poggenpohl, S. (1986). On design education: The case for professionalism. In Heller, S. & Finamore, M. (Eds.), Design culture: An anthology of writing from the AIGA journal of graphic design (pp. 184-186). New York: Allworth Press.

Postman, N. (1993). Technopoly: The surrender of culture and technology. New York: Vintage Books.

Purcell, A. T. & Gero, J. S. (1998). Drawings and the design process. Design Studies, 19, 389-430.

Rossman, M. (1998). Are our schools unknowingly becoming emissaries for the values of the new technology? Art & Academe, 10(2), 32-44.

Rubinstein, R. (1994). Designers on a disk®. In Heller, S. & Finamore, M. (Eds.), Design culture: An anthology of writing from the AIGA journal of graphic design (pp. 24-26). New York: Allworth Press.

Runco, M.A. (1989). Parents' and teachers' ratings of the creativity of children. Journal of Social Behavior and Personality, 4, 73-83.

Salchow, G.(1993). Graphic design is not a profession. In Heller, S. & Finamore, M. (Eds.), Design culture: An anthology of writing from the AIGA journal of graphic design (pp. 83-84). New York: Allworth Press.

Sappington, A.A., & Farrar, W.E. (1982). Brainstorming v. critical judgment in the generation of solutions which conform to certain reality constraints. Journal of Creative Behavior, 16, 68-73.

Sawahata, L. (1999). Creativity: Innovative ways to build great design. Gloucester, MA.: Rockport Publishers.

Schreuders, P. (1977). Lay in—lay out. In Bierut, M, Helfand, J Heller, S. & Poynor, R. (Eds.), Looking closer 3: Classic writings on graphic design (pp. 260-266). New York: Allworth Press.

Schwartz, H., & Jacobs, J. (1979). Qualitative sociology: A method to the madness. New York: The Free Press.

Sebastian, L. (2001). Digital design business practices: For graphic designers and their clients. (3rd ed.). New York: Allworth Press.

Simons, T (2001). Mastering the art of metaphor. Presentations, June 2001, 44, 46, 48, 52.

Spencer, H. (1964). The responsibilities of the design profession. In Bierut, M, Helfand, J Heller, S. & Poynor, R. (Eds.), Looking closer 3: Classic writings on graphic design (pp. 156-160). New York: Allworth Press.

Strauss, A. & Corbin, J. (1990). Basics of qualitative research: Grounded theory procedures and techniques. Newbury Park, CA: Sage Publications.

Starko, A. J. (2001). Creativity in the classroom:Schools of curious delight. (2nd ed.) Mahway, NJ: Lawrence Erlbaum Associates.

Sternberg, R.J. (1988). The nature of creativity. New York: Cambridge University Press.

Sullivan, P. (1988). Desktop publishing: A powerful tool for advanced composition courses. College Compositions and Communications, 39, 344-347.

Swanson, G. (1995). Is design important?. In Heller, S. & Finamore, M. (Eds.), Design culture: An anthology of writing from the AIGA journal of graphic design (pp. 167-169). New York: Allworth Press.

Swanson, G. (1998). Graphic design education as a liberal art: Design and knowledge in the university and the "real world." In Heller, S. (Ed.), The education of a graphic designer (pp. 13-23). New York: Allworth Press.

Swann, A. (2000). The new graphic design school. New York: John Riley & Sons.

Treffinger, D.J., & Isaksen, S.G., & Firestein, R.L. (1983). Theoretical perspective on creative learning and its facilitation. Journal of Creative Behavior, 17, 9-17.

Truckenbrod, J. (1990). Computers as a vehicle for integrated creativity. Leonardo, 23, 440.

Vermaas, C. (1995). Sketching: Conversations with the brain. In Heller, S. & Finamore, M. (Eds.), Design culture: An anthology of writing from the AIGA journal of graphic design (pp. 174-175). New York: Allworth Press.

Volti, R. (2001). Society and technological change. New York: Worth Publishers.

Verstijnen, J. M., Henessey, J. M. & van Leeuwen, C. (1998). Sketching and creative discovery. Design Studies, 19, 519-546.

Wake, W. K. (2000). Design paradigms: A sourcebook for creative visualization. New York: John Wiley & Sons, Inc.

Walker, D., & Herman, M. (1994). Image appropriation: On the rise? Photo District News, 14(5), 1, 30-32.

Webster, Jr. F. E. (1999). Market-driven management: Using the new marketing concept to create a customer-oriented company. New York: John Wiley & Sons, Inc.

Wiesner, J. B. (1967). Education for creativity in sciences. In Kagan, J (Ed.), Creativity and learning (pp. 92-102). Boston: Houghton Mifflin Company.

Wild, L. (1998). That was then: Corrections and amplifications. In Heller, S. (Ed.), The education of a graphic designer (pp. 39-52). New York: Allworth Press.

Winnicott, D. W. (1971). Playing and reality. London: Tavistock/Routledge.

APPENDIX A

HUMAN SUBJECTS APPROVAL LETTER

TEXAS TECH UNIVERSITY

Office of Research Services

Box 41035
Lubbock, TX 79409-1035
(806) 742-3884
FAX (806) 742-3892

January 24, 2002

Mr Dennis E. Fehr
Mr. Kok Cheow Yeoh
Art
MS 2081

RE: Project 02001   The Impacts of Computer Usage on Creativity: A Case Study of
Undergraduate Graphic Design Students in a Major University in
Southwest United States

Dear Mr Fehr:

The Texas Tech University Committee for the Protection of Human Subjects has approved
your proposal referenced above. The approval is effective from January 1, 2002 through
December 31, 2002. You will be reminded of the pending expiration one month prior to
December 31, 2002 so that you may request an extension if you wish.

The best of luck on your project.

Sincerely,

Dr. Richard P. McGlynn, Chair
Human Subjects Use Committee

APPENDIX B

INSTRUCTIONAL SHEET

HELLO, Fellow Educators!

Please help me gather data for my research. My name is Kok Cheow Yeoh and I am one of the instructors in the Design Communication program. I am also a doctoral student in the Visual Studies program at the School of Art. The chairperson is Dr. Dennis Fehr and Prof. Carla Tedeschi also serves on my committee. The title of my research is *The Impacts of Computer Usage on Creativity: A Case Study of Undergraduate Graphic Design Students in a major University in Southwest United States.*

i

YOUR CONTRIBUTIONS AS AN EDUCATOR

1. To understand if computer technology can impact the students' creativity especially in the design process. And by doing so, the study may also define the strengths and limitations of computers in design education.
2. To investigate how graphic design students construct and visualize (problem-solve) their concepts and solutions in visual discourse.
3. To construct a theory about the practice of graphic design by expressing in systematic terms or concepts the analysis of the design process in order to give it meaning, significance, and legitimacy in service-oriented and market driven contexts.

CONTENT

In this package, you will find:

- _____ sets of Questionnaire (10 questions each) printed on a 11" x 17" sheet.i
- **Recruiting Statement** Displayed on the front page of the questionnaire, entitled "**YOUR OPINION**, Please!" all participating students are required to read them before answering the questionnaire.

BEFORE YOU DISTRIBUTE QUESTIONNAIRES

1. Let the students know how important it is that they contribute to the research by referring to "**YOUR CONTRIBUTIONS**" on the first page of the questionnaire for guidance.
2. Because some participants may have contributed in this survey in another class, please make sure that they do not repeat the survey.
3. Although I ask for participation from every student, his or her participation is voluntary and their identities are anonymous. This is explained on the front page of the questionnaire.
4. Every Design Communication student's participation is expected in order to strengthen this research because this is a chance for them to express their opinion about the relevancy of their graphic design education and their design processes. Please explain to them that the research is important to our field and I appreciate every effort they can contribute towards the research.

PLEASE MAKE SURE OF THE FOLLOWING

1. Please make sure you have a full class attendance since participation from every student is encouraged for this survey. Responding to all the questions usually last from 20-30 minutes. Do not allow the students to take this survey home. It must be completed in the classroom.
2. They need to write legibly and thoroughly. Each student should express reflectively or personally because the qualitative interpretation of data relies on their words. Make sure they refrain from answering simply "yes" or "no." Rather, they should explain their responses and make sure they write legibly.
3. Because of the necessary time to codify the questionnaire by early April of 2002, I would appreciate it if you could get them to me at your earliest convenience.
4. When you are done with the questionnaires, please put them back into the envelope provided,**seal it,** and leave them in my mailbox (YEOH K.C.) opposite the door of our art department office.

THANK YOU FOR YOUR HELP

If you wish a copy of the results in this research, please contact me at kcyeoh@yeoh.com or you can call (806) 763-1998. Feel free to visit me online at http://www.yeoh.com. Once, again, thank you very much for your help. You and your students' contributions are valuable to our field.

Yeoh, Kok Cheow, B.F.A., M.A.
Ph.D. Candidate

APPENDIX C

SAMPLE OF QUESTIONNAIRE

YOUR OPINION, Please!

YOUR CONTRIBUTIONS _____

This research is being conducted as part of a doctoral dissertation of the Texas Tech University School of Art'

Please answer 1-10 thoroughly because the result of this survey is highly dependent on your written response. You may use a separate piece of paper for more space. There are no right or wrong answers but please refrain from answering simply "yes" or "no." Rather, explain your responses and please write legibly.
Please use a separate piece of paper if necessary and remember to indicate the number of the question.

PLEASE CHECK ONE

You are a ☐ female ☐ male participant.

1. Do you sketch* with pencil and paper during the early phase of your design process?
    If you do please explain how it can be beneficial to your work.
    If you don't, please explain how it is **not** beneficial to your work.
    If you **don't sketch with pencil and paper**, you use the computer to sketch instead?
    If you use the computer to sketch, please explain how is the computer beneficial.
    *Sketching is defined as a rough or tentative drawing representing the ideas often made as a preliminary study in a des

_____

_____

_____

_____

_____

2. Depending on which medium you are comfortable with, how does sketching **either by** pencil and paper **or** the computer influence your design process?

_____

_____

_____

_____

_____

3. As you go through the process of searching for a solution and alternative designs are generated, do you rely on your intuition or common sense? Please explain.

_____

_____

_____

_____

_____

4. Do you discover anything new while working on your computer in terms of idea generation? Please describe.

_____

_____

_____

_____

_____

_____

_____

5. Which area do you find yourself worrying about more: the early idea generation aspects **or** the later production (mockup, software knowledge, technical information, presentation) aspects?

_____

_____

_____

_____

_____

_____

_____

6. Briefly **list** and **describe** each step involved in solving your design project from the beginning to finish. Indicate any tools, artifacts, or devices that are important at each step.

_____

_____

_____

_____

_____

_____

_____

PLEASE TURN OVER

158

7. Do you think computer technology is maximizing or minimizing (enhancing or impeding) your creativity? In other words, what are the pros and cons of using a computer to execute your project?

_____

_____

_____

_____

_____

8. How do you find your initial concepts in relation to your end result? In other words, does your final solution match your initial sketches or ideas? Please explain how it does or how it does not.

_____

_____

_____

_____

_____

9. In relation to question #8, what factors influenced or changed your initial sketches or ideas?

_____

_____

_____

_____

_____

10. Do you feel prepared to enter the field of graphic design? Please explain why you are and why you are not.

_____

_____

_____

_____

_____ **Thank you for your participation!**

Table D.1 Data analysis of respondents for question #1

Class	Respondents	Direct quote(s)	Pencil/ Computer	Keywords
ART 4356-390 (PAC-390)	1 male 0 female	Pencil it gives me the time to do a lot of thought process quickly by jotting down ideas. Computer because everything you can get to look more like you want it quicker (M-1, PAC-390).	Pencil & Computer	Do a lot of thought process down quickly
ART 4352-390 (POR-390)	3 males 4 females	I sketch some small ideas & then transfer them to the computer. It is 50/50 in the inital [sic] process (M-1, POR-390).	Pencil & Computer	Sketch small ideas to transfer to computer
		Yes, it helps to brainstorm and work out ideas. It focuses your mind to get an idea of what might work and what doesn't. Also, it allows for spontaneity, I might randomly sketch something I wouldn't never thought of before (M-2, POR-390).	Pencil	Helps to brainstorm and work out ideas
		Yes I do sketch before, NOW When I started doing graphics, I used to "sketch" using the computer but now I've learned that it is generally faster and more accurate to what I invision [sic] in my head now that I know how to use the computer (M-3, POR-390).	Pencil	Generally faster and more accurate
		When working on layout, composition, form (logos) and the overall flow of a piece, I sketch w/pen and paper because it keeps me from being gimmicky and from forgetting to consider basic formal concerns. When sketching out fonts and considering colors, I use the computer b/c it speeds up the process (F-1, POR-390).	Pencil & Computer	The computer speeds up the process
		I always try to sketch first with a pencil - I find that it always turns out better if I start at that stage (F-2, POR-390).	Pencil	It always turn out better
		Yes, but I tend to use pen b/c of the way it moves on the paper - I find it very beneficial - it really helps you to get an in depth understanding of what you are exactly creating before you get on the computer (F-3, POR-390).	Pencil	To get an in depth understanding of one's exact creation

160

Table D.1 cont.

Class	Respondents	Direct quote(s)	Pencil/ Computer	Keywords
		It helps the creative process & gets ideas going, when you develope [sic] ideas and explore as a visual person. Applying two kinetic senses (F-4, POR-390).	Pencil	Gets ideas going
ART 3350-390 (SYM-390)	7 males, 3 females	Yes, because it works faster, quick changes, nothing is deffinate [sic] (M-1, SYM-390).	Pencil	Works faster
		I do use a pencil to sketch in the first phase. By doing so I am able to see a fixed image of my idea and it is easily altered, thereby making it a method that is the least time or effort consuming (M-2, SYM-390).	Pencil	Able to see a fixed image and it is easily altered
		Yes, I do. I feel that it lets you get an idea of what something will look like much faster and easier than a computer can in the early stages of design (M-3, SYM-390).	Pencil	Much faster and easier than a computer
		Yes, I use a pencil and paper. I think that it is necessary to sketch before you work on the computer so that it will not look completely digitized (M-4, SYM-390).	Pencil	So that it will not look completely digitized
		I always sketch prior to my use of the computer. A computer can never draw, or translate any idea as well as it can with a pencil. I use the computer to simply sharpen and refine my own drawn images (M-5, SYM-390).	Pencil	A computer can never draw or translate any idea
		Yes, I begin my design process by doing pencil sketches. It's easier to begin with in order to thouroughly [sic] try out ideas (M-6, SYM-390).	Pencil	Easier to begin with sketching
		Yes, I do sketch in the early phase of my design process. I think its [sic] absolutely necessary to try out different solutions by hand rather than just limiting yourself to the computer. No one can draw on th ecomputer as good as by hand. I come up with more ideas through sketching than through the computer (M-7, SYM-390).	Pencil	Try out different solutions by hand rather than to the computer

Table D.1 cont.

Class	Respondents	Direct quote(s)	Pencil/Computer	Keywords
		If I sketch w/pencil paper I can get more ideas out more quickly (F-1, SYM-390).	Pencil	Get more ideas out quickly
		I sketch with pencil and paper in order to compose a # of ideas quickly, which could not be accomplished on the computer at the time. After sketching out ideas I refine the "top choices" with pen and ink making it as clean as possible in order to easily recreate it on the computer (F-2, SYM-390).	Pencil	To compose a number of ideas quickly
		Yes, I do sketch with a pencil and paper. It is the easiest way to get your ideas down usually (F-3, SYM-390).	Pencil	Easiest way to get ideas down
ART 3350-391 (SYM-391)	1 male 0 female	Yes, sketching with pen and paper is quicker than the computer in most cases and allows me to visualize ideas and how well they work before translating the drawings on the computer (M-1, SYM-391).	Pencil	Quicker than the computer, visualize ideas
ART 3351-390 (TYP-390)	2 males, 1 female	I do but it just forms a direction to take or a framework to start from. It's a fast way to start and see (M-1, TYP-390).	Pencil	Fast way to start and see
		Yes I sketch - it is beneficial to me because I can see and get on idea of what might work and what might not. It does sometimes suck because it is time if I have very little time to work on it (M-2, TYP-390).	Pencil	Can see what might work and what might not
		Yes I sketch with pencil, it benefits my work because it helps set the project up for preliminary problems. I can resolve some problems before I even get to the computer (F-1, TYP-390).	Pencil	Can see what might work and what might not
ART 3351-391 (TYP-391)	6 males, 6 females	I am required in all of my classes to make pencil sketches for thumbnail roughs. I believe it is beneficial to the idea process. What can be a mistake with a pencil can lead to another good idea, plus it helps me to quickly sketch my idea while brainstorming for quantity of solutions (M-1, TYP-391).	Pencil	Mistakes can lead to another good idea. Quantity of solutions
		I sketch before I use a computer because it doesn't limit your creativity or your design (M-2, TYP-391).	Pencil	The computer does not limit creativity

162

Table D.1 cont.

Class	Respondents	Direct quote(s)	Pencil/ Computer	Keywords
		Yes with pencil because I like to brainstorm in a messy but organized fashion (M-3, TYP-391).	Pencil	Like to brainstorm
		Sketching is a quick way of finding out if an idea is worth expanding on. Drawing is easier with a hand than a computer any way unless you have a computer drawing pad (M-4, TYP-391).	Pencil	A quick way to find out if an idea is worth expanding
		Yes I do sketch in the early phases of my design process. The reason I do so is because it helps with the production of ideas and also makes it easier to put those ideas into the computer (M-5, TYP-391).	Pencil	Helps with the production of ideas
		I feel that sketching out ideas with pencil/paper gives me a nice change (being more tactile) from the world of computer generated imagery. Pencil/pen also seems to be more flexible (M-6, TYP-391).	Pencil	Tactility Pencil/pen more flexible
		Yes, b/c doing many thumbnails benefits you later in your designs, using a process notebooks [sic] helps you look back & combine old ideas w/new ones (F-1, TYP-391).	Pencil	Benefits you later when using a process notebook
		I do sketch with pencil & paper, it helps generate ideas and put my thoughts on paper quickly, so I can get multiple ideas out of just one quick sketch (F-2, TYP-391).	Pencil	Multiple ideas out of one quick sketch
		Yes - sketching helps get ideas out of my head quickly before I forget them. It is easier to translate from head to paper to computer, than straight from head to computer because technological aspects are sometimes distracting (F-3, TYP-391).	Pencil	Easier to translate from head to paper
		I sketch when computer is not available but prefer the comp b/c it is faster & you can make changes more easily. Although for independant [sic] work I do like to sketch - it causes you to look more closely & notice more things when sketching a specific object, person, etc. (F-4, TYP-391).	Pencil	Faster and can make changes easily. Also causes you to look more closely when sketching

Table D.1 cont.

Class	Respondents	Direct quote(s)	Pencil/Computer	Keywords
		I do sketch w/pencil & paper. I can generate ideas quicker w/this old fashioned method & I tend to create work that is more original (F-5, TYP-391).	Pencil	Like to brainstorm
		yes, I do sketch with pencil and paper as part of my design process! I think it s a lot more flexible then [sic] just getting on the computer as well as lets you get your ideas out fast, it also allows for trial & error so you learn what works & what doesn 't (F-6, TYP-391).	Pencil	Allows for trial and error so you learn what works and what does not
ART 3352-390 (TY1-390)	4 males, 3 females	Yes I think it helps to put ideas down, much quicker to brainstorm (M-1, TY1-390).	Pencil	Helps to put ideas down
		Yes - Sometimes you can accomplish nice elements that you might have overlooked if you had worked w/a computer from the beginning (line quality, color, etc.) (M-2, TY1-390).	Pencil	Might overlooked elements if worked on the computer
		Yes, I do sketch. I do no like doing it on the computer because I feel restrained & limited. I feel limited from what the computer will allow me to do. Its [sic] beneficial to my work because in these steps I need the full freedom & open creativity (M-3, TY1-390).	Pencil	Feel restrained and limited from what the computer will allow me to do
		I personally use sketches first. I feel it gives me a direction & a stranger thought process than the computer does. The comp. may be faster @ generating ideas/sketches, but I think the theory & conceptualization of the project gets pushed aside. Sketching helps me organize a more all around thought process (M-4, TY1-390).	Pencil	Gives a direction and a stranger thought process than the computer does. Sketching helps to organize thought process
		Occasionaly [sic] if ever do I sketch. I don 't know that it isn't beneficial I just feel it is faster to sketch on the computer. My ideas sometimes come so fast this way I can capture them all (F-1, TY1-390).	Computer	Faster to sketch on the computer. Ideas come fast this way

Table D.1 cont.

Class	Respondents	Direct quote(s)	Pencil/ Computer	Keywords
		I sketch w/a pencil initially so that I will not forget some different ideas that I formulated (brainstorming, etc.) These sketches are very rough and usually make sense to me. Lots of time I just make notations (F-2, TYI-390).	Pencil	Sketch so that I will not forget some different ideas, for making notations
		Sometimes, I vaguely sketch out ideas basically so I can remember ideas as opposed to helping to develop my concept. Concept for me comes to me while I work on the computer. It is an additive process - I like to add & take away quickly. Drawing take [sic] too much time (F-3, TYI-390).	Pencil	To remember ideas. Concept for me comes while I work on the computer. It is an additive process
ART 3352-391 (TYI-391)	1 male, 1 female	Yes I think that it allow [sic] your creativity to come out better. Sketching is a quick way to express your ideas and seems to build the more you do it. It can become very clean or stay rough and depending on what you're working on (M-1, TYI-391).	Pencil	Allows creativity to come out better. A quick way to express ideas
		Yes, I do. It helps by providing a quick way to get your ideas down on paper. It also provides a quick way to experiment with layout design (F-1, TYI-391).	Pencil	Sketching provides a quick way to experiment with layout design
ART 4381-390 (PSS-390)	4 males, 10 females	Because of my pers. [sic] preference & instructors assignments, I usually start with 1 set of hand drawn sketches before going to the computer. This usually gives me good direction and a starting point (M-1, PSS-390).	Pencil	Hand drawn sketches before going to the computer, gives good direction
		I do sketch in the preliminary process of design. I believe that this causes me to give more consideration to form and composition as well as style. When I am ready to move to the computer I am more focused and able achieve a better design. By Being Focused [sic] on the overall goal I am able to make better decisions about design (M-2, PSS-390).	Pencil	Sketching gives more consideration to form composition and style

165

Table D.1 cont.

Class	Respondents	Direct quote(s)	Pencil/ Computer	Keywords
		Yes, as of late I am starting to lose the benefit behind drawing. I have always used drawing to express feeling & emotion but never to formulate ideas. I formulate before drawing and build as I go. It is hard to work in reverse when you can formulate on the computer, because of the luxury of being able to move objects around (M-3, PSS-390).	Pencil	Used drawing to express feeling & emotion but never to formulate ideas. Hard to work in reverse when you can formulate on the computer
		I always prefer to sketch out my work because then I am only limited by my imagination. When try to use the computer for sketches, I find that I am confined by the tools and my work tends to lack individuality or serious ingenuity (M-4, PSS-390).	Pencil	When using the computer for skeches, confined by the tools and my work tends to lack individuality or ingenuity
		To begin my initial work I like to start with pencil and paper (F-1, PSS-390).	Pencil	Like to start with pencil and paper
		Sometimes - it depends on the piece ... if it will have illustration I definitely do. I usually do to help with the layout. It just makes you come up with a lot of different ideas to work with (F-2, PSS-390).	Pencil	It depends. It makes you come up with a lot of different ideas to work with
		I sketch with pencil & paper. It helps me get ideas & work out possible problems before going to the computer. Once I get on the computer, I find it harder to see things (F-3, PSS-390).	Pencil	Get ideas and work out possible problems
		Sketching does not always help. It depends really on what I want at first. If I have a good idea, I go straight to the computer (F-4, PSS-390).	Computer	It depends on what I want first
		I sketch w/pencil & paper. I have to sketch out everything before getting on the computer - it saves a lot of time if I work out most problems on paper, rather than trying to work through everything on the computer (F-5, PSS-390).	Pencil	Saves a lot of time, work out most problems on paper

Table D.1 cont.

Class	Respondents	Direct quote(s)	Pencil/ Computer	Keywords
		I sketched with a pencil and paper primarily because a pen or marker would have distracted me to think about details, where it is a time to concentrate on ideas and gets as many out as possible. The same applies to the computer (F-6, PSS-390).	Pencil	A pen or marker would have distracted me to think about details
		I sketch with pencil and paper, it is easier for me to get my ideas down faster. It is beneficial to my work because by being able to do things faster. The faster I get on the computer to refine my ideas and get my work done (F-7, PSS-390).	Pencil	Easier for me to get ideas down faster. Able to do things faster
		I sketch w/pen & paper. I find it much easier to quickly explore idesa on paper. Then I am not restricted by the computer. This happens when I can not or do not know how to translate an idea with a program (F-8, PSS-390).	Pencil	Much easier to quickly explore idesa on paper. Not restricted by the computer
		I don't sketch as much as I should. I feel I have most some of my drawing skills because it is not required anymore (well, as much). Sometimes it is easier to get or give a vivid picture from the computer at the start (F-9, PSS-390).	Pencil	I have most some of my drawing skills because it is not required anymore It is easier to get a vivid picture from the computer
ART 3352-392 (SYS-392)	5 males, 3 females	Lets me get different ideas (F-10, PSS-390).	Pencil	To get different ideas
		yes I sketch with pencil any [sic] paper, but it allows me to explore many ideas and compositions quickly and cheaply before moving to the computer (M-1, SYS-392).	Pencil	It allows me to explore many ideas and composition quickly and cheaply before moving to the computer
		Yes I do - the computer has to be managed and requires a process to create even the simplest of images, but with paper and a pencil, you are able to lay out plans in a quick manner that has a personal interpretation and allows continuous re-verification of the image (M-2, SYS-392).	Pencil	The computer has to be managed and requires a process to create. With paper and a pencil, one can lay out plans in a quick manner that has a personal interpretation and allows continuous re-verification

167

Table D.1 cont.

Class	Respondents	Direct quote(s)	Pencil/ Computer	Keywords
		I do sketch with pencil and paper first because you can up down on paper many idea in a little amount of time. Then, you choose the best Idea and refine it to perfection. Most people get an idea in their head and run with it, even through [sic] it is not their strongest idea (M-3, SYS-392).	Pencil	With pencil and paper first you can up down on paper many idea in a little amount of time
		I use pencil or pen just to do rough sketches and thumbnails. It helps me because with the lack of detail it provides a good view for the layout (M-4, SYS-392).	Pencil	It helps me because with the lack of detail it provide a good view for the layout
		Sketches help you to explore ideas quickly, as they come to mind (M-5, SYS-392).	Pencil	Sketches help you to explore ideas quickly
		Yes I do - but it doesn't always help me if I don't know what images, what font, or what size I am going to use - but I think sketching just gets me in the mode to design more than anything (F-1, SYS-392).	Pencil	Gets me in the mode to design more than anything
		I do sketch, but only because thumbnails seem to be required for class. When I get an idea it is generally easier for me to use the actual objects that would appear in the project. It is easier to move the objects and designing on the computer allows me to try different ideas easier (F-2, SYS-392).	Pencil	It is easier to move the objects and designing on the computer allows me to try different ideas easier
		Yes, I sketch w/pencil first @ [sic] thumbnail size. It helps me get my idea down quickly before I forget it. Once getting on the computer I may or may not reference [sic] the original sketch, depending on what I'm doing (F-3, SYS-392).	Pencil	It helps me get my idea down quickly before I forget it
ART 3352-393 (SYS-393)	2 males, 0 female	Yes I love sketches because it helps broaden my ideas (M-1, SYS-393).	Pencil	It helps broaden ideas
		Yes, in the initial stages. to develop ideas (M-2, SYS-393).	Pencil	To develop ideas
ART 4352-392 (PUB-392)	1 male, 0 female	I use [sic] to sketch all the time, as my skills progressed on the computer, I find myself using the computer more. I use it to get more of the design decisions out of the way, but not the concept (M-1, PUB-392).	Computer	Use it to get design decisions out of the way, but not the concept

168

Table D.2 Data analysis of respondents for question #2

Class	Respondents	Direct quote(s)	Pencil/ Computer	Keywords
ART 4356-390 (PAC-390)	1 male 0 female	It allows you to come up with a lot of ideas so that you can place bits & pieces to get the end result (M-1, PAC-390).	Pencil	Place bits and pieces to get the end result
ART 4352-390 (POR-390)	3 males, 4 females	It is easier to convey what you want to in the beginning process (M-1, POR-390).	Pencil	Easier to convey
		I'll start out by brainstorming w/pencil & paper and then go on to the computer to get a more accurate image of what the idea will look like later (M-2, POR-390).	Pencil	Computer to get a more accurate image
		Now that I more fully understand the computer, I can use the sketch as a "template" for the design (M-3, POR-390).	Computer	Using sketch as a "template"
		I notice when I sketch first on paper, there are less formal design concerns later and my ideas are usually more varied and creative than when I start on the computer (F-1, POR-390).	Both	Ideas are more varied and creative on the computer
		It just gives me a starting point and a guide (F-2, POR-390).	Pencil	A starting point
		Like I said in #1 it helps you to become a part of your piece and understand its [sic] make up a little more before you jump on the computer - They are 2 separate pieces (F-3, POR-390).	Pencil	Sketching helps in piecing and understanding
		It influences the way my design will process. No matter where you start - there will be a working process that develops [sic] and if sketching doesn't happen, the rest of the process may just take longer to get there (F-4, POR-390).	Pencil	If sketching does not happen, the rest may just take longer
ART 3350-390 (SYM-390)	7 males, 3 females	I like the computer to influence my design by different strokes and colors (M-1, SYM-390).	Computer	To influence design by different strokes and colors
		Sketching on paper allows the ideas to generate more quickly, and I feel that it helps my creative process to get fired up (M-2, SYM-390).	Pencil	Ideas generate more quickly
		I do not think the sketches really change the design. In order to sketch the idea must be there first (M-3, SYM-390).	Pencil	The ideas must be there first

Table D.2 cont.

Class	Respondents	Direct quote(s)	Pencil/Computer	Keywords
		I use my other sketches to give me inspiration for new ones (M-4, SYM-390).	Pencil	Sketches to inspire new ones
		I believe each medium influences your design. I actually think that the pencil gives the most personal design(M-5, SYM-390).	Pencil	Pencil gives the most personal design
		It helps in tweaking the project. It makes it easier to continuously fix or tighten up the project (M-6, SYM-390).	Pencil	Makes it easier to continuously fix project
		I get more ideas working with brushstrokes [sic]. It is looser and less controlling. It influences my design process because the more I sketch the more I get to choose from (M-7, SYM-390).	Brush strokes	Looser and less controlling
		It makes it more interesting and raw - if you only work on the comp. It can look too contrived w/out personality (F-1, SYM-390).	Pencil	Makes it more interesting and raw
		I am better at sketching and not at skilled at the pen tool in Illustrator. I get very frustrated w/the computer so I make sure my final sketch is clean to be traced on the computer w/a fair amount of ease (F-2, SYM-390).	Pencil	Final sketch is clean for tracing on the computer
		It is easier for me to allow my ideas to evolve (F-3, SYM-390).	Pencil	Allow ideas to evolve
ART 3350-391 (SYM-391)	1 male 0 female	After looking over my drawings on paper, I can see how well the concepts are working within them. Then, I can either refine my sketches or put them on the computer (M-1, SYM-391).	Pencil	Can see how well the concepts are working
ART 3351-390 (TYP-390)	2 males, 1 female	It provides a creative path to follow but some things can't be rendered how the computer can (M-1, TYP-390).	Computer	Some things cannot be rendered how the computer can
		Well with sketching my designs usually suck, but with computer they are visually stronger (M-2, TYP-390).	Computer	With computer, they are visually stronger
		Pencil influences my design because sometimes I scan in drawn elements in a piece (F-1, TYP-390).	Pencil	Pencil influences my design

Table D.2 cont.

Class	Respondents	Direct quote(s)	Pencil/ Computer	Keywords
ART 3351-391 (TYP-391)	6 males, 6 females	I am more confident about my computer skills than my hand skills, and I can generate better work on computer than by hand. Use my handwriting for instance, I would have rather typed this out because it's cleaner and neater than by hand (M-1, TYP-391).	Computer	Confident about computer skills. Cleaner and neater
		Pencil influences the design process by making everything more different which a computer makes everything the same (M-2, TYP-391).	Pencil	Pencil makes everything more different
		It helps me to develop a concept when I sketch in pencil (M-3, TYP-391).	Pencil	Helps to develop a concept
		I feel that using pencil will allow you to explore more possibilities and when you refine a sketch it require [sic] less time on the computer to clean up. Being able to draw is an important part of any field of art (M-4, TYP-391).	Pencil	Allow you to explore more possibilities
		It allows me to create a fair amount of ideas in a short amount of time. I also know that not all my designs have to be good, and I don't need to spend a lot of time worrying about it (M-5, TYP-391).	Pencil	Create a fair amount of ideas a short amount of time
		Yes, starting off either way effects a piece drastically. Using pencil seems to lend itself to more linear designs. Especially with type. It also lends itself to a more "organic" feel. (M-6, TYP-391).	Pencil	More linear designs. Lends itself to an "organic" feel
		Sketching on paper helps b/c you can include more detail in your ideas & can scan in your thumbnails & trace right over the image (F-1, TYP-391).	Pencil	Can include more detail in ideas
		I am allowed to put something on paper quickly. I can take the initial design and change it in various ways (F-2, TYP-391).	Pencil	Allowed to put something on paper quickly
		Computer helps more because trying different options is much less time consuming. You can more easily compare very similar ideas to make decisions (F-3, TYP-391).	Computer	Trying different options is less time-consuming

171

Table D.2 cont.

Class	Respondents	Direct quote(s)	Pencil/ Computer	Keywords
		Computer - you move quicker through your design, see more alteranives, variations of our design. It is easier to keep up w/your own thoughts w/a computer (F-4, TYP-391).	Computer	Move quicker through designs. Easier to keep up with thoughts
		Sketching, I feel is necessary to developing an idea. However, I only use pencil & paper in the begining [sic] stages, then I do more sketching on the computer to further my hand drawn ideas (F-5, TYP-391).	Pencil	Necessary for developing an idea
		By sketching as part of my process, I am able to try anything. The more I do the better off I am. It allows me to get my mind flowing, to get to those ideas which will work, not just settling for an "ok" idea (F-6, TYP-391).	Pencil	Able to try anything. Allows for mind flowing
ART 3352-390 (TYI-390)	4 males, 3 females	I think the comp. helps, but if you can't get the idea down on paper, then it won't help to start from the comp (M-1, TYI-390).	Pencil	If ideas are not on paper, it does not help to start from the computer
		Its [sic] a good starting to then figure out how to translate the idea into my piece, depending on the parameters (M-2, TYI-390).	Pencil	A good starting to figure out how to translate the idea
		It helps me to explore more options/solutions to problems before I try applying them on the comp. (M-3, TYI-390).	Pencil	Helps to explore more options/solutions to problems
		Sketching makes me think more. My decisions are more concious [sic] instead of an impluse to what I see on the screen. Sketcing threnghtens [sic] my design. It makes my comp. work more organized (wasting less time) (M-4, TYI-390).	Pencil	Sketching makes the computer work more organized, wasting less time
		A great deal - how else would you design if you didn't sketch. - explore ideas + layouts (F-1, TYI-390).	Pencil	Explore ideas and layouts
		I am less inclined to feel obligated to finish a piece if I sketch in pencil, which is good, because then I have more freedom to branch off into different directions, paying less attention to the initial stages looking "perfect" (F-2, TYI-390).	Pencil	Have more freedom to branch off into different directions

Table D.2 cont.

Class	Respondents	Direct quote(s)	Pencil/ Computer	Keywords
ART 3352-391 (TYI-391)	1 male, 1 female	It helps you to see how a certain element might aide or hinder your design. It allows you to through out all your ideas whether good or bad (F-3, TYI-390).	Pencil	To see how a certain element might aide or hinder your design
		Pencil is easier for me to use. It is more natural. I've been sketching forever where the computer is more confining (M-1, TYI-391).	Pencil	Pencil is more natural. The computer is more confining
		It helps to refine your design. The sketches can provide a good framework for your design. I believe that the overall quality of the final piece will be enhance by using sketches (F-1, TYI-391).	Pencil	Helps to refine design. Provide a good groundwork for the design
ART 4381-390 (PSS-390)	4 males, 10 females	It just gives me a good grounding, a place for my ideas to grow M-1, PSS-390).	Pencil	A good grounding for ideas to grow
		Sketching by hand. Lets [sic] me see exactly what is in my mind's eye. There are no distractions or outside influence M-2, PSS-390).	Pencil	To see exactly what is in the mind
		Same answer as above. Drawing inhanses [sic] hand skills and helps figure the look you want, but the computer helps more with layout through the flexibility of moving images (M-3, PSS-390).	Pencil	Enhances hand skills, figure out the look you want
		When sketching, my design is free to roam and do whatever I want, with the computer as a supplemental tool, whereas sketches on the computer allow the programs to dictate my design and direction. Making it look generic and uncreative (M-4, PSS-390).	Pencil	Programs on the computer can dictate design, make it look generic and uncreative
		I feel that pen & paper provide a blueprint. If I go immediately to the computer, I often get stuck and lazy (F-1, PSS-390).	Pencil	Pen & paper provide a blueprint
		You are able to make changes easily & see your ideas FAST -> determine which you like & which you don't before even starting on the computer (F-2, PSS-390).	Pencil	Able to make changes easily & see ideas fast

Table D.2 cont.

Class	Respondents	Direct quote(s)	Pencil/Computer	Keywords
		I think sketching allows more creativity. You don't have to think about margins [sic], rules, leading, kerning, ect [sic]. You can just design (F-3, PSS-390).	Pencil	Don't have to think about margins, rules, leading, kerning. You just design
		It only helps to get me going. I feel like I always start on my "final" design the first time I start designing on the computer (F-4, PSS-390).	Pencil	Feel like I always start on my "final" design the first time I start on the computer
		I can get more ideas out more quickly w/pencil & paper. The computer limits my idea generation (F-5, PSS-390).	Pencil	Can get more ideas out quickly. The computer limits my idea generation
		The design process seems to be more complete when the early sketch phases are approached with pencil & paper (F-6, PSS-390).	Pencil	Design process seems more complete when approached with pencil and paper
		Sketching on paper helps me visualize and improve the next idea. By being able to see it done quickly I am able to improve that idea and go on to the next step (F-7, PSS-390).	Pencil	Sketching on paper helps to visualize and improve the next idea
		Paper sketch allows me to figure out basic design solutions before getting caught up on the computer, where one can easily get distracted and focus too much on "perfecting" before a successful design has been worked out (F-8, PSS-390).	Pencil	To figure out basic design solutions before getting caught up on the computer, easily distracted, focus too much on "perfecting"
		Pencil helps get out the most obvious ideas first. It is hard to get a layout from pencil to computer makes everything drawn is too scale. That can be an advantage through because you can see more variations that way (F-9, PSS-390).	Pencil	Get out the most obvious ideas first. Can see more variations
		Pencil is faster & easier to make changes (F-10, PSS-390).	Pencil	Faster and easier to make changes

174

Table D.2 cont.

Class	Respondents	Direct quote(s)	Pencil/ Computer	Keywords
ART 3352-392 (SYS-392)	5 males, 3 females	Very much, often I will rework ideas with pencil and paper during the design process (M-1, SYS-392).	Pencil	Often I will rework ideas with pencil and paper
		it lets me try ideas quickly and with indications of the whole (M-2, SYS-392).	Pencil	Try ideas quickly with indications of the whole
		It will refine any idea to perfection (M-3, SYS-392).	Pencil	It will refine any idea to perfection
		A great amount because I can always go back to my thumbnails and use other sketches for layouts (M-4, SYS-392).	Pencil	Can always go back to thumbnails and use other sketches for layouts
		Sketching ideas gives you an [sic] quick visual of what you want to accomplish or convey in your design (M-5, SYS-392).	Pencil	A quick visual of what you want to accomplish or convey in your design
		It somewhat steers the direction of what I end up doing. Sometimes I make thumbnails (mainly to placate the instructor) and then ignore them & start designing on the computer & then by the final draft I realized how closely it resembles an initial sketch (F-1, SYS-392).	Pencil	It steers the direction of what I end up doing. Start designing on the computer and then by the final draft I realized how closely it resembles an initial sketch
		By using the computer I feel like I can be more creative because ideas seem to come to me when I have the different component in front of me. Rather than when I am starring [sic] at a blank piece of paper (F-2, SYS-392).	Computer	Ideas seem to come to me when I have the different component in front of me
		My sketch is phase 1 of getting an idea out; phase 2 through whatever is almost always on the computer. My ideas further develop once on the computer & I can do so much more there that I never go back to sketching for that project. A lot of teachers make students do 30-50 thumbnails for a project. This seems like a waste of time because after eeking [sic] out #50 I have lost all inspiration for the project & 99% of the time my first few sketches are the ones I use (F-3, SYS-392).	Computer	My ideas further develop once on the computer and I can do so much more there that I never go back to sketching for that project

Table D.2 cont.

Class	Respondents	Direct quote(s)	Pencil/Computer	Keywords
ART 3352-393 (SYS-393)	2 males, 0 female	The sketches help develop a concept or a stylized look to my design (M-1, SYS-393). by helping me quickly brainstorm and easily create new ideas (M-2, SYS-393).	Pencil Pencil	Help develop a concept or a stylized look to my design by helping me quickly brainstorm and easily create new ideas
ART 4352-392 (PUB-392)	1 male, 0 female	I can get a solid mental picture of what I want as well as what changes are possible (M-1, PUB-392).	Pencil	Can get a solid mental picture as well as what changes are possible

Table D.3 Data analysis of respondents for question #3

Class	Respondents	Direct quote(s)	Intuition/ Common sense	Keywords
ART 4356-390 (PAC-390)	1 male 0 female	Both - intution because we as artist rely on what we think looks good. Common sense because as designers we are to keep up with the trends and new ones (M-1, PAC-390).	Both	Rely on what looks good
ART 4352-390 (POR-390)	3 males 4 females	I rely on both to reach my goal - they are both necessary (M-1, POR-390).	Both	Both are necessary
		Intuition first but then I'll use analysis and "common sense" to tweak the design (M-2, POR-390).	Intuition	Analysis and common sense to tweak the design
		Both - depending on what my specific goal is: I might use my "gut" to pick what feels best and my common sense to what looks best (M-3, POR-390).	Both	Common sense to what looks best
		I rely on intuition and naturally draw from my life and experiences (F-1, POR-390).	Intuition	Draw from life experiences
		Intuition - it is always stronger & more creative than common sense (F-2, POR-390).	Intuition	Intuition always stronger and creative than common sense
		I rely on intuition after a certain point - Once I have my research and lived w/it a little. I always in all walks of life rely on common sense. There is a happy medium between the two (F-3, POR-390).	Intuition	Happy medium between the two
		Intuition mostly - common sense plays part depending on the design project there are certain areas to go, but one should not be limited to explore & push the envelope (F-4, POR-390).	Intuition	Depending on the design project
ART 3350-390 (SYM-390)	7 males, 3 females	Intuition, thoughts just come in my head (M-1, SYM-390).	Intuition	Thoughts come in my head
		[Left blank] (M-2, SYM-390).	Intuition	[No response to code]
		I rely on intuition at first, going on sure gut feeling. After that I try to apply what limited graphic design knowledge I have in order to critique my own ideas (M-3, SYM-390).	Intuition	Gut feeling

177

Table D.3 cont.

Class	Respondents	Direct quote(s)	Intuition/ Common sense	Keywords
		I try to design what is pleasing to me and hope other will like it also (M-4, SYM-390).	Both	To design what is pleasing to me
		Common sense, as designers we are creating artwork that is to be understood by the general public. The general public understands common sense, but not necessarily intuition (M-5, SYM-390).	Common sense	We are creating artwork that is to be understood by the general public
		Both, I use common sense to develop initial ideas, and from there intuition helps me to make a project look better or try new things (M-6, SYM-390).	Both	Intuition helps me make a project look better
		Both, Common sense helps you with the obvious and the obvious can be good in design it helps people understand your design. Through intuition however I come up with ideas that are more complex & subtle and this can be good too (M-7, SYM-390).	Both	Common sense helps with the obvious. Intuition is for ideas that are more complex
		I guess both (F-1, SYM-390).	Both	
		Common sense, what is easily readable and not far-fetched. When I'm stuck on 2 designs I factor in pros and cons and pick the best (F-2, SYM-390).	Common sense	Easily readable and not far-fetched
		Both. I work on ideas that catch my eye, but I also think about how the public would see it (F-3, SYM-390).	Both	Think about how the public would see it
ART 3350-391 (SYM-391)	1 male 0 female	Intuition, I've found that research and development of ideas works better than just trying to come up with something off the top of my head (M-1, SYM-391).	Intuition	Research and develop- ment of ideas work better
ART 3351-390 (TYP-390)	2 males, 1 female	I rely more on intuition and feelings first I look for balance a lot (M-1, TYP-390).	Intuition	Look for balance
		Both - common sense because if you know some what about the company you just go off on your own and see what you come up with. Intuition - after you research and learn about something then come up with a design - it is cool to compare the different ways (M-2, TYP-390).	Both	Cool to compare the different ways

Table D.3 cont.

Class	Respondents	Direct quote(s)	Intuition/ Common sense	Keywords
ART 3351-391 (TYP-391)	6 males, 6 females	Both compliment my work because intuition gives a personal feel where as common sense is more based off knowledge of the public (F-1, TYP-390).	Both	Intuition gives personal feel and common sense is based off the public
		I rely more on my common sense for idea generation. I try to find a logical related path for generating multiple ideas (M-1, TYP-391).	Common sense	Try to find a logical related path for generating ideas
		both, I do what every seems to be working the best at the time (M-2, TYP-391).	Both	Do what seems to be working
		My intuition because most of the time my common sense fails me (M-3, TYP-391).	Intuition	Common sense fails me
		Both, commen [sic] sense is always factor because things have to be logical (there has to be a reason for what you do.) but intuition is also important because you will experiment more without thinking and you don't see your reason for it until after you've already done it (M-4, TYP-391).	Both	Because things have to be logical
		I believe I rely on a little of both. Intuition tells me what I can do, and common sense tells me whether or not it will work (M-5, TYP-391).	Both	Intuition for what I can do and common sense for whether or not it will work
		Definitely intuition. I'm the type of person that goes by a "gut reaction." If I like the way something looks on paper or on a computer screen, I have a tendency to want to leave it that way (M-6, TYP-391).	Intuition	Goes by "gut reaction"
		Intuition because for me your ideas become more original & not as generic being more common sense bound (F-1, TYP-391).	Intuition	Ideas become more original and not as generic
		I go on my intuition. I want my design to be unique and different. Common sense is a good thing, but what I feel will help my design personally is what matters most to me (F-2, TYP-391).	Intuition	What I feel will help my design matters to me

179

Table D.3 cont.

Class	Respondents	Direct quote(s)	Intuition/Common sense	Keywords
		Both - if I intuitively like one solution better but it is not logical enough for an audience to understand, then I will go with the commen [sic] sense idea (F-3, TYP-391).	Both	If not logical enough for an audience, I will go with common sense
		Intuition - sometimes Im [sic] not really sure why a design works. When you look at it, it is complete, nothing can be added or taken away (F-4, TYP-391).	Intuition	Not sure how a design works
		It depends. I usually let intuition drive me and later edit while using comon [sic] sense (F-5, TYP-391).	Both	Intuition first and common sense later
		I think its [sic] most times intuition in that I am looking for my design to look a certain way or the way I want it to go. But often times common sense steps in and decides for me. So I probably use both (F-6, TYP-391).	Both	Looking for designs to look a certain way through intuition first and common sense later
ART 3352-390 (TYI-390)	4 males, 3 females	Some intuition w/ some common sense of design helps to get other solutions. I definitely rely more on intuition (M-1, TYI-390).	Intuition	Intuition and common sense of design helps to get other solutions
		Intuition, if I don't feel right w/ my direction, I won't be into my work (M-2, TYI-390).	Intuition	Intuition if do not feel right with direction
		A little of both. You have to be sensative [sic] to design, but you can't help how you feel about a certain piece/quality. Maybe it could be re-visited & a better solution could come about (M-3, TYI-390).	Both	Have to be sensitive to design
		At first I rely on common sense (theoretical concepts) Artistically, I rely on my intuition because it helps me design for the sake of art (that's important to me) (M-4, TYI-390).	Both	Common sense (theoretical concepts) Artistically on intuition
		Yes a bit - mixed w/ the objective factors such as balance, hierarchy, focal pt. etc. All subjective or all objective doesn't seem to work - we are trained professional (F-1, TYI-390).	Both	All subjective or all objective does not seem to work - mixed

Table D.3 cont.

Class	Respondents	Direct quote(s)	Intuition/ Common sense	Keywords
		My design is based mostly on intuition and the concept behind synesthesia. Good designs are often stimulated by some inherent quality - after this is when I begin to think more formally (layout/precision, etc) (F-2, TYI-390).	Intuition	Based mostly on intuition and the concept behind synesthesia
		Intuition. Design should never be common sense. Design is an individuals [sic] own - therefore intuiton plays a key role in my design. It sets everything apart (F-3, TYI-390).	Intuition	Design should never be common sense. Intuiton plays a key role in my design
ART 3352-391 (TYI-391)	1 male, 1 female	I think both are necessary common sense give you direction but you have to expand upon that for creativity. Intuition does the same but in a different way. Maybe in deeper thought (M-1, TYI-391).	Both	Common sense gives direction
		Both. My intuition usually serves me well, but you must use common sense, too. What may be obvious to you or other designers may not be obvious to the average viewer. You must put yourself in the viewer's place (F-1, TYI-391).	Both	What may be obvious to you may not be obvious to the average viewer
ART 4381-390 (PSS-390)	4 males, 10 females	Intuition is my common sense. They go hand in hand & influence each other (M-1, PSS-390).	Both	Intuition is my common sense
		I rely on intuition for decision making. I think that this pushes boundaries and gives my design personality and character (M-2, PSS-390).	Both	Gives my design personality and character
		Intuition because you have to know the target audience and do research to know more about them. This helps you formulate ideas, needs, and stategies [sic] which develop the idea. Common sense is not a factor. Some ideas have to break away from the norm to catch the viewers [sic] eye (M-3, PSS-390).	Intuition	Have to know the target audience. Common sense is not a factor. Some ideas have to break away from the norm

181

Table D.3 cont.

Class	Respondents	Direct quote(s)	Intuition/ Common sense	Keywords
		A little bit of both. As a designer, there must be an intuitive ability to decide where things should go, often only later to find out that if your decision was in-line with some obscure rule of design, but there must always be a reason for choice. A client & a client's needs should dictate how design is done, whether or not it is appropriate, and other such matters (M-4, PSS-390).	Both	Must be an intuitive ability to decide where things should go. A client & a client's needs should dictate how design is done
		I tend to use common sense once I have formulated an idea (F-1, PSS-390).	Common sense	Common sense after formulation of an idea
		Both, intuition and what I think will look good. And then common sense on what does work (F-2, PSS-390).	Both	Common sense for what does work
		I rely more on intuition. I like to go by what looks better to me and my ability to explore new ideas (F-3, PSS-390).	Intuition	Go by what looks better
		Really both. If not for both, one would be lopsided (F-4, PSS-390).	Both	If not for both, one would be lopsided
		I rely on both, but I rely on intuition more. I use common sense to develop a concept; intuition to elaborate on it (F-5, PSS-390).	Both	Use commonsense to develop a concept, intuition to elaborate
		I combine both because both produce creativity when used together (F-6, PSS-390).	Both	Both produce creativity when used together
		Yes I rely on both and on knowledge of desing [sic]. By going with what I belive [sic] the target audience will be more attracted to [sic] (F-7, PSS-390).	Both	Going with what the target audience will be attracted to
		I tend to go with my intuition initially and perhaps use more common sense when refining (F-8, PSS-390).	Both	Use more common sense when refining
		I think I rely on my intuition. It can bring out new ideas (F-9, PSS-390).	Intuition	It can bring out new ideas
		Mainly intuition (F-10, PSS-390).	Intuition	[Response too short to code]

182

Table D.3 cont.

Class	Respondents	Direct quote(s)	Intuition/ Common sense	Keywords
ART 3352-392 (SYS-392)	5 males, 3 females	Common sense, it seems design is meant to be viewed by non artists and designers, so it should be read easily and common sense lend itself to that (M-1, SYS-392).	Common sense	Design is meant to be viewed by non artists and designers, so it should be read easily
		Both. There are certain rules that govern design, but most of these are pulled from what can be called intuition, which is formed from visual perception and memory (M-2, SYS-392).	Both	There are rules that govern design, but most of these are from intuition, which is formed from visual perception and memory
		I rely on my education of design, what I've been taught the last 4 years (M-3, SYS-392).	Both	Rely on my education of design
		I use whatever is visually pleasing to the eye and whatever has a deeper meaning (M-4, SYS-392).	Both	Use whatever is visually pleasing to the eye and whatever with a deeper meaning
		Somewhat intuition, because sometimes different aspects in your design just feel right and best conveys your ideas (M-5, SYS-392).	Intuition	Because different aspects in design just feel right and best conveys your ideas
		I rely heavily on my intuition I know somewhere inside of me what looks "good" or "bad" ... I realize that what I am constantly learning always help change & evolve this internal sense - but the gut instinct is strongest (F-1, SYS-392).	Intuition	I realize that what I am constantly learning always help change and evolve this internal sense
		A little of both. At first I rely on intuition but as I start to fine tune my ideas I incorporate common sense in with intuition (F-2, SYS-392).	Both	I rely on intuition but as I start to fine tune my ideas I incorporate common sense
		I think common sense is a big part of intuition, so I would say both (F-3, SYS-392).	Both	common sense is a big part of intuition

Table D.3 cont.

Class	Respondents	Direct quote(s)	Intuition/ Common sense	Keywords
ART 3352-393 (SYS-393)	2 males, 0 female	I rely on my common sense the most although my common sense is not always there (M-1, SYS-393).	Common sense	Rely on common sense though it is not always there
		both, I draw from all my experiences in life, as well as my morals, beliefs, and influences. I sometimes try to twist common sense and intuition to create a new look at my design (M-2, SYS-393).	Both	Twist common sense and intuition to create a new look at my design
ART 4352-392 (PUB-392)	1 male, 0 female	The common sesnse, it may not sound right bur it is taught. Elements such as readibility [sic], eye moment smoothly, continuity, and eye catching. The intuition is more personal (the fun part, its [sic] what you want just because) (M-1, PUB-392).	Common sense	The common sesns is taught. Intuition is more personal

Table D. 4 Data analysis of respondents for question #4

Class	Respondents	Direct quote(s)	Discover anything?	Keywords
ART 4356-390 (PAC-390)	1 male	The set up of the project, tools, thought process, angles (M-1, PAC-390).	Yes	Miscellaneous
ART 4352-390 (POR-390)	3 males 4 females	You see things in a whole new light. & see things that you have never seen before & implement them (M-1, POR-390).	Yes	See things in a whole new light
		I never stop thinking of alternatives of new direction in the design process I've completely changed designs the night before they're due (M-2, POR-390).	Yes	Never stop thinking
		The computer helps when you want to explore compositional changes (M-3, POR-390).	Yes	Compositional changes
		Not so much in terms of idea generation. This is one thing that I think computer can limit (F-1, POR-390).	No	Computer can limit
		It is just easier to change color & type & image fast - so you can compare easily [sic] what looks the best (F-2, POR-390).	Yes	Easier to change color & type
		Yes, because there are a lot of things w/ typography that can be achieved through the computer more easily than the paper, but you should always start on the paper in my opinion. Also the computer is just part of the process and it helps to take your work to the next level (F-3, POR-390).	Yes	The computer is part of the process
		Yes - b/c ideas on paper may not work out on the computer. You have to trouble shoot & try other ways to present the idea in a way that the computer can execute it the most (F-4, POR-390).	Yes	Ideas on paper may not work out on the computer
ART 3350-390 (SYM-390)	7 males, 3 females	Yes, sometimes the gradient tool, or blending is generated into my ideas (M-1, SYM-390).	Yes	Tools generated into ideas
		Not normally, normally when I use the computer it is to make a finished product of something I have drawn (M-2, SYM-390).	No	Use the computer to make a finished product
		Yes. Many times a mistake will spark an idea, or can see something in the design during developement [sic] on the computer that can spark ideas also (M-3, SYM-390).	Yes	Mistake will spark an idea

Table D.4 cont.

Class	Respondents	Direct quote(s)	Discover anything?	Keywords
		Yes. It is easier to manipulate the designs once they are on the computer (M-4, SYM-390).	Yes	Easier to manipulate the designs
		Yes, but it is not always wise to take ideas from the computer. It heads you in new ways that you might not want to go (M-5, SYM-390).	Yes	Heads you in new ways
		Yes, new ideas are always being discovered. Working on the computer is no different (M-6, SYM-390).	Yes	New ideas are always being discovered
		Sometimes, when you are working with a program and you see how a filter or tool affects a drawing that can be useful in coming up with ideas, but that is very limiting. I can do anything by hand that I can do on a computer and a lot more (M-7, SYM-390).	Neutral	Filter of tool affecting a drawing
		Yes. Once you do your preliminary sketches the comp. can enhance your ideas (F-1, SYM-390).	Yes	The computer can enhance your ideas
		No, except the fact my ideas are always altered in the computers cleaner output, and some level of hand skill and 'man made' quality is taken from the idea (F-2, SYM-390).	No	Ideas are always altered in the computers cleaner output
		Yes, because with all the different tools available, ideas keep popping into my head for different solutions (F-3, SYM-390).	Yes	Different tools, ideas keep popping
ART 3350-391 (SYM-391)	1 male 0 female	Yes, the computer allows you to move elements around and clean things up. In doing so, you can then see if there is some change that needs to be made or that there is something missing (M-1, SYM-391).	Yes	Allows you to move elements around and clean things up
ART 3351-390 (TYP-390)	2 males, 1 female	As stated above there are some things the computer can do that may be difficult to render (M-1, TYP-390).	Yes	Some things the computer can do
		All the time, my design usually comes together when on the computer. I would say 75% of the time I acomplish [sic] the final piece on the pc/mac (M-2, TYP-390).	Yes	Design usually comes together when on the computer
		Yes because sometimes I cannot control the computer better than a hand drawn piece (F-1, TYP-390).	Yes	Cannot control the computer

Table D.4 cont.

Class	Respondents	Direct quote(s)	Discover anything?	Keywords
ART 3351-391 (TYP-391)	6 males, 6 females	Yes, one mistake can lead to the "oops ... wait, That kinda looks neat" factor. Plus I can manipulate objects text and ideas easier and faster, plus use the tools that the programs provide for new ideas (M-1, TYP-391).	Yes	One mistake can lead to ...kinda looks neat factor
		yes, sometimes certain things that the computer can do turn out nice even though I may not have thought of it in pencil roughs (M-2, TYP-391).	Yes	Certain things a computer can do turn out nice
		Yes, because you can add, subtract, multiply, or divide to anything that you have created which in turn expands your ideas (M-3, TYP-391).	Yes	Add, subtract, multiply or divide which expands your ideas
		The clean surface sometimes allows you to see things better and after it is put on the computer and saved it is easier to explore new possibilities such as type and image placement (M-4, TYP-391).	Yes	It is easier to explore new possibilities such as type and image
		I usually do because with the computer you can make slight, or major changes to a sound idea rather quickly due to the fact that you do not have to redraw every time you make a change you want to make (M-5, TYP-391).	Yes	Do not have to redraw every time you make changes
		In a way I feel that the computer can be very limiting for just "pure" design or idea generation. On the other hand, I wouldn't want to live without it for magazine, newspaper, etc. layout (M-6, TYP-391).	No	Would not want to live without the computer for page layout
		Yes, placement & type choice particulary b/c free hand sketches cannot have the precision & capability the computer has. Color choice as well - Pantone helps (F-1, TYP-391).	Yes	Placement, type, precision, and color choices
		The computer allows me to think more simplistically. I honestly don't get ideas from working with the computer unless it is dealing with type or fonts. Seeing the fonts on the computer help [sic] with differentiation and positioning (F-2, TYP-391).	Yes	To think more simplistically. Help with differentiation and positioning

Table D.4 cont.

Class	Respondents	Direct quote(s)	Discover anything?	Keywords
		YES - it is easy to change colors & shades, to tweake [sic] shapes and to move things slightly. Changing a small detail that easily can inspire new ideas. A slight change might remind me of something I had not thought of before (F-3, TYP-391).	Yes	Changing a small detail can inspire new ideas
		Yes, I dont [sic] know what every tool can do but every now & then I'll do something by accident & it will take my design in a completely different direction (F-4, TYP-391).	Yes	An accident takes my design in a completely different direction
		I find myself making my sketches less accurate especially w/ geometric shapes b/c I know I could just easily do it on the computer. I do enjoy the way computers allow you to try many variations of the same idea quite easily (F-5, TYP-391).	Yes	Purposely make sketches less accurate. Computers allow you to try many variations
		Only sometimes do I discover new ideas or alternatives when on the computer. Most times, I will discover more when looking at the printout then [sic] when I am working on the screen. But often times an idea is generated through a slight change on the computer (F-6, TYP-391).	Neutral	Discover more when looking at the printout. Idea generated through a slight change on the computer
ART 3352-390 (TYI-390)	4 males, 3 females	W/comp [sic] you can do things easier than on paper & getting the output wanted. So yes the comp helps me take some ideas further (M-1, TYI-390).	Yes	The computer helps take some ideas further
		No, or hardly ever. My concept will be the same but little aspects of it might change. Color, font ... (M-2, TYI-390).	No	My concepts will be the same
		Yes - it is a lot like sketching. Whether its [sic] accidental or on purpose, things happen & new ways are learned. Through this exploration - the discovery varies & the final benifits [sic] greatly (M-3, TYI-390).	Yes	Accidental or on purpose, things happen and new ways are learned
		Yes, there are many processes it is hard to visualize w/out a computer. Filters are a good example (Photoshop) Sometimes to help get an idea moving more I run through the filters to see what it can stimulate visually (M-4, TYI-390).	Yes	Hard to visualize without a computer. I run through the filters to see what it can stimulate visually

Table D.4 cont.

Class	Respondents	Direct quote(s)	Discover anything?	Keywords
		Sure, happy accidents all the time. The other day I forgot to move the ruled box that defines my working area - it was 2/3 of the way off. I printed it all way by accident and it looked good so I added rules in those areas. (F-1, TYI-390).	Yes	Happy accidents all the time
		The computer allows for so manipulation of text/image that often "happy accidents" occur. It is also nice to know that with a simple command, ⌘Z, a mistake can be "undone." This makes the sense of freedom w/out messing up and getting stuck/ruining an idea broad (F-2, TYI-390).	Yes	occur. A mistake can be "undone." The sense of freedom
		Always. The computer gives ease to additive & deconstructive elements. It allows you to play & always reverse back to where you started. Various filters also give ideas that you might have never considered (F-3, TYI-390).	Yes	Additive & deconstructive elements. To play & reverse back. Various filters give ideas that you might have never considered
ART 3352-391 (TYI-391)	1 male, 1 female	Yes the computer provides ways of doing things that you could not do without it. Easy manipulation and color change, screening back. I think all of those tools and more can produce ideas (M-1, TYI-391).	Yes	The computer provides ways of doing things that you could not do without it. The tools and more can produce ideas
		Yes when I'm working on the computer, new ideas usually come to me. Actually seeing the layout on screen can give you ideas that you haven't had before. Strengths & weaknesses of layout can be more clearly seen (F-1, TYI-391).	Yes	Seeing the layout on screen can give you ideas. Strengths and weaknesses of layout can be more clearly seen
ART 4381-390 (PSS-390)	4 males, 10 females	Yes. Because my brain & my computer work different, different solutions arise. Because of the limitations of the computer different solutions are more applicable than what you can do in your head (M-1, PSS-390).	Yes	Brain & computer work differently, different solutions arise

Table D.4 cont.

Class	Respondents	Direct quote(s)	Discover anything?	Keywords
		Yes. New ideas a [sic] discovered on the computer however I do not think that you could come to these conclusions are the result of the predesign process on an actual sketch book. Both are needed for good design (M-2, PSS-390).	Yes	New ideas are discovered on the computer
		Happy accidents. As you learn more about programs you can develope [sic] mistake that really push other ideas (M-3, PSS-390).	Yes	Happy accidents
		When it comes to layout, I can generate many ideas very quickly and options that would normally take longer to do by hand, and when doing photo adjustments, there are happy accidents, but more often then not, idea generation must come before you get on the computer (M-4, PSS-390).	Yes	Happy accidents, idea generation must come before you get on the computer
		I don't really gain ideas from the programs. However, I often get ideas for layout, colors, type, imagery, etc from the internet and observation (F-1, PSS-390).	Yes	Often get ideas for layout, colors, type, imagery, etc
		Yes - when you work on actually putting things on the computer things change - you can try more stuff - a little change can completely make your design (F-2, PSS-390).	Yes	When on the computer, things change
		I think the computer helps me come up with new ways to improve an idea. The computer allows me to nail down details - fonts, colors, ect [sic]. I get a basic idea on paper and the computer is where the idea comes alive (F-3, PSS-390).	Yes	New ways to improve an idea. Get a basic idea on paper and the computer is where the idea comes alive
		Yes, filters help me so much. I like to make collages w/my work, & this allows me to make great collages (F-4, PSS-390).	Yes	Filters help
		Its [sic] easier to do variations. It's also easier to see what's working (F-5, PSS-390).	Yes	Easier to see what's working
		Yes - usually, it is with layout and type - with ideas & concept. I usually think of new ideas when I am away from the computer (F-6, PSS-390).	Yes	With layout, type, ideas, and concept

190

Table D.4 cont.

Class	Respondents	Direct quote(s)	Discover anything?	Keywords
		Sometimes, happy mistakes happen and it makes my idea better but not all the time does something like that happen. I put in what I thought up in paper. It is just a more cleaner and modified version (F-7 PSS-390).	Yes	Happy mistakes, it makes my idea better. I put in what I thought up in paper
		I find it is much easier to explore color options & reversals on the computer. Specific copy to headline sizes are also easier to work on the computer. Therefore I do often explore totally new ideas once I have moved onto the computer (F-8, PSS-390).	Yes	Easier to explore color options, reversals, specific copy to headlines are easier too
		It's easier to go through several ideas at a time by clicking (F-9, PSS-390).	Yes	Several ideas at a time by clicking
		[Left blank] (F-10, PSS-390).		[No response to code]
ART 3352-392 (SYS-392)	5 males, 3 females	Yes, in terms of color, filters, and font the idea can change dramatically (M-1, SYS-392).	Yes	In terms of color, filters, and font the idea can change dramatically
		The computer's ability to perfect rough drawings allows it to be seen to better relate to the rest of the image (M-2, SYS-392).	Yes	The computer's ability to perfect rough drawings
		Well, I do if I leave a while and then come back to it (M-3, SYS-392).	Yes	I do if I leave a while and then come back to it
		Going from paper to computer is a great change. You can manipulate images on the computer and you can't do that on paper (M-4, SYS-392).	Yes	Can manipulate images on the computer and cannot do that on paper
		Sometimes you can discover something new they may inhance [sic] your design (M-5, SYS-392).	Yes	Sometimes you may discover something new
		No - not really - lots more ideas are gained by interaction throughout the process w/ teachers & peers (F-1, SYS-392).	No	More ideas are gained by interacting with teachers and peers
		I feel like there are more often available in the creative process while on the computer (F-2, SYS-392).	Yes	More often available while on the computer

Table D.4 cont.

Class	Respondents	Direct quote(s)	Discover anything?	Keywords
		Beneficial "accidents" are more likely to happen @ [sic] the computer - those "accidents" usually result in better idea generation. Many effects can not be obtained w/a sketch or other mediums [sic] (F-3, SYS-392).	Yes	Beneficial "accidents" are more likely to happen. Many effects cannot be obtained with a sketch
ART 3352-393 (SYS-393)	2 males, 0 female	Yes I always about 98% of the time discover something new when I translate my ideas to the computer because many times I change something little about the design giving it a whole new meaning (M-1, SYS-393).	Yes	Discover something new when I translate my ideas to the computer
		Sometime, b/c a computer can generate looks and effects not easily created by hand (M-2, SYS-393).	Yes	A computer can generate looks and effects not easily created by hand
ART 4352-392 (PUB-392)	1 male, 0 female	I do, because the computer teaches you everyday. By playing with it on an everyday basis you experiment constantly, what can I do that the guy next to me doesn't know how to do (M-1, PUB-392).	Yes	By playing with it on an everyday basis you experiment constantly

Table D.5 Data analysis of respondents for question #5

Class	Respondents	Direct quote(s)	Idea generation/ Later production	Keywords
ART 4356-390 (PAC-390)	1 male 0 female	The later production - ideas come to artist but the other stuff we have to learn (M-1, PAC-390).	Later production	Learn other stuff
ART 4352-390 (POR-390)	3 males 4 females	Actually I am very strong at both ends (M-1, POR-390).	Both	Strong at both ends
		Later production (M-2, POR-390).	Later production	
		- idea generation - 5 yrs of using the computer has made me profisient (sp?) [sic] in that area (M-3, POR-390).	Idea generation	Computer has made me proficient
		Idea generation. Anything can be made to look pretty, but if the idea sucks, the final piece will suck (F-1, POR-390).	Idea generation	If the idea sucks, the final piece will suck
		Idea generation - I always second guess my concepts (F-2, POR-390).	Idea generation	Always second guess concepts
		I would say that I am more comfortable with early idea generation, but if it is not there the latter does not even matter. If you have a great idea though it can be destroyed by poor print production, mock-ups, etc. (F-3, POR-390).	Later production	Ideas can be destroyed by poor print production
		Idea generation: due to the fact that this is where the process starts it is more difficult - it is hard to begin - well not starting, but coming up w/the idea that works, is unique, complete executable is more difficult (F-4, POR-390).	Idea generation	Idea generation is hard to begin
ART 3350-390 (SYM-390)	7 males, 3 females	Mock up, to have a good idea to generate or start from (M-1, SYM-390).	Idea generation	To have a good idea to start from
		Early idea generation. I don't believe I can have a good design without a good concept in the beginning (M-2, SYM-390).	Idea generation	A good concept in the beginning

193

Table D.5 cont.

Class	Respondents	Direct quote(s)	Idea generation/ Later production	Keywords
		The late production I think is more important. After all that is what everyone sees, so I think I worry about how it will look and how I can get the computer to do what I am hoping for (M-3, SYM-390).	Later production	That is what everyone sees
		I worry more about the early idea generation because ideas don't always come quickly when you are first starting out (M-4, SYM-390).	Idea generation	Ideas do not always come quickly
		Early ideas come easily for me, but the final touches and messing w/ the computer seem to get in the way many times (M-5, SYM-390).	Later production	Messing with the computer seem to get in the way
		The hardest part is getting started. The early idea generation can take a while to develop [sic], but once the idea is discovered it becomes easier to try in different ways and finish up in all stages (M-6, SYM-390).	Idea generation	Once the idea is discovered, it becomes easier
		The early ideas, because they are the base of your work, if that's not good nothing in the final stages will be. I worry more about the idea, rather than I can generate what I've already done (M-7, SYM-390).	Idea generation	They are the base of your work
		Both actually. Sometimes it's hard to get started and sometimes it's hard to finish up w/a bang (F-1, SYM-390).	Both	Hard to get started and to finish up
		Later production - technical/software knowledge - creating an idea that is just as strong on the computer as it was on sketch paper. This is probably due to lack of experience in the 'Illustrator' program (F-2, SYM-390).	Later production	Lack of experience in the 'Illustrator' program
		The early idea generation worries me the most. Sometimes it is difficult to think of something original (F-3, SYM-390).	Idea generation	Difficult to think of something original

Table D.5 cont.

Class	Respondents	Direct quote(s)	Idea generation/ Later production	Keywords
ART 3350-391 (SYM-391)	1 male 0 female	Both, new ideas are not always easy to come by, and I often find myself worrying about it constantly at the beginning (and sometimes even throughout the project). Production is a concern because it takes a lot of concentration to present everything cleanly, and without any smudges. Getting everything to print out right is another big problem (M-1, SYM-391).	Both	Production is a concern. Getting everything to print out right is a big problem
ART 3351-390 (TYP-390)	2 males, 1 female	I feel I spend more time on later production. The finish is more exciting (M-1, TYP-390).	Idea generation	The finish is more exciting
		Early more than anything. I am a strong public speaker so I never worry about that - I always know once I get on the Mac I will create something visual appealing - but when sketching things first out is probably my most problematic stage (M-2, TYP-390).	Idea generation	Sketching things is my most problematic stage
		Early idea, and also presentation (F-1, TYP-390).	Both	[Response too short to code]
ART 3351-391 (TYP-391)	6 males, 6 females	I worry more about the early idea aspect. Once I get the good idea and figure out what I want, I know I can get it on the computer (M-1, TYP-391).	Idea generation	The finish is more exciting
		Actually I worry about it all a lot, but if it gets close to being due and I am not satisfied then I will worry even more (M-2, TYP-391).	Both	Worry about both a lot
		Probably with the later production. It is hard for me to actually make the finished product where its [sic] professionally constructed or designed (M-3, TYP-391).	Later production	Hard to make the finished product professionally constructed
		I worry more about the initial design idea. When painting the longest part of it is figuring out what you want to paint, the same goes for a design. A good foundation is always the toughest to find (M-4, TYP-391).	Idea generation	A good foundation is always the toughest to find

Table D.5 cont.

Class	Respondents	Direct quote(s)	Idea generation/ Later production	Keywords
		I find myself worrying more about the later production aspects because that is what the professor or client sees (M-5, TYP-391).	Later production	That is what the professor or client sees
		I am definitely one to say that "process is the most important aspect of design ". I think that if the end result is good it does not matter whether or not I spent a half an hour or 4 months on it (M-6, TYP-391).	Idea generation	process is the most important aspect of design
		The software knowledge because I had this great idea once with masking images into letters & ect. [sic]. And not with the knowledge first hand it took me twice as long to provide the image (F-1, TYP-391).	Later production	It took twice as long to produce the image without software knowledge
		I always find it more difficult to put my idea on the computer in a way that suits me best. I know a lot about the software, but the updates and technical aspects of it are somewhat difficult (F-2, TYP-391).	Later production	The updates and technical aspects of it are somewhat difficult
		The early idea generation aspects - once I come up with an idea it is simple to make it look good on the computer but if there is a no idea to start with then every other step is harder (F-3, TYP-391).	Idea generation	If there is a no idea to start with then every other step is harder
		Production freaks me out a bit. I'll have this great this idea but not the time or money to do it like I want or I'll get stumped on how my idea or if it will be clear (F-4, TYP-391).	Later production	Not the time or money to do it like I want
		Definitely the later stages. There is still a lot that I don't know about computers & they still intimidate me. I feel I have control of traditional mediums [sic] & can make them do what I want. I don't feel I've mastered the computer enough to have those same feelings (F-5, TYP-391).	Later production	Still a lot that I don't know about computers

196

Table D.5 cont.

Class	Respondents	Direct quote(s)	Idea generation/ Later production	Keywords
		It [sic] most situations I get more anxious about taking my ideas to the computer. The amount of things to do & you can use in the software & my knowledge of that causes some intimidation. It then causes me to worry about presentation, thinking I am limited as to what I could do, or knowing it could be better (F-6, TYP-391).	Later production	The amount of things to do in the software causes some intimidation
ART 3352-390 (TYI-390)	4 males, 3 females	The early is usually the hardest step. Once an idea gets formulated the rest falls into place (M-1, TYI-390).	Idea generation	Once an idea gets formulated the rest falls into place
		Early idea generation, the foundation needs to be laid out first, the rest technical & tangible in it's [sic] resolution (M-2, TYI-390).	Idea generation	The foundation needs to be laid out first
		Early idea - I try to look for originality & then shoot for creativity (M-3, TYI-390).	Idea generation	Look for originality and then creativity
		Early ideas are harder for me. Once I get a strong idea I'm comfortable w/ it's easy for me to execute it. I don't have many comp/technical problems. (M-4, TYI-390).	Idea generation	Once a strong idea is found, it is easy to execute it
		I think I panic in the beginning that I won't be able to come up w/ something (F-1, TYI-390).	Idea generation	Panic in the beginning
		The early idea generations are vital for conceptual development. Other later production aspects help to sell a design/idea, but the real talent lies within (F-2, TYI-390).	Idea generation	Early idea generations are vital for conceptual development
		idea generation! Without a clear definate [sic] concept later production & craft - no matter how remarkable - are insignificant (F-3, TYI-390).	Idea generation	Without a clear concept later production & craft are insignificant

Table D.5 cont.

Class	Respondents	Direct quote(s)	Idea generation / Later production	Keywords
ART 3352-391 (TYI-391)	1 male, 1 female	I worrie [sic] more about the idea generation because I find it to be the most challenging part of the process. Its [sic] also the part that the rest of the piece leans on to make it work (M-1, TYI-391).	Idea generation	The most challenging part of the process, the rest leans on it
		Idea generation usually gives me more problems. I 'm used to thinking traditionally and have trouble coming up with unique & unusual ideas (F-1, TYI-391).	Idea generation	Used to thinking traditionally
ART 4381-390 (PSS-390)	4 males, 10 females	Later production. The idea generation is easier, its [sic] making them into effective designs that are hard (M-1, PSS-390).	Later production	Making effective designs are hard
		I worry more about the end of the process. I always forget a little details a cap here or there, or my alignment will be off just a bit. I am great with ideas and concepts but weak when it comes to little details (M-2, PSS-390).	Later production	Weak when it comes to little details
		Later production (M-3, PSS-390).	Later production	[Response too short to code]
		For me, the early idea generation and concept development is [sic] fundamentally crucial. I am sometimes to eager to get to the computer because I am excited to implement my ideas, but one should never go to the computer looking for idea generation because you 'll find nothing but redundant layout and Photoshop files (M-4, PSS-390).	Both	Early idea generation and concept development are crucial. Never go to the computer looking for ideas because you 'll find redundant layout and Photoshop files
		I tend to worry more about the idea generation. Sometimes stressing about this leads to later procrastination (F-1, PSS-390).	Idea generation	Stressing about it leads to procrastination
		Idea generation --> then printing!! (F-2, PSS-390).	Both	[Response too short to code]

Table D.5 cont.

Direct quotes(s)	Idea generation/ Later production	Keywords
My worst fear is printing problems. I am always worrying about program version problems, paper problems, weird printer colors, font output problems ect [sic] It is so frustrating to be finished but not able to get it into a hard copy form (F-3, PSS-390).	Later production	Frustrating to be finished but not able to get it into a hard copy form
Early idea generation. If it wasn 't for Ken, the lab technician) I might have more problems w/ my printing. I wish I knew more about technical information (F-4, PSS-390).	Idea generation	I wish I knew more about technical information
I worry about early idea generation. Once I have a strong idea, the development is much easier (F-5, PSS-390).	Idea generation	Once I have a strong idea, the development is much easier
Both - it varies depending on the project, but with time it always works out in the end (F-6, PSS-390).	Both	With time it always works out in the end
The early Idea [sic] comes fast because one can get all kinds of Ideas [sic] at one time. The process of production is more time consuming. This is because one wants it to be perfect for presentation. And has to look into every detail (F-7, PSS-390).	Later production	Production is more time consuming. One wants it to be perfect for presentation
I tend to work out more about the later production because I may not be able to create the design I have visualized with a particular program. For me the paper designing (when working with layouts) tends to help me start out & organize my thoughts - all refining is done on the computer (F-8, PSS-390).	Later production	Paper designing helps me to start out and organize my thoughts, all refining is done on the computer
Early idea generation. For me it takes longer for me to develop an idea into a good one. The software makes it easier to explore new and numerous ideas (F-9, PSS-390).	Idea generation	The software makes it easier to explore new and numerous ideas
Later production (F-10, PSS-390).	Later production	[Response too short to code]

199

Table D.5 cont.

Class	Respondents	Direct quote(s)	Idea generation/Later production	Keywords
ART 3352-392 (SYS-392)	5 males, 3 females	early idea generation (M-1, SYS-392).	Idea generation	[Response too short to code]
		the later production, even though I realize the early idea generation is extremely important (M-2, SYS-392).	Later production	Idea generation is extremely important
		the later production worries me, sometimes it is a mystery to me of what to do, because I think about that first (M-3, SYS-392).	Later production	It is a mystery to me
		I worry most about quantitive [sic] process and software knowledge. I know what I want to do most of the time but I always have trouble executing (M-4, SYS-392).	Later production	Always have trouble executing
		I worry most about quantitive [sic] process and software I worry about the complete knowledge of the software (M-5, SYS-392).	Later production	Worry about the complete knowledge of the software
		More concerned w/later production ie: getting the ideas I have translated on paper - BUT if early ideas are not present then the whole process WILL LAG and production is not even a worry - idea generation is (F-1, SYS-392).	Later production	If early ideas are not present then the whole process will lag and production is not even a worry
		I think my level of stress stays fairly the same. Maybe I stress more on presentation (in craftsmanship) (F-2, SYS-392).	Later production	Stress more in craftsmanship
		I think the basic "sketch/early computer" stage is the one I worry most about because you have to have a good idea in the beginning to have any hope of getting a good result/ solution. Also, most clients/teachers do not say to totally change your idea - they beat around the bush and you never have a chance to start over (F-3, SYS-392).	Idea generation	Have to have a good idea in the beginning to have a good result/ solution. Most clients/ teachers beat around the bush

200

Table D.5 cont.

Class	Respondents	Direct quotes(s)	Idea generation/ Later production	Keywords
ART 3352-393 (SYS-393)	2 males, 0 female	The later production because my problem is putting everything together and making it come out the way I want it to (M-1, SYS-393).	Later production	My problem is putting everything together
		Neither, I like the challenge of both. but I worry more about later production. Time management, printing etc (M-2, SYS-393).	Later production	Like the challenge of both. Time management, printing, etc.
ART 4352-392 (PUB-392)	1 male, 0 female	I personally worry about the idea generation aspect. You get burned out all the time and sometimes an idea thats [sic] original is extremely dificult [sic] to come up with (M-1, PUB-392).	Idea generation	An original idea is extremely difficult to come up with

Table D.6 Data analysis of respondents for question #6

Class	Respondents	Direct quotes(s)	Keywords
ART 4356-390 (PAC-390)	1 male 0 female	Pencil/paper - jotting down ideas and working from there, computer roughs, color mock-ups, layout (M-1, PAC-390).	Pencil sketches, computer roughs later
ART 4352-390 (POR-390)	3 males 4 females	Initial project - think about a concept & then draw & design on the computer initially to come up w/ this. After this I refine my ideas & come up with a look I want to give the piece (M-1, POR-390).	Conceptual development first then work on computer later
		Sketch, brainstorm, sketch, computer, sketch, computer, etc. Doodling on my notes in other classes is great (M-2, POR-390).	Intermediary sketchings
		1. 15 - 20 thumbnails - pen & paper (usually ball point - don't like to erase) 2. 5 - 10 sketches - rough explorations of specific ideas (pencil/paper) 3. 2 - 3 roughs - explore color media (various media/paper) 4. 1 - 2 comps - print outs from computer 5. final - saved/ready to print (M-3, POR-390).	Pen & paper, explorations, computer
		1. pen & paper ... sketch inital [sic] ideas 2. research ... library, antique shop, looking around me all the time 3. pen & paper ... sketch more refined ideas, begin to consider media 4. design on computer ... scan a lot of crap, computer 5. print management ... stay involved in production TO THE END (F-1, POR-390).	Sketch ideas, research, pay attention to surrounding, refine sketches, design on computer, print
		look - and get inspired by everything and anything sketch - with pencil to get ideas computer sketch - playing with small changes to find out the best solution. refine - making changes print out - for final presentation (F-2, POR-390).	Get inspired by everything. Sketch, refine, make changes, print for final presentation

Table D.6 cont.

Class	Respondents	Direct quote(s)	Keywords
		I start w/research. I mean learning, reading, visually looking at other things. Idea generation starts there. I then sketch usually w/a pen in a book. Computer comes next. Usually trying to render the sketches. Once that stage is done you just keep on pushing it until your concept is completely done (F-3 POR-390).	Be attentive. Research, sketch, computer
		- brainstorming - sketching/research - feedback - materials/media/ * - type/image * - layout* - critique* - mock up - complete * usually repeated more than once (F-4 POR-390).	Materials/media/layout/critique are iterative in the design process Brainstorm, sketching/research, critique, mock up
ART 3350-390 (SYM-390)	7 males, 3 females	Research, pencil & paper, more defining pencil & paper. Computer roughs, computer roughs, computer final. Presentation (M-1, SYM-390).	Research, pencil & paper, computer roughs and final, presentation
		Brainstorm - Think of related words Search - Go through my collection & look for visual ideas Develope [sic] - Design a lot & narrow down to the best Render - Make a finished drawing of best few Present - Present my best, single idea (M-2, SYM-390).	Brainstorm, research, develop, render, present
		Brainstorm - list out ideas, keywords, concepts Sketch - trying to put ideas down quickly Refine sketch - developing an idea further Computer - putting design into computer Computer Refinements - modifications to design Comp - turning it in (M-3, SYM-390).	Brainstorm, sketch, refine, computer computer refinements, comp

Table D.6 cont.

Class	Respondents	Direct quote(s)	Keywords
		I start by creating small rough thumbnails and then refine the best thumbnails before put them in the computer. I will usually do several versions once on the computer and then pick one and refine it more until I am pleased with the final comp (M-4, SYM-390).	Rough thumbnails, refine thumbnails, several computer versions, pick one, refine
		I start with small pencil sketches. I then refine and enlarge the sketches. Then, I use my pen to add value ranges. If I like the design, I will attempt to put it on the computer (M-5, SYM-390).	Small pencil sketches, refine and enlarge, use pen to add value ranges, computer
		I usually begin with pencil sketches, critic those & choose a few of the best roughs. From there I will do a tighter ink version, then put on computer w/refinements on the ink drawing. Then refine the computer rough & usually finish from there (M-6, SYM-390).	Pencil sketches, critic, choose, tighter ink version, computer refinements, refine computer rough
		sketch (pencil) - to get going think up ideas by listing ideas sketch those use computer to see if it works sketch through the entire process computer for finished product (M-7, SYM-390).	Pencil sketch to get started, list ideas, sketch listed ideas, computer, more sketches, computer for finished product
		Brainstorm, write down anything & everything you can think of. Then make connections and start sketching. Pick best ideas and really work on them. Pick the best 3 and work them on comp. Then go w/the best one (F-1, SYM-390).	Brainstorm, write down ideas, make connections, start sketching, pick best three, refine and go with the best one
		Thumbnails - Research - More thumbnails w/mechanical pencil on graph paper - inked top thumbnails - xerox copier - changes w/white out and pen - scan into computer - pen tool in Illustrator (F-2, SYM-390).	Thumbnails, research, more thumbnails, ink thumbnails, copier, refine, scan into computer

Table D.6 cont.

Class	Respondents	Direct quote(s)	Keywords
ART 3350-391 (SYM-391)	1 male 0 female	1. rough sketches - pencil & paper 2. research of what things look like - library & internet 3. list of associated items/terms 4. more rough sketches - pencil & paper 5. clean sketches 6. scan into computer & work in photoshop or illustrator 7. final presentation (F-3, SYM-390). Research: knowledge of the client and their service/nature of business helps a lot in the way of idea generation Thumbnails: quickly sketched ideas to determine what might work and what won't Roughs: refining the best thumbnails, adding details, fixing placement, etc. Computer Roughs: putting the roughs on the computer and further arranging and fixing Presentation: printing and mounting (M-1, SYM-391)	Rough sketches with pencil & paper, library and Internet research, list associated terms, more sketches, refine, scan into computer, presentation Knowledge of the client helps in idea generation, thumbnails to determine what works, refine roughs, computer roughs and presentation
ART 3351-390 (TYP-390)	2 males, 1 female	Brainstorm -> use research and look at things to get quick ideas. Sketch -> quick pencil drawing I sometimes use tracing paper & x-acto knives to simplify the process Review -> look to sketches and find what works & make changes Import -> scan sketches or use digital camera Refine -> apply the computer to edit and create (M-1, TYP-390). thinking pondering sketch - paper/pen/eraser project brief examples of the idea - pc - rough on mac - thinking/pondering -> teachers [sic] feedback - final process on mac - boards/cutting/matting - presentation (M-2, TYP-390).	Using traditional media: tracing paper and x-acto knives to simplify the process. Use digital camera, scanner, and computer to edit Think, sketch, rough on computer feedback, mount for presentation

Table D.6 cont.

Class	Respondents	Direct quote(s)	Keywords
		research, thumbnails, production, presentation research - looking for criteria which will inspire your product thumbnails - working through ideas to get to a finish product production - working through a finished product presentation - ready for public (F-1, TYP-390).	Research, thumbnails, production, presentation
ART 3351-391 (TYP-391)	6 males, 6 females	1. Accept the problem and understand what the project is & requires 2. Analyze and research materials about the project. Brainstorm ideas and use groups to help generate more & also use old advertising books and internet commercials for idea generation. The start to thumbnail with a pencil then take roughs to computer. Throughout this process have others look at it to gain a different perspective than yours (M-1, TYP-391).	Accept and understand the project, analyze and research materials, brainstorm ideas, thumbnails, roughs to computer
		Pencil roughs, computer roughs, refined computer roughs, finished products. Pencil, paper, computers are all important when making a design (M-2, TYP-391).	Pencil, paper, computers are all important when making a design
		Brainstorm, develop concept, project brief, thumbnails, roughs on computer, then refine roughs until finished (M-3, TYP-391).	Brainstorm, develop concept, project brief, thumbnails, roughs on computer, refine roughs
		First I will research the company (project) and look for insparation [sic] then I will do many many sketches thumbnails. Then Two will be chosen and I will explore, expand, and refine those ideas, then they go into the computer and more exploring, expanding and refining occurs. Until finally I am truly happy with my work (M-4, TYP-391).	Research, thumbnails, explore, expand, refine ideas, then go into the computer to explore, expand, and refine.

Table D.6 cont.

Class	Respondents	Direct quote(s)	Keywords
		Brainstorming of ideas which sometime occurs during the rough sketching of ideas. Next comes choosing two or three designs that have potential and refining the rough sketches. Then I put the images into the computer, scanning them and redrawing them with Adobe Illustrator. Those are the computer roughs. Next they go through several stages of refinement before they are finally printed out neatly and mounted (M-5, TYP-391).	Brainstorming, choose two or three designs, refine rough sketches, put images into the computer, scan and redraw with Illustrator, refine computer roughs, print and mount
		1. Idea generation - Usually I go by "whatever looks best in my head" although thumbnails have contributed as well.	Go by "whatever looks best in my head," pick a direction with help from colleagues, instructors, refine 3 -5 through constructive criticism, final piece
		2. Picking a direction - Pick (with help from colleagues, instructors) from best generated ideas & begin refining it.	
		3) Refinement - I usually refine 3-5 times on any given piece through constructive criticism.	
		4. Final piece (M-6, TYP-391).	
		• accept idea • analyze - thumbnails • define • ideate • select • implement • evaluate (F-1, TYP-391).	Accept idea, analyze thumbnails, define, ideate, select, implement evaluate
		1) pencil & paper, rough sketches 2) pencil - refined sketches of my favorite 3 designs 3) pick one design, make a tight comp 4) scan design into the computer 5) redraw the design onto the computer 6) make small changes - clean it up 7) print (F-2, TYP-391).	Pencil & paper rough, refine and pick three designs, tight comp from one tight design, scan into the computer, redraw in the computer, clean up, print

207

Table D.6 cont.

Class	Respondents	Direct quote(s)	Keywords
		1. make lists of ideas & things related, 2. draw thumbnails with pen and paper until I cannot think of more, ask others (teacher's student's friend's) opinions and then do more thumbnails, 3. transfer ideas to computer, 4. refine idea creatively & technically until satisfied 5. ask opinions of others then refine if needed 6. print & mount (F-3, TYP-391).	List ideas, thumbnails, ask others, more thumbnails, transfer ideas to computer, refine creatively and technically, refine, print & mount
		idea (brainstorm) materials composition placement presentation (F-4, TYP-391).	Idea (brainstorm), materials, composition, placement, presentation
		Brainstorm - various methods of webing [sic], connecting, & generating ideas Sketching - pencil & paper making rough thumbnails Refining - sharpie marker - cleaning up pencil drawings scan - bring image into computer redraw- convert image to vectors (unless photo) edit - refine image & explore placement & color options final desicon [sic] (F-5, TYP-391).	Brainstorm, sketching, refining, scan into computer, redraw, edit, and finalize
		First, I research, see what I need to know about the client or the anticipated design. Then I brainstorm for ideas by means of words or by starting my sketches. From here I sketch until I have two or three strong ideas, then I take it to the computer. Here I work & refine the designs, print them out, work on the prints then go back to the computer and refine my changes. In the end, if I am satisfied I print of prints and look & then one more time for last min. revisions (F-6, TYP-391).	Research, brainstorm, sketch until I have two or three strong ideas, take it to computer, refine designs, print, work on prints, back to computer, refine, print out, last minute revisions

Table D.6 cont.

Class	Respondents	Direct quote(s)	Keywords
ART 3352-390 (TYI-390)	4 males, 3 females	brainstorm ideas pull a good conceptual plan work on & elaborate from that plan research ditto put the pieces together (M-1, TYI-390).	Brainstorm, plan, elaborate plan, research, put pieces together
		general discussion words/written as tangents ideas thumbnails refinement of ideas sketches refinement layout actual output critique refinement critique final product (M-2, TYI-390).	Brainstorm, thumbnails, refinements, sketches, more refinements, critique, refinements, critique, final product
		Brainstorm - word associations, lists, free write Sketch - pencil, pen, paper Comp - play around w/tools to create the idea/wanted/look I was shooting for Break down/build - tweak small problems, take away & Add to composition, deconstruct/reconstruct Mockup - watch for craftsmanship (M-3, TYI-390).	Brainstorm, sketch, comp, deconstruct/reconstruct, mockup
		1. sketches - ideas, brainmapping, listing thoughts 2. generalized outline w/image selections/sketches 3. computer process 4. critique 5. revise computer process (M-4, TYI-390).	Sketches, brainmapping, generalized outline, computer process, critique revise computer process

Table D.6 cont.

Class	Respondents	Direct quote(s)	Keywords
		sketching on the computer - tons of it. Carla calls it seriation and I never know when to stop. I use the scanner, collage, digital camera, paint, etc. whatever seems appropriate. I love to experiment, Oh - the photocopy machine is one of my favorite took after taking this class. Printing is a bit of a problem sometimes - matching screen color to the different printers in the lab (F-1, TYI-390).	Sketching, seriation, use the scanner, collage, digital camera, paint, etc. whatever seems appropriate. Printing is a problem - matching screen color to the different printers in the lab
		accept assignment brainstorm/ideate possible client brief/research (library/internet) thumbnails (pencil) @ least 30 computer roughs - not attention to perfection -- mainly just layout perfect output -- this stage takes longest presentation ideas combine present (F-2, TYI-390).	Accept assignment, brainstorm/ideate, client brief, research (library/internet) thumbnails (pencil), computer roughs, perfect output, presentation of ideas combine, present
		Get stable stance on project at hand, write down things that come to mind - relative & arbitrary, research for those ideas you might not have gotten (library, friends, internet) put elements together, ask friends again, render idea on computer, get viewer input (use only if you feel necessary), print (F-3, TYI-390).	Write down things that come to mind, research, put elements together, ask friends, render ideas on computer feedback, print
ART 3352-391 (TYI-391)	1 male, 1 female	sketches, ideas, painting drawings ect. [sic] putting them together in computer, critiquing [sic] them, making changes, again again and again (M-1, TYI-391).	Sketching, ideas, put them together in computer, critique, make changes
		1) brainstorming --> list any idea or imagery or related topics that I can think of 2) Thumbnails --> begin to sketch out layouts & begin to choose imagery & fonts	Brainstorm, thumbnails, computer roughs, refine, final presentation

Table D.6 cont.

Class	Respondents	Direct quote(s)	Keywords
		3) Computer roughs --> convert thumnail [sic] ideas to computer 4) Design roughs --> refine roughs 5) Final Presentation --> Mount final presentations on boards (F-1, TYI-391).	
ART 4381-390 (PSS-390)	4 males, 10 females	- Usually sketches, research & brainstorming. - sketch books - first computer roughs & critique, computer ILL & Photoshop - then just refining & revamping ideas (M-1, PSS-390).	Sketches, research, brainstorming, computer roughs, critique, refining, revamping
		The problem Certify what conclusion you kneed [sic] to satisfy Brain storm - Free association - Alphabet - Lists Concept Thumbs Roughs Computer (M-2, PSS-390).	Identify the problem, brainstorm, free association, concept development, thumbnails, roughs, computer layout
		Research, research, research, design loyot [sic], font search, image search, outside review, revise, outside review, revise, presentation (M-3, PSS-390). 1. Research - a designer must know their client/topic. Ignorant design is useless design 2. Idea generation/thumbnails - Concept is good. Here, along with generating sketches, it is imperative to create reason for design 3. Refinement - process of retooling and eliminating ideas and finding the one that is the best 4. Implementation - last & final is going to the computer and making the design tangible 5. Refinement - critiquing design - making it free of small inconsistencies (M-4, PSS-390).	Research, design layout, font & image search, outside review, revise, presentation Research, a designer must know their client/topic. Idea generation/thumbnails, create a reason for design. Refinement, process of retooling and eliminating ideas and finding the one that is the best. Implementation, use computer to make the design tangible. Refinement, critiquing design making it free of small inconsistencies

Table D.6 cont.

Class	Respondents	Direct quote(s)	Keywords
		1. get assignment/project 2. collect information/research 3. thumbnail sketches 4. begin computer work 5. refine & critique (F-1, PSS-390).	Assignment/project, research, thumbnail sketches, begin computer work, refine & critique
		Research & brainstorming --> sketching w/pencil & paper --> translating to computer (F-2, PSS-390). 1. research 2. concept generation 3. thumbs 4. computer roughs 5. computer refinements 6. refine 7. refine (F-3 PSS-390).	Research, brainstorm, sketch, translate to the computer research, concept generation, thumbnails, computer roughs and refinements
		concept (creative workplan), thumbnails (LOTS!), design on computer, import any scanned images, print (F-4 PSS-390).	Concept, thumbnails, design on the computer, import any scanned images, print
		1. Research - internet, library 2. conceptual work plan 3. lots of thumbnails (hand) 4. computer roughs 5. mock ups 6. final (F-5 PSS-390).	Research, conceptual work plan, lots of thumbnails by hand, computer roughs, mock ups, final
		1. idea generation: mind map, word association 2. thumbs (hand) 3. thumbs & layout (computer) 4. refine 5. critique 6. due & mount (F-6 PSS-390).	Idea generation using mind map, word association, thumbnails (by hand), thumbnails and layout (in computer), refine, critique, mount for presentation

Table D.6 cont.

Class	Respondents	Direct quote(s)	Keywords
		Research, coming up with a concept, thumbnails of concept, refind [sic] thumbnails, computer to size roughs of concept, Imagery research, coming up w. body copy or deciding what will be used, put in imagery and body copy into computer. Several refinements of layouts, print critique work, and decide on final project, print, mount and present (F-7, PSS-390).	Research, coming up with a concept, thumbnails of concept, refine thumbnails, computer to size roughs of concept, imagery research, body copy, put imagery and body copy into computer, refinement, print, mount and present
		Thumbnails - pen & paper, many idea generations, lists of related words, ideas, formulation of a concept & translation to thumbnails. For logos, thumbnails tend to last much longer than w/layout design. Mock-ups- computer, Illustrator, Photoshop, Quark, find images to match thumbnail ideas, translate copy & headlines into computer layouts & begin more exploration leading to finalization of design (F-8, PSS-390).	Thumbnails, many idea generations, list of related words, ideas, formulation of a concept & translation to thumbnails. Mock-ups, Illustrator, Photoshop, Quark. Find images to match thumbnail ideas, translate copy & headlines into computer layouts & begin more exploration leading to finalization of design
		That's hard because I go by the requirements of the class. When the projects are faster I find myself refering [sic] back to the pencil & paper for association list (F-9, PSS-390).	When the projects faster, refer to pencil & paper for association lists
		Sketching on paper, translate to computer, modify on computer (F-10, PSS-390).	Sketching on paper, translate to computer, modify on computer
ART 3352-392 (SYS-392)	5 males, 3 females	sketching, revising, color roughs (computer roughs), revising and producing a final comp (M-1, SYS-392).	sketching, revising, color computer roughs, revising and producing a final comp
		scribble on paper then attempt to derive meaning from it (M-2, SYS-392).	Scribble and derive meaning from it
		Usually, however the teacher or instructor make us do it. We are in the process of learned this stuff (M-3, SYS-392).	In the process of learning
		Thumbnails, Printouts and more Printouts (M-4, SYS-392).	Thumbnails and printouts
		Research material (loads of information) Thumbnails to formulate ideas Sketches to put your ideas together to better form your design	Research, thumbnails, sketches, computer generated copies, computer revisions, finalize

213

Table D.6 cont.

Class	Respondents	Direct quote(s)	Keywords
		Computer generated copies for a better visual of design More computer revisions to give you different variations of your design Final attributes to your design (M-5, SYS-392). Brainstorming - Bouncing ideas off other people References (Print design annuals are good) Right programs - which software is best to use (F-1, SYS-392).	Brainstorming, bounce ideas off people, references, select the right computer programs
		Its [sic] different for each project. Basically starts with ideas, roughs, select, refine, refine, refine (F-2, SYS-392). • Conceptualization - thinking of elements/images I want to use then I will lay them out • Sketches - a few w/pencil just to get them down so I don't forget • non-computer creating/finding - produce/find textures/images I want to use • computer - scan thing in –> create –> print –> revise (F-3, SYS-392).	Basically starts with ideas, roughs, select, refine, refine, refine Conceptualization, sketches, non-computer creating/finding, computer to scan, print, revise
ART 3352-393 (SYS-393)	2 males, 0 female	Brainstorm on the project such as getting references Project Brief to find out who the client or project is about Sketches to get an idea or concept Computer Roughs Putting it together (M-1, SYS-393) 1. Sketch - brainstorming 2. Computer roughs 3. Put it together 4. look at it as a whole and re-evaluate my choice, Show Someone I Trust! 5. Make changes 6. Turn in (M-2, SYS-393)	Brainstorm, project brief, sketches, computer rough, putting it together Sketch, brainstorm, computer roughs, show someone trusted, make changes, turn in

Table D.6 cont.

Class	Respondents	Direct quote(s)	Keywords
ART 4352-392 (PUB-392)	1 male, 0 female	Thumbnails, research, thumbnails, research, scan or illustrate, work, print, work, print, ... (M-1, PUB-392).	Thumbnails, research, thumbnails, research, scan or illustrate, work, print, work, and print

Table D.7 Data analysis of respondents for question #7

Class	Respondents	Direct quote(s)	Maximizing/ Minimizing	Keywords
ART 4356-390 (PAC-390)	1 male 0 female	It makes the work look cleaner and more professional. Using a computer to do roughs hinders the ability to draw ideas (M-1, PAC-390).	Minimize	Makes the work look professional
ART 4352-390 (POR-390)	3 males 4 females	Maximizing if you use it right (M-1, POR-390).	Maximize	If used correctly
		The computer definitely facilitates my design but I think too many rely on it as an exclusive method and it becomes a crutch that limits the possibilities (M-2, POR-390).	Maximize	Facilitates design
		Once past the "exploration" phase - the computer enhances the "final" stages in that you can change colors, papers, and composition w/copy (M-3, POR-390).	Maximize	"exploration" phase before the "final" stage with computer
		Impinding [sic]. already answered this question (F-1, POR-390).	Minimize	
		Minimizing - we seem to jump to computer too soon & it henders [sic] design (F-2, POR-390).	Minimize	Use computer too soon
		I think that computer technology can minimize your creativity if you do not realize its powers. Cons can be that you do not fully take advantage of your idea generation w/ the pen and paper to fully create your concept before jumping on the computer (F-3, POR-390).	Minimize	Take advantage of idea generation to fully create concepts before using a computer
		Like #4 - can do both depending on what you are trying to acomplish [sic] - since I am a graphic designer it is my tool - & it is my job/goal like any medium is to make the medium I choose inhance [sic] my art (F-4, POR-390).	Both	The computer is a tool to enhance art creations
ART 3350-390 (SYM-390)	7 males, 3 females	Maximizing, the colors, moving and tools are greatly appreciated. The many things it allows me to do gets my creativity flowing (M-1, SYM-390).	Maximize	Tools are greatly appreciated
		I haven't played a major role on the kind of work I have done in the last year, but I believe it would help more than not (M-2, SYM-390).	Maximize	It would help more than not

Table D.7 cont.

Class	Respondents	Direct quote(s)	Maximizing/ Minimizing	Keywords
		I think the computer helps. Pros - helps generate new ideas, easily reprinted, speed of final design and modifications. Cons - awareness of all computer can do, getting to know programs (M-3, SYM-390).	Maximize	Pros and cons
		I don't think that the computer henders [sic] my creativity. I use it as a tool for refinement (M-4, SYM-390).	Maximize	Use it as a tool for refinement
		For me, the computer should never be part of the creativity. It helps to clean things up and make drawings look more professional, nothing more (M-5, SYM-390).	Minimize	Computer should never be part of creativity
		It helps maximize time used on projects, as well as help out the designer in the process if he/she aren't the best at using their hands. It also helps us to do things that you just can't do anywhere else but on the computer (M-6, SYM-390).	Maximize	Help out the designer in the process
		It enhances it I guess because it is just another tool. The pencil & paper will never be replaced by the computer. But to depend totally on the computer is impending [sic] creativity (M-7, SYM-390).	Maximize	Pencil & paper will never be replaced by the computer
		Maximizing (F-1, SYM-390).	Maximize	[Response too short to code]
		Takes that hard done feel away from the piece, minimizing - people jump right to the computer when sketching numerous ideas usually derives the best solution (F-2, SYM-390).	Minimize	People jump right to the computer when sketching
		It is maximizing, because you can do so much more with it, but one also doesn't have to use it. Pros: clean images, various tools, easy to experiment. Cons: not so sure now (F-3, SYM-390).	Maximize	Clean images, various tools, easy to experiment
ART 3350-391 (SYM-391)	1 male 0 female	Pros: allows for cleaner out-put and quicker adjustments. Cons: If you jump onto the computer too soon, you tend to generate fewer ideas, and therefore you may miss a solution to the problem that would work better (M-1, SYM-391)	Both	Cleaner out-put and adjustments. Might miss a solution

217

Table D.7 cont.

Class	Respondents	Direct quote(s)	Maximizing/ Minimizing	Keywords
ART 3351-390 (TYP-390)	2 males, 1 female	I feel it maximizes right now some things come to me on the computer that I haven't thought of before (M-1, TYP-390).	Maximize	Things come to me on the computer
		Mac = enhancing and maximizing. pros = makes me work harder con = printing stuff out is a damn hassel [sic] (M-2, TYP-390).	Both	Computer makes me work harder, difficulty in printing
		Computer technology maximizes my work because I can do things on the computer that can not be done by hand (F-1, TYP-390).	Maximize	Can do things that can not be done by hand
ART 3351-391 (TYP-391)	6 males, 6 females	I think it is definitely maximizing my creativity. It is helping me with manipulation, idea generation, and craftsmanship. I have great craftsmanship on a computer because I can use it greatly, and w/out it I would definitely suffer as a designer (M-1, TYP-391).	Maximize	Helping with manipulation, idea generation, and craftsmanship
		Computers limit you because they make it harder to destigush [sic] bad design from good design. Computers help because they make good designs cleaner and more professional (M-2, TYP-391).	Minimize	Harder to distinguish bad design from good design
		I think it maximizes my creativity for the fact that it helps you broaden your ideas with colors, shape, and live (M-3, TYP-391).	Maximize	Broaden your ideas with colors, shape, and live
		A. pro is that designs are very clean and sharp. It takes a lot less time to do something on the computer. B. con is that I feel that people are relying less and less on artistic and drawing skills. With computer we're getting closer for any John Doe to be able to do what we do (M-4, TYP-391).	Both	Takes a lot less time to do something on the computer. Getting closer for any John Doe to do what we do
		I believe that a computer helps to maximize my creativity because of the ability to change things quickly and the neatness of the final product. A con might be when the computer freezes or the printer won't work (M-5, TYP-391).	Maximize	The ability to change things quickly and the neatness of the final product

Table D.7 cont.

Class	Respondents	Direct quote(s)	Maximizing/ Minimizing	Keywords
		Pros - instant type, instant visuals, many possibilities of the manipulation of type & imagery. Excellent for layouts. Cons - can become a "crutch" for many people. Although helpful with imagery still cannot replace ALL ASPECTS of handmade imagery (M-6, TYP-391).	Both	Instant type, visuals, manipulation of type & imagery. Cannot replace all aspects of handmade imagery
		Yes, b/c finding a certain color, or having a certain idea - can be minimized by the computer. For some reason a lot of graphic works come out looking the same or a lot alike (F-1, TYP-391).	Minimize	A lot of graphics come out looking a lot alike
		I think the computer is maximizing my creativity. It allows quick change of color and shape. The world is all computer-based, current and future knowledge is necessary. Tools are hard sometimes, but gets easier w/practice (F-2, TYP-391).	Maximize	Allows quick change of color and shape.
		Maximizing - I have a very rough drawing style and tend to prefer very simple clean designs so that the computer helps me refine my hand drawn designs. Sometimes though there are computer problems that hold me back whether it is lack of knowledge or computer gliches [sic] (F-3, TYP-391).	Maximize	The computer helps to refine hand drawn designs
		The computer is good in that it allow you to see your work before you begin, ex-sculpture [sic]. But it takes you away from your craft on the other hand (F-4, TYP-391).	Maximize	Allow you to see your work before you begin
		Both. At first I would say it was hindering my creativity because I had limited knowledge of how to use many programs. Now I feel it is helping me (F-5, TYP-391).	Both	Had limited knowledge of how to use many programs

Table D.7 cont.

Class	Respondents	Direct quote(s)	Maximizing/ Minimizing	Keywords
		I think the computer gives a [sic] incredible look to designs and allows freedom for you to do things you wouldn't acomplish [sic] otherwise, but it also gives limitation, it's really hard to keep up with the software or even the point that someone's who's [sic] idea isn't as strong as yours can make theirs work through the program when your idea & sketch loose in the comp design (F-6, TYP-391).	Both	Gives incredible look to designs, freedom to do things. Hard to keep up with the software or compete without someone with strong program knowledge
ART 3352-390 (TYI-390)	4 males, 3 females	Well the computer seems to maximize my creativity, but the comp should not be the only tool. Computers are helpful in making small changes & fine tuning work. They allow the designer to work in a virtual field (M-1, TYI-390).	Maximize	Computers are helpful in making small changes & fine tuning work. Allows the designer to work in a virtual field
		Pro's Con's Efficient Limiting to capability of CPU Professional look unreliable Easy reproduction, output too technical (M-2, TYI-390).	Both	Efficient, professional look, easy reproduction, limiting to capability of central processing unit (CPU), unreliable, too technical
		Maximizing - fast, convenient, - You can still incorporate things you used/made w/o a computer and you can build onto them --> simplify or enhance variaty [sic] (M-3, TYI-390).	Maximize	Fast, convenient
		Both, as a web designer it helps me review new sites. Therefore, I can generate/analyze the competitors. On my personal work it hinders me until I know what I'm doing. I feel more confident wasting time sketching than I do playing w/ideas on the comp (M-4, TYI-390).	Both	Analyze competitors. Feel more confident wasting time sketching than playing with ideas on the computer
		Maximizing w/out a doubt, pros - faster, maybe for some the [sic] don't add extras such as their own designs, use real brushes etc. but NOT me (F-1, TYI-390).	Both	Faster

220

Table D.7 cont.

	Respondents	Direct quote(s)	Maximizing/ Minimizing	Keywords
		I like to have a nice blend of hand/computer skills. The computer helps to maximize my creativity with its infinite options, but a major thing to note is: never EVER overdesign. This is a con to the computer -- there are almost too many options (F-2, TYI-390).	Maximize	Infinite options, there are almost too many options
		Both, while the computer allows for quick, easy explorations & a broader range of ideas, it makes it easier for the designer just to use a few filters & crazy type & say they're done (F-3, TYI-390).	Maximize	The computer allows for quick, easy explorations & a broader range of ideas
ART 3352-391 (TYI-391)	1 male, 1 female	I see the computer mostly as a tool. I very seldom get inspired by the computer but it does make the process much quicker in the end changes are easier. I think it can hinder creativity in it's [sic] excessability [sic]. People don't have the time and won't take the time if they do have to (M-1, TYI-391).	Minimize	Infinite options, there are almost too many options
		Using the computer definitely speeds up the whole process. I don't think that physical work (collage, sketch, etc) can be totally abandoned. A combination of the two must be used, I think (F-1, TYI-391).	Maximize	Using the computer speeds up the whole process. Physical work can't be totally abandoned
ART 4381-390 (PSS-390)	4 males, 10 females	Maximizing, I am not able to draw as well as I see things in my head. The computer allows me to "cheat" & cover up my lack of drawing skills (M-1, PSS-390).	Maximize	The computer allows me to "cheat" and to cover up any lack of drawing skills
		Maximizing By allowing for quick exploration of type & layout (M-2, PSS-390).	Maximize	By allowing for quick exploration of type & layout
		Layout it helps Ideals and creativity - neutral Diminishes the art for hand design feal [sic] (M-3, PSS-390).	Both	Diminishes hand design

221

Table D.7 cont.

Class	Respondents	Direct quote(s)	Maximizing/ Minimizing	Keywords
		In many ways, using computers can be extremely debilitating to designers, especially younger ones because it will totally direct their design, but with proper preparation and research before sitting down at the computer. They can do nothing but amplify and allow for more idea generation very quickly - as long as one doesn't depend on computers for implementation (M-4, PSS-390).	Minimize	Computers can be extremely debilitating to designers, it will totally direct their design. They do nothing but amplify and allow for more idea generation very quickly
		Pros: speed, overall cleanliness Cons: laziness (F-1, PSS-390).	Both	Speed, cleanliness, and laziness
		Maximizing --> neat. clean fast to make changes (F-2, PSS-390).	Maximize	Neat, clean, fast to make changes
		I think computers allow you to do things you could never do with out them. They def. enhance design, I think they can become a con if you jump straight to the comp. (F-3, PSS-390).	Maximize	Definitely enhance design
		Maximizing! It really helps to quickly change an idea by the push of a button. Sometimes computer work takes longer than you think though (F-4, PSS-390).	Maximize	Quickly change an idea by the push of a button
		I can start on the computer because the blank screen is daunting. However, once I have decided on a concept, sketched it out on paper, the computer then enhances my creativity. I get more detailed ideas once I'm using the computer (F-5, PSS-390).	Maximize	The blank screen is daunting. Once sketched out on paper, the computer then enhances my creativity
		Neither one - I don't use any "special new features" when designing. I try to rely on type & design characteristics because anyone can use filters etc. and create something that has been seen before (F-6, PSS-390).	Both	Anyone can use filters etc. to create something that has been seen before
		Computer only proves the speed of the production. In some instances it does improve creativity by the happy mistakes (F-7, PSS-390).	Both	It does improve creativity by the happy mistakes

222

Table D.7 cont.

Class	Respondents	Direct quote(s)	Maximizing/ Minimizing	Keywords
		I think the computer aides because it is easier to visualize the design in a more final appearance throughout the process enabling the designer to see design flaws & successes easier. It is also easier to see how alterations will affect the design (F-8, PSS-390).	Maximize	Easier to visualize the design in a more final appearance throughout the process, can see design flaws and successes
		I think slowly my creativity is diminishing. Things off the computer start to all look the same. Nothing is new any more, at least if you are drawing it, it has a diff. feel (F-9, PSS-390).	Minimize	Things off the computer start to all look the same. Nothing is new anymore
		Maximizing (F-10, PSS-390).	Maximize	[Response too short to code]
ART 3352-392 (SYS-392)	5 males, 3 females	Maximizing as long as one remembers the computer is only a tool and cannot design for you (M-1, SYS-392).	Maximize	The computer is only a tool and cannot design for you
		Enhancing - pencil and paper is good for quick idea generation, but the computer allows me to carry to an extent I couldn't do without (M-2, SYS-392).	Maximize	The computer allows me to carry to an extent I couldn't do without
		Maximizing technology can minimize your creativity if you don't know how to use it (M-3, SYS-392).	Maximize	Technology can minimize your creativity if you don't know how to use it
		The computer has the ability to maximize my work but since there is always new software coming out it is hard to keep up with (M-4, SYS-392).	Maximize	Always new software coming out it is hard to keep up
		The computer helps to expand your ideas. A student can use sketches along w/the computer when manipulating work on the computer (M-5, SYS-392).	Maximize	Can use sketches along with the computer when manipulating work on the computer
		Its [sic] just there as a tool - I sometimes choose to use it and often times I don't (F-1, SYS-392).	Minimize	Just there as a tool

223

Table D.7 cont.

Respondents	Direct quote(s)	Maximizing/ Minimizing	Keywords
	Pros - work is faster, easier Cons - work is faster, keeping up w/technology (F-2, SYS-392).	Both	Work is faster, keeping up with technology
	I think the computer maximizes my creativity because so many things happen there that cannot happen w/other mediums [sic] - things I didn't even think of. I have already been trained in other mediums [sic] so I know their limits - I can then combine these medium [sic] w/the computer to explore my options more creatively (F-3, SYS-392).	Maximize	Many things happen that cannot with other media. Can then combine these media with the computer to explore creatively
ART 3352-393 (SYS-393)	2 males, 0 female	I definitely think it maximizes my creativity. I like the computer because it explores areas I might not have thought of (M-1, SYS-393).	Maximize	It explores areas that I might not have thought of
	Depends on the designer, I think every good designer knows the importance of art, and texture, and actual hands on feel that you can't get w/a computer, but good designer use both to push design (M-2, SYS-393).	Both	A good designer uses both to push design
ART 4352-392 (PUB-392)	1 male, 0 female	I believe it is maximizing, the problem is that in a town like Lubbock it is hard to find business [sic] including Tech that has updated software, its [sic] great when its [sic] available, but its [sic] not unless you have 10,000 grand to spend for your home equipment (M-1, PUB-392).	Maximize	It is hard to find businesses with updated software or spend a lot of money for home equipment

224

Table D.8 Data analysis of respondents for question #8

Class	Respondents	Direct quote(s)	Match/ Not matching	Keywords
ART 4356-390 (PAC-390)	1 male 0 female	No because it is a process to get the best ideas to coincide together (M-1, PAC-390).	Not matching	A process
ART 4352-390 (POR-390)	3 males 4 females	I think the progress all the way through comes to a conclusion & is always better in the end (M-1, POR-390).	Match	Progress Conclusion
		I usually find that my initial ideas work the best, but I allow myself to consider everything, which has inspired me at times (M-2, POR-390).	Not matching	Initial ideas work the best
		Now that I'm more experienced, almost exactly (M-3, POR-390).	Match	Experienced
		Sometimes yes, sometimes no. Often an idea continues to evolve as you are forced to address specific issues and concerns (F-1, POR-390).	Depends	Ideas continue to evolve. Forced to address issues
		Never - I always change things during my process - I am always experiencing new things (F-2, POR-390).	Not matching	Always experience new things
		Yes, the concept usually matches, but almost never do the sketches match identically. The concept has just been pushed farther on the computer (F-3, POR-390).	Match	Concept usually matches
		Usually not - the developement [sic] involved in the process may come out w/the hint of initial idea/design - but it has been altered considerably to develope [sic] the design (F-4, POR-390).	Not matching	Initial idea is altered considerably
ART 3350-390 (SYM-390)	7 males, 3 females	With a few changes here and there the idea is generally the same (M-1, SYM-390).	Match	Idea is generally the same
		They are similar, just more developed (M-2, SYM-390).	Match	Just more developed
		Usually my final solution resembles my sketches, unless an idea is sparked while applying sketches to computer (M-3, SYM-390).	Match	Unless an idea is sparked

Table D.8 cont.

Class	Respondents	Direct quote(s)	Match/ Not matching	Keywords
		The end results look close to the original but I usually have to change small things to get the look I want (M-4, SYM-390).	Match	Look close to the original
		If I am successful, the final images will not look much different from what I have drawn (M-5, SYM-390).	Depends	If successful, final images should match
		Only if I get it perfect from the start does my final solution match my initial sketch. That rarely happens (M-6, SYM-390).	Depends	Only if it is done right from the start
		Well there is only so much you change about a good idea. To keep changing usually makes it more complex and that's not good for me. I change things and come up with a lot of ideas, but I don't continually change those ideas (M-7, SYM-390).	Match	There is only so much in changing a good idea
		Not always (F-1, SYM-390).	Depends	[Response too short to code]
		It changes quite dramatically - It usually starts as a fairly complicated sketch and is simplified on or by the computer creation (F-2, SYM-390).	Not matching	Starts as a complicated sketch and becomes simplified on the computer
		They usually do match pretty well. The final is tweaked and clean of course (F-3, SYM-390).	Match	The final is tweaked and clean
ART 3350-391 (SYM-391)	1 male	It varies from project to project. My initial drawings are not usually very details, I use them to jot down ideas so that I don't forget them later. Sometimes refinements completely change the original ideas, but not always (M-1, SYM-391).	Depends	Use initial drawings to jot down ideas
ART 3351-390 (TYP-390)	2 males, 1 female	For the most part they are strikingly similar (M-1, TYP-390).	Match	For the most part
		Sometimes - depends if I like a sketch or not. If I do I will go with it. If not I will just go solo with the computer (M-2, TYP-390).	Depends	Dependent on the sketch
		Sometimes my drawn elements are better than my finish product (F-1, TYP-390).	Not matching	Drawn elements are better

Table D.8 cont.

	Respondents	Direct quote(s)	Match/ Not matching	Keywords
ART 3351-391 (TYP-391)	6 males, 6 females	The sketches show very rough examples and just hints to the final design. I end up coming up or/better work than my sketches because it's easier to manipulate on the computer and duplicate your work (M-1, TYP-391)	Not matching	Show very rough examples and just hints to the final design
		Yes, except that they are improved because I have worked out the problems of the design (M-2, TYP-391).	Matching	Worked out the problems
		Most of the time my end result very much represents my concept. I try to stay as close to the sketches as I can (M-3, TYP-391).	Matching	Try to stay as close to the sketches
		It depends, half of the time my finished result will look almost identical to my first drawings, sometimes they will change a little but still retain most of the same forms, but sometimes the initial idea and the finished project looking nothing alike and all they share was an idea (M-4, TYP-391).	Depends	Sometimes the initial idea and the finished project looking nothing alike and all they share was an idea
		Usually my end result resembles my initial idea fairly well. Most of my ideas I have not had to make drastic changes to for a strong final product (M-5, TYP-391).	Matching	I have not had to make drastic changes
		I would say that a final piece matches original concepts 75%. The rest comes in the refinement where tweaks are made, however there have [sic] been a few times where I think a rough has been superior visually or by layout (M-6, TYP-391).	Matching	There have been a few times where I think a rough has been superior visually or by layout
		No, b/c your original idea is a starting point & you do not take in to factor the other implementations that are in effect. Placement of type, color choice, ect ... [sic] (F-1, TYP-391).	Not matching	Original idea is a starting point
		My sketches are rough and usually get more conceptual as they progress (F-2, TYP-391).	Not matching	Sketches are rough and usually get more conceptual

Table D.8 cont.

Class	Respondents	Direct quote(s)	Match/Not matching	Keywords
		Not usually - usually my original sketches evolve into completely different sketches (once I get the most obvious solutions out of the way). My final sketches usually look very similar to the computer drawings (F-3, TYP-391).	Not matching	Original sketches evolve into completely different sketches
		No the design is constantly changing. From beginning to end even after I have finished I see alternatives. But it is usually done (F-4, TYP-391).	Not matching	Design is constantly changing
		Actually, usually not. Lately I've ended up w/much different results on the computer than my original sketches. My sketches are free-form & my computer images are much more controled [sic] (F-5, TYP-391).	Not matching	Different results on the computer than original sketches
		A lot of the time my ideas will all in all resemble their original sketch but there are always revisions & refinements that cause it to stray from the original (F-6, TYP-391).	Match	There are always revisions and refinements
ART 3352-390 (TYI-390)	4 males, 3 females	Yes the link is there, but they should not look exactly like the original sketches because w/more research the idea should be refined (M-1, TYI-390).	Match	Because with more research the idea should be refined
		Most of the time, but not a too direct translation if they don't I'm not disappoint [sic] because my sketches were just starting points, open to tangents in the process (M-2, TYI-390).	Match	Sketches were just starting points, open to tangents in the process
		No - things happen along the whole process - parts are removed, things are added - sometimes ideas are remodeled. There is so much on the comp that the original idea can develope [sic] far more than it would have w/o a computer (M-3, TYI-390).	Not matching	Parts are removed, things are added, sometimes ideas are remodeled
		Mostly it does. In well planned areas like logo design the output matches the initial idea. (M-4, TYI-390).	Match	Logo design matches the initial idea

Table D.8 cont.

Class	Respondents	Direct quote(s)	Match/ Not matching	Keywords
		It seems to work very systematically, one sketch builds off the other. It is so interesting to look back at the process notebook Carla makes up keep (F-1, TYI-390).	Not matching	It works very systematically, one sketch builds off the other
		Usually my initial sketches are vague and only hint to a concept. my initial concept usually does not match the end result because there is such an evolution during the different stages between (F-2, TYI-390).	Not matching	Initial sketches are vague and only hint to a concept. There is such an evolution during the different stages
		Concept usually remains the same, but often the layout will be altered. Through exploration you can often find a better solution (F-3, TYI-390).	Match	Concept usually remains the same. Through exploration you can find a better solution
ART 3352-391 (TYI-391)	1 male, 1 female	My concepts stay basically the same but grow through out the process with the computer as part of the process (M-1, TYI-391).	Match	Grow through out the process with the computer as part of the process
		The final product usually is related to my initial idea in the same way. Of course, the idea undergoes changes along the way (F-1, TYI-391).	Match	The final product usually is related to my initial idea. The idea undergoes changes along the way
ART 4381-390 (PSS-390)	4 males, 10 females	No. My projects usually take a huge turn before the end (M-1, PSS-390).	Not matching	Projects usually take a huge turn
		I find that I tend to have a little bit of a shift in my idea but the overall concept stays the same (M-2, PSS-390).	Match	Overall concept stays the same
		Final is always a serious more [sic] of the original idea, but the original idea is the seed (M-3, PSS-390).	Not matching	The original idea is the seed
		Overall, they tend to turn out nicely in relation to my sketches. I find improvement and generally in the end, better design. Now, but in the past, even with clean sketches and paper research, heavy dependency on the computer to help generate my design and a tendency to forget the power of real design (or design done hand) would tend to produce results far below the quality expressed in my thumbnails (M-4, PSS-390).	Match	Heavy dependency on the computer to help generate design tend to produce results far below the quality expressed in my thumbnails

229

Table D.8 cont.

Respondents	Direct quote(s)	Match/ Not matching	Keywords
	Generally things (concepts) don't change often. But type and layout often get modified based on critiques (F-1, PSS-390).	Match	Type and layout often get modified based on critiques
	You can definitely see some relation (F-2, PSS-390)	Match	Can see some relation
	My final concept usually matches the initial sketches. It doesn't visually look like the sketches, but the general idea is the same (F-3, PSS-390).	Match	Doesn't visually look like the sketches, but the general idea is the same
	My final solution never matches my initial sketches. All initial sketches are done by hand, but when I go to the computer, they always change (F-4, PSS-390).	Not matching	All initial sketches are done by hand, but when I go to the computer, they always change
	The final looks nothing like the 1st couple ideas - I have to get all the bad stuff out of my head before I can get to the good stuff. Once I develop a concept, those stronger thumbs are more closely related to the final (F-5, PSS-390).	Not matching	Once I develop a concept, those stronger thumbs are more closely related to the final
	Not always. As the design process proceeds, new ideas are generated changing the original concept (F-6, PSS-390).	Not matching	New ideas are generated changing the original concept
	Yes my final solution does match my initial idea, but improved (F-7, PSS-390).	Match	My final solution does match my initial idea, but improved
	Quite often my initial sketches relate distinctly to the final design. Since I formulate my concept before paper thumbnails & refine as I continue to sketch, my ideas are usually fairly solid before starting to translate onto the computer (F-8, PSS-390).	Match	My ideas are usually fairly solid before starting to translate onto the computer
	It always changes. I think it would also if I did pencil (F-9, PSS-390).	Not matching	Always changes
	No, they don't always match up. I think of new ways to improve as I go along (F-10, PSS-390).	Not matching	Always think of new ways to improve

230

Table D.8 cont.

	Respondents	Direct quote(s)	Match/ Not matching	Keywords
ART 3352-392 (SYS-392)	5 males, 3 females	No, it changes throughout the course, as new ideas are generated, the sketches give you a good over all direction (M-1, SYS-392).	Not matching	It changes throughout the course, as new ideas are generated
		It usually matches at several ideas, but not one in particular (M-2, SYS-392).	Match	It usually matches at several ideas
		No, my final product is always more refine. you can picture an image is [sic] your head but it is not perfect (M-3, SYS-392).	Not matching	My final product is always more refine
		It has similarities but I wouldn't say that it matches. After critiques there are so many new ideas that I have (M-4, SYS-392).	Not matching	It has similarities
		My final work has none relation to my initial ideas, but as you mark through the processes your discover ideas that will work more efficiently and makes for a better design (M-5, SYS-392).	Not matching	Discover ideas that will work more efficiently
		It depends on the project (F-1, SYS-392).	Depends	It depends on the project
		No, my final results always differ from the initial ideas. Very different (F-2, SYS-392).	Not matching	Always differ
		Depending on what I'm doing, my initial concept rarely matches the end result exactly. From sketches to computer my ideas grow, concepts strengthen, and at the end I have a much better solution that what I started with (F-3, SYS-392).	Not matching	Ideas grow, concepts strengthen, and at the end, a much better solution
ART 3352-393 (SYS-393)	2 males, 0 female	Most of the time my final result relates to one of my sketches but it is different or is stylized (M-1, SYS-393).	Match	The final result relates to one of the sketches
		Usually pretty close (conceptually), but the end results always surprise me (M-2, SYS-393).	Match	The end result always surprises me
ART 4352-392 (PUB-392)	1 male, 0 female	Sometimes they do but for the most part they constantly change throughout the creative process (M-1, PUB-392).	Not matching	For the most part they constantly change throughout the creative process

231

Table D.9 Data analysis of respondents for question #9

Class	Respondents	Direct quote(s)	Influential factors
ART 4356-390 (PAC-390)	1 male 0 female	Bits and pieces of each sketch combined w/what look good together and what doesn't (M-1, PAC-390).	Bits and pieces of sketches
ART 4352-390 (POR-390)	3 males 4 females	[Respondent draws an arrow to suggest his intention of repeating the same answer in #8] (M-1, POR-390).	
		Looking through design annuals and then media (M-2, POR-390).	Reference books and media
		The only thing that MIGHT influence a change in mass production limitations (M-3, POR-390).	Production limitations
		[Respondent draws an arrow to suggest his intention of repeating the same answer in #8] (F-1, POR-390).	
		Daily experiences - Everything in this world - I just keep my eyes open (F-2, POR-390).	Daily experiences
		The way that the type usually works. Changes because my sketches of type usually work differently than the actual layout on the computer (F-3, POR-390).	Sketches of type work differently on the computer
		Process, ideas from others, influence other prof. designers, working progress, me deciding to to change - seeing what works better (F-4, POR-390).	Seeing what works better, influenced by professors, working progress
ART 3350-390 (SYM-390)	7 males, 3 females	Colors, pen tool curves, gradients, copy & paste and sometimes filters (M-1, SYM-390).	Influenced by computer tools and filters
		[Left blank] (M-2, SYM-390).	[No responses to code]
		Most of the time accidents on a program change my idea (M-3, SYM-390).	Accidents on a program can change an idea
		Suggestions for my classmates and my profesor usually help me find the best comps (M-4, SYM-390).	Peers and professors
		The factor I most consider are the useability [sic] of the design (M-5, SYM-390).	Usability of the design

Table D.9 cont.

Class	Respondents	Direct quote(s)	Influential factors
		Critics of [sic] looking at project and the opinions of teachers, and my peers influence how my ideas are changed (M-6, SYM-390).	Opinion of teachers and peers
		Just things that are related to design. What makes a better design? Changing negative space, composition, tweaking little things to make a better design, etc. (M-7, SYM-390).	Opinion of teachers and peers
		More ideas - diff. ideas that are better (F-1, SYM-390).	More better ideas
		Simple idea is more readable and memorable (F-2, SYM-390). Other people's input ideas that come up later experimentation (F-3, SYM-390).	Simple, readable, memorable ideas people's input, latent ideas, experimentation
ART 3350-391 (SYM-391)	1 male 0 female	How well the idea comes across, How good the idea is in the first place, How well the idea solves the problem (M-1, SYM-391).	How well the idea is in the first place and how well the idea solves the problem
ART 3351-390 (TYP-390)	2 males, 1 female	Feed back mostly from other designers and wether [sic] I thought it worked (M-1, TYP-390).	Feedback from other designers, self evaluation
		Teacher's opinion - how it would look or the computer after scanned in (M-2, TYP-390).	Teacher's opinion, how it looks, and also how it looks after scanned into the computer
		I like a pen mouse rather than a regular mouse, I can control a pen mouse like a pencil (F-1, TYP-390).	Pen mouse
ART 3351-391 (TYP-391)	6 males, 6 females	As I get it on to the computer, I know there are things that I can do on the computer that I couldn't dream of doing by hand. I am more skilled on the computer than by hand (M-1, TYP-391).	There are things on the computer that cannot be done by hand
		Friends, class mates, instructors, and even my own good judgement (M-2, TYP-391).	Friends, class mates, instructors, own good judgement
		Maybe noticing something minor that could be changed such as type or color (M-3, TYP-391).	Something minor such as type or color

Table D.9 cont.

Class	Respondents	Direct quote(s)	Influential factors
		Usually peers and instructors comments, sometime I might see something just doing my normal routine that changes my mind. I like to take my work to people and friends that aren't in design or art and see what they think and listen to any ideas they may have (M-4, TYP-391).	Peers, instructors, normal routine, people, and friends that aren't in design or art
		Some factors might be the strength of the ideas, the practicality of it, the practicality of elements within the design (lines, shapes, colors, ect [sic], and the overall concept of the work (M-5, TYP-391).	The strength of the ideas, the practicality of it, the practicality of elements within the design, and overall concept
		I would definitely have to list the variety of media used and how much critiquing & criticism has gone into the work (M-6, TYP-391).	The variety of media used and critiquing and criticism
		Not having a sloppy design, as roughs resemble. Placement & font choice usually change for me & positioning of logo uses as well (F-1, TYP-391).	No sloppy design, placement, font choice
		Others opinions, my own opinion, deeper concept, deeper understanding, etc. (F-2, TYP-391).	Others opinions, own opinion, deeper concept, deeper understanding,
		Ideas from others, books I looked at, different solutions I tried that inspired me to other solutions (F-3, TYP-391).	Ideas from others, books, other different solutions
		As you work you still think about alternatives your ideas just grows as you research & work thru the design (F-4, TYP-391).	Alternatives ideas, research
		My lack of knowledge of ways I can use different computer programs & the time it takes me to figure out how to do what I want to (F-5, TYP-391).	Lack of different computer program knowledge
		The factor of what works or looks better then [sic] what 's there. Opinion of those around me. Most times, it 's just the elements that cause improvement (F-6, TYP-391).	What works or looks better, opinion, and the elements that cause improvement

234

Table D.9 cont.

Class	Respondents	Direct quote(s)	Influential factors
ART 3352-390 (TYI-390)	4 males, 3 females	The incorporation of new info, or angles, on the subject, possibly it just did not work when it was pieced together (M-1, TYI-390).	Incorporation of new info, or angles on the subject
		Spurr [sic] of the moment ideas, thoughts (M-2, TYI-390).	Spur of the moment ideas
		tools that otherwise would have been overlooked/difficult color/opacity/layers/filters etc. (M-3, TYI-390).	Tools, color, opacity, layers, filters, etc.
		Usually it's processes not easily sketched than can be created on a comp that change my ideas. ie motion blurs, (M-4, TYI-390).	Processes not easily sketched such as motion blur
		I don't think it did - it developed a progression isn't that a natural part of the process? (F-1, TYI-390).	A progression
		My peers/co-designers influence me the most during critiques/discussions. A lot of times I will have a moment of insight or I will re-brainstorm (F-2, TYI-390).	Peers, co-designers, moment of insight, re-brainstorm
		Computer. Input from friends. If I could actually render my idea the way I thought it would look (F-3, TYI-390).	Computer, input from friends
ART 3352-391 (TYI-391)	1 male, 1 female	The computer does change the idea because of the tools involved (M-1, TYI-391).	Computer tools involved
		Input of fellow students, teachers, & friends who are not designers help a great deal. I take everyone's opinion seriously. This helps me break out of I'm in a rut & see the project from someone else's point of view (F-1, TYI-391).	Input of fellow students, teachers, and friends who are not designers. See the project from someone else's point of view
ART 4381-390 (PSS-390)	4 males, 10 females	Usually during the long arduous hours of staring at my computer a breakthrough occurs & something changes. My computer is magic (M-1, PSS-390).	Long arduous hours of staring at my computer a breakthrough occurs

Table D.9 cont.

Class	Respondents	Direct quote(s)	Influential factors
		Type style location layout (M-2, PSS-390).	Type style, location, layout
		Seeing the way others react to it. It is all about societies view as to how well it works (M-3, PSS-390).	It is about societies view as to how well it works
		The factor that has most directly influenced my design is having too much dependency on the computer to realize my design. Despite proper research and thumbnail/idea generation, if you go to the computer solely depending on it to produce your design, forgetting [sic] hand made design on things created by hand, and abandoning our artistic skills, then the end design, I have found, suffers detrimentally from the original concepts/sketches (M-4, PSS-390).	Too much dependency on the computer to realize the design. End design suffers if you go to the computer solely to produce designs
		People (instructors, peers, classmates) always influence my ideas (F-1, PSS-390).	People always influence my ideas
		Mock-ups ... Actually translating to computer --> more time to think & come up with better stuff --> PEERS (F-2, PSS-390).	Mock-ups, translation to the computer
		Peer input teacher's comment solutions (F-3, PSS-390).	Peer input, teacher's comment, solutions
		New ideas, new things to try on the computer (F-4, PSS-390). [Left blank] (F-5, PSS-390).	New ideas, new things on the computer [No responses to code]
		More research, other designers work in magazines (F-6, PSS-390).	Research, other designers work in magazines
		Several printouts and critiques of how can I improve the work that has already been done (F-7, PSS-390).	Printouts and critiques of how to improve the work
		Ability to translate may affect some designs, but I find that by combining programs, almost any idea can be translated to computer. Actually the computers [sic] ease of change in design has often left [sic] to design changes that were unexpected & successful changes (F-8, PSS-390).	By combining programs, almost any idea can be translated to computer. The computer's ease of change has often led to design changes that were unexpected & successful

Table D.9 cont.

Class	Respondents	Direct quote(s)	Influential factors
ART 3352-392 (SYS-392)	5 males, 3 females	Other works, changing ideas (F-9, PSS-390).	Other works, changing ideas
		Professor/classmate's inputs (F-10, PSS-390).	Professor and classmate's inputs
		Teachers, my own ideas, the development of a new direction while exploring another, and by creating multiple ideas (M-1, SYS-392).	Teachers, my own ideas, the development of a new direction, and by creating multiple ideas
		The computer's ability to perfect it and manipulate it (M-2, SYS-392).	The computer's ability
		The creative processes, sketching out ideas, refining, revising (M-3, SYS-392).	The creative processes, sketching, refining, revising
		critiques and opinions (M-4, SYS-392).	critiques and opinions
		Different teachers influence each design. There could be changes in text or the images you choose to use in the design (M-5, SYS-392).	Different teachers, changes in text or the images you choose
		Feedback from classmates/peers/instructors (F-1, SYS-392).	Feedback from classmates, peers, instructors
		I see new things, get better ideas. Time affects my work the most (F-2, SYS-392).	Time affects my work the most
		• critique feedback - I feed off of others ideas while in process • possibilities - computer offers gradients, layering, fading, etc. • color - I do not sketch in colors • fonts - hard to sketch & play w/size/position in a sketch (F-3, SYS-392).	Feedback, possibilities from the computer, fonts
ART 3352-393 (SYS-393)	2 males, 0 female	Maybe simplify one of my sketches or adding to one of my sketches (M-1, SYS-393).	Simplify or add to one of my sketches
		Critiques, looking at my project after a day or two, looking at art (M-2, SYS-393).	Critiques, looking at my project after a day or two

Table D.9 cont.

Class	Respondents	Direct quote(s)	Influential factors
ART 4352-392 (PUB-392)	1 male, 0 female	This is really simple. You design for what the professor wants, his or her tastes. The problem is every prof has different tastes. What might be genius to one might be total crap to another. Catch 22 (M-1, PUB-392).	Design what the professor wants. The problem is that every professor has different tastes. Catch 22

Table D.10 Data analysis of respondents for question #10

Class	Respondents	Direct quote(s)	Prepared/ Not prepared	Keywords
ART 4356-390 (PAC-390)	1 male 0 female	Yes, because I've done it in the real world and no, because the economy for graphic designers is real poor right now (M-1, PAC-390).	Prepared	Done it in real world
ART 4352-390 (POR-390)	3 males 4 females	Yes, b/c if you have concept (thought process) down first you will always come up w/a good result (M-1, POR-390).	Prepared	[Response not usable ::irrelevant]
		Yes, I feel I've gained a lot from all my teachers and I realize that my first job will be a continuation of my education (M-2, POR-390).	Prepared	First job will be a continuation of education
		Yes, I do, I have had every experienced teachers that are very knowledgable [sic] in the field prepare me in my portfolio class (M-3, POR-390).	Prepared	Experienced teachers
		Yes, I have a good basic knowledge of fine art and handskills [sic], as well as an understanding of the computer's role and printing techniques (F-1, POR-390).	Prepared	Basic knowledge of art and understanding technical skills
		No - well I just don't feel that I know the technical (printing) info (F-2, POR-390).	Not prepared	Not knowing printing skills
		Yes, as much as I can be, but honestly I am a little scared. Just basically of the unknown. I feel as though I have gained the basic tools to help start me (F-3, POR-390).	Prepared	Scared of the unknown
		Yes - I do b/c I have worked in it a bit, but I have had reviews of my work that lead me to believe I am on the right track. By no means I feel I have learned everything, there will be a big learning curve - but I look forward to it & I enjoy design which makes me feel I am in the right area (F-4, POR-390).	Prepared	There will be a big learning curve
ART 3350-390 (SYM-390)	7 males, 3 females	No, I have a growing knowledge but not quite at the top to go on my own yet. I need to learn different aspects and possible assignment solutions first (M-1, SYM-390).	Not prepared	Need to learn different aspects
		Yes. I realize that most of what I will need to know, I will learn on the job (M-2, SYM-390).	Prepared	Will learn on the job

Table D.10 cont.

Class	Respondents	Direct quote(s)	Prepared/ Not prepared	Keywords
		I feel prepared to enter certain areas of graphic design partly because I think I can do it and partly because I am just ready to move t o the next step. I am worried that I am not good enough or creative enough to become successful (M-3, SYM-390).	Prepared	Worried about not good or creative enough
		I hope I am ready, I do not know if I am or not. Once I get out there it will be a different story (M-4, SYM-390).	Not sure	Once out there, a different story
		I still have a lot of learning to do (M-5, SYM-390).	Not prepared	A lot of learning to do
		Yes. I feel I've been here long enough & learned enough to do well. My design skills are good & I'm open to learning more. The world of design is always changing & you have to know how to constintly [sic] learn (M-6, SYM-390).	Prepared	The world of design is constantly changing
		I'm learning, but I have a lot more to learn. I feel I have the drawing skills and the creativity, but I need to learn more about type and the printing process and what goes on in the design world more (M-7, SYM-390).	Not prepared	Need to learn more about type, printing process and the design world
		Not yet. I need to take portfolio? really spend individual time w/each project. Also I don't really know how to deal w/a client (F-1, SYM-390).	Not prepared	Don't know how to deal with a client
		At this time no, not only just really learning what it is all about but I am not as computer literate as I would hope to be I rely on my drawing sills as the primary factor in ideas creations (F-2, SYM-390).	Not prepared	Not as computer literate. Rely on drawing skills
		Yes and no. I need to learn more about the programs, but my ideas are usually pretty good (F-3, SYM-390).	Not sure	Need to learn more about the programs
ART 3350-391 (SYM-391)	1 male 0 female	Not at the moment. I still don't feel comfortable with my type choices. I don't know of even a few companies that are currently hiring. I would like to know what jobs are out there as well as which ones I am qualified for (M-1, SYM-391).	Not prepared	Not comfortable with type choices. Companies not hiring.

Table D.10 cont.

Class	Respondents	Direct quote(s)	Prepared/ Not prepared	Keywords
ART 3351-390 (TYP-390)	2 males, 1 female	Yes even though there is a lot of competition and closeness in the skill of my peers, everyone has their own approach and style. I feel I have what I will need when I make place in the world (M-1, TYP-390).	Prepared	Competition and closeness in skill of peers
		Yes because the faith in me to achieve my ultimate goal "being happy in life" designing in the real world - I know my client will be happy with my work. If not - I will work harder, until I bleed damn it! (M-2, TYP-390).	Prepared	Will work harder
		Not really, only because I am still unclear how a firm would work, maybe, an internship will make me feel more comfortable (F-1, TYP-390).	Not prepared	Internship can help
ART 3351-391 (TYP-391)	6 males, 6 females	Yes I believe I am prepared because of my experience and knowledge I have learned through life & college. Even though some of the classes we have to take don't make sense as why we have to take them, I am ready to enter the field (M-1, TYP-391).	Prepared	Experience and knowledge learned through life and college
		Some what, but I feel finishing my degree first would be a good idea (M-2, TYP-391).	Not prepared	Need to finish degree first
		Yes, because I have an understanding of how to come up with a concept and how to apply my concept to come up with my final product (M-3, TYP-391).	Prepared	Know how to come up with concepts and how to apply them
		Not yet, but, I feel that I'm getting a lot closer. After taking symbols and typography I have begun to get a taste for the pace and type of work involved. I've learned a lot more about process [sic], but I still have a couple years hear [sic] at Tech (M-4, TYP-391).	Not prepared	Still have a couple of years at Tech
		I don't feel I am ready just yet because I have not learned all of what the university offers to teach me, but I am confidant [sic] that when I am finished I will be well prepared to enter the field of graphic design (M-5, TYP-391).	Not prepared	Have not learned all of what the university offers to teach

Table D.10 cont.

Class	Respondents	Direct quote(s)	Prepared/Not prepared	Keywords
		I think that I am beginning to grow into that stage where I could be successful as a designer, although I know there is always more to learn (M-6, TYP-391).	Prepared	There is always more to learn
		No, b/c I need more experience with the computer. I am very familiar with art itself, but technically I need to learn more (F-1, TYP-391).	Not prepared	Need more experience with the computer.
		I feel prepared and knowledged [sic]. I do think that more computer design classes would have been beneficial but not always necessary (F-2, TYP-391).	Prepared	More computer design classes would be beneficial
		Sometimes - I feel more prepared every semester but I don't think I will feel ready when I graduate, it will take lots of experience to feel comfortable in the field (F-3, TYP-391).	Not prepared	Takes experience to feel comfortable
		I start to feel that way but when I begin a new class or new assignment I am humbled once again & realise [sic] there is so much more to the field than a good idea or concept (F-4, TYP-391).	Not prepared	Much more to the field than a good idea or concept
		No. I still feel afraid of the computer. There are many terms that I don't know & I feel the tool keeps changing & I can't seem to catch up (F-5, TYP-391).	Not prepared	Many unfamiliar terms, the tool keeps changing, can't seem to catch up
		No. Right now I think I am at turtle speed compared to those that are out really working. I dont [sic] feel I am prepared to do what is needed to be successful or work in the programs (F-6, TYP-391).	Not prepared	At turtle speed compared to those that are out really working.
ART 3352-390 (TYI-390)	4 males, 3 females	I think I will be ready to enter graphic design field, w/the knowledge I have gained & the resources I have required (M-1, TYI-390).	Prepared	Knowledge gained and resources required
		Not yet, I don't think I will ever be. There's a lot out there I will always be unprepared for (M-2, TYI-390).	Not prepared	A lot out there, always unprepared

242

Table D.10 cont.

Class	Respondents	Direct quote(s)	Prepared/ Not prepared	Keywords
		I feel I am some what prepared. Everything is so overwhelming that my confidence is the only thing I feel will hold me back (M-3, TYI-390).	Prepared	Everything is so overwhelming. Confidence will hold me back
		Yes, No. Technically & design wise, yes. Business wise, no. But my internships & freelance jobs are changing that (M-4, TYI-390).	Not sure	Internships and freelance job are changing that
		not yet, but when I complete my next year and a halve [sic] I will. I love design. I love this class. Carla wouldn't let us get away w/out pushing ourselves, not doing the best we can. I still need to learn about printing and hope to get an internship for that (F-1, TYI-390).	Not prepared	Need to learn about printing and hope to get an internship
		I feel that if I maintain my own style and respect for sensitivity of design, then I am ready. I do not want to fall into the melting pot of designers that only cater to client wants without keeping in mind that they have to be satisfied with their work, too. Also I feel prepared b/c I do not let works of others over-influence me -- I do not copy (F-2, TYI-390).	Not sure	Maintain own style and respect for sensitivity of design, not let others over-influence
		Yes. I feel I make reasonable decisions in relation to design. I have learned much about design in school, but I feel its [sic] a learn as you go process, won't actually do it until you get there (F-3, TYI-390).	Prepared	Have learned much about design in school, a learn as you go process
ART 3352-391 (TYI-391)	1 male, 1 female	I feel like on the way to being ready to enter the design world, but I not there yet (M-1, TYI-391).	Not prepared	On the way to enter the design world
		I don't think I'm prepared yet. I don't feel that I have enough experience working with actual clients. I am confident, however, that my remaining classes and an internship or two will equip me with the tools I need for this field (F-1, TYI-391).	Not prepared	Not enough experience working with actual clients. Remaining classes and an internship or two will equip me with the tools I need

Table D.10 cont.

Class	Respondents	Direct quote(s)	Prepared/ Not prepared	Keywords
ART 4381-390 (PSS-390)	4 males, 10 females	Yes. Although I would of [sic] liked more exposure to the business/marketing side of design (M-1, PSS-390).	Prepared	More exposure of the business/marketing side of design
		Yes I am, I feel that I have pushed many boundaries in design I also have been given a good knowledge of myself what I am strong & weak in. I know the program (M-2, PSS-390).	Prepared	Pushed many boundaries in design. A good knowledge of myself
		For the most part I am interested in pushing on into the real workplace to see if my views and learning will work together well (M-3, PSS-390).	Prepared	Interested in pushing on into the real workplace to see if my views and learning will work together well
		Yes. I have invested (at this point) at least a good 5 yrs of my life, three at college, to making design my everything. I've wanted nothing more than to be a good designer & have applied myself as such, seeking to get all the experience I can. And now, although I am not too close to graduation, I feel confident in my design abilities and I am even more eager to get out there and learn more (M-4, PSS-390).	Prepared	Making design my everything. Confident in my design abilities and I am eager to get out there and learn more
		Not all the time. From the business end and printing (as in print shops) I feel like their [sic] is a lot yet to learn (F-1, PSS-390).	Not prepared	A lot yet to learn from the business end and printing (as in print shops)
		I think I need more refinements on stuff & a better portfolio & more computer skills ... but I'm well on my way (F-2, PSS-390).	Not prepared	Need more refinements on stuff & a better portfolio & more computer skills
		I feel prepared design wise, but not company wise. I don't feel I know enough about collecting for output, sending to press, etc. (F-3, PSS-390).	Not prepared	Prepared design wise, but not company wise
		Yes & No. Yes, because I know how to design & feel that my designs are effective, & No - because I'm afraid of not being able to reproduce something that someone has done before. I feel like they wouldn't be happy with my work (F-4, PSS-390).	Not sure	Afraid of not being able to reproduce something that someone has done before

Table D.10 cont.

Class	Respondents	Direct quote(s)	Prepared/ Not prepared	Keywords
		Yes. I have developed strong skills in time management, research, conceptual development, the actual process of design (F-5, PSS-390).	Prepared	Strong skills in time management, research, conceptual development, the actual process of design
		Yes - well, after portfolio I will. I think students feel scared until they re-visit their work in portfolio class (F-6, PSS-390).	Prepared	Students feel scared until they re-visit their work in portfolio class
		Yes because I feel that I have the enough experience with the desing [sic] proces [sic] and tools. And the knowledge of how the process of decission [sic] is (F-7, PSS-390).	Prepared	Have enough experience with the design process and tools
		I do feel prepared to enter the field, especially since I had done 2 internships in addition to several free-lance jobs while still in school. However I am planning to attend grad school to further my design experience in a non-constricting environment (F-8, PSS-390).	Prepared	Prepared to enter the field, had done two internships, several free-lance jobs while in school. Planning to attend graduate school
		NO I always feel my work is never good enough. We need a class on how to be confident about your work (F-9, PSS-390).	Not prepared	Need a class on how to be confident about your work
		Somewhat ... there is always something that could be learned and improved (F-10, PSS-390).	Not sure	There is always something that could be learned and improved
ART 3352-392 (SYS-392)	5 males, 3 females	Yes, this program has been hard enough and challenging enough to prepare me for a job in computer grafix [sic] (M-1, SYS-392).	Prepared	This program has been hard and challenging
		No, the teachers spoon-feed us design ideas and teach us to use other's ideas altered to fit our own (M-2, SYS-392).	Not prepared	Teachers spoon-feed us design ideas and to use other's ideas
		Not just yet, I feel I have more to learn in the classes I have left (M-3, SYS-392).	Not prepared	Have more to learn in the classes left

245

Table D.10 cont.

Class	Respondents	Direct quote(s)	Prepared/ Not prepared	Keywords
		not yet but I will be once I have time to sit at a computer for a long time (M-4, SYS-392).	Not prepared	I will be once I have time to sit at a computer for a long time
		Right this moment I do not feel that I am ready, because I feel that I have so much to learn about the programs (M-5, SYS-392).	Not prepared	Have so much to learn about the programs
		Yes & No - But I have one more year & I think I will be prepared by then - I am also an above average age student so ?!? [sic] (F-1, SYS-392).	Not sure	Have one more year, above average age student
		I am almost there. Although there is some pretty bad design out there. I think right now I'm somewhere in the middle (F-2, SYS-392).	Not prepared	Somewhere in the middle
		I have already done graphic design on a lower level successfully and have an Associate degree in it. I feel very prepared (F-3, SYS-392).	Prepared	Have done graphic design on a lower level successfully, have an Associate degree
ART 3352-393 (SYS-393)	2 males, 0 female	At first I had doubts, but now that I am getting better at it I am starting to love it (M-1, SYS-393).	Prepared	I am starting to love it
		I do feel prepared to enter the field, but I want to grow more as an artist/designer. I feel my technical skills are ready. But I want to experience more before I start working (M-2, SYS-393).	Prepared	My technical skills are ready. I want to experience more before I start working
ART 4352-392 (PUB-392)	1 male, 0 female	I feel prepared to do the job but not get the job. Aparently [sic] work is scarce for us, and thats [sic] heart breaking when you love design (M-1, PUB-392).	Prepared	Work is scarce for us